# God and Subjectivity

# American University Studies

Series V
Philosophy
Vol. 99

PETER LANG
New York • Bern • Frankfurt am Main • Paris

Gerald J. Galgan

# God and Subjectivity

PETER LANG
New York • Bern • Frankfurt am Main • Paris

**Library of Congress Cataloging-in-Publication Data**

Galgan, Gerald J.
  God and subjectivity / Gerald J. Galgan.
    p. cm. — (American university studies. Series V, Philosophy ; vol. 99)
  Includes bibliographical references.
   1. First philosophy—History.  2. Anselm, Saint, Archbishop of Canterbury, 1033-1109.  I. Title.  II. Series.
BD331.G25        1990        110—dc20        90-33276
ISBN 0-8204-1339-9                             CIP
ISSN 0739-6392

© Peter Lang Publishing, Inc., New York 1990

All rights reserved.
Reprint or reproduction, even partially, in all forms such as microfilm, xerography, microfiche, microcard, offset strictly prohibited.

Printed in the United States of America.

*To Joseph J. Carpino*

# Acknowledgments

I wish to thank Ann Hartle, Joseph Carpino, Peter Leonard, Robert Sokolowski, and John J. McDermott for their suggestions for the improvement of the manuscript. A sabbatical for research and writing was granted by St. Francis College, Brooklyn, N.Y. during the Fall semester of 1982, for which I am grateful.

# Contents

**Prologue**..................................................................... xi

**I. The Aristotelian Founding of First Philosophy**............ 1
    i.    Essence as Substance ........................................ 1
    ii.   Divine Substance .............................................. 4
    iii.  First Philosophy as Theology ........................... 8
    iv.  The Being of Beings ........................................ 14
    v.   Aristotle and Anselm........................................ 17

**II. Anselm's Meditation on First Philosophy** ................. 23
    i.    The Being Among Beings................................. 24
    ii.   Substance as Essence ........................................ 29
    iii.  Created and Uncreated Essence ..................... 35
    iv.  First Philosophy as Trinitarian Theology ...... 39
    v.   The Being Beyond Beings ............................... 45
    vi.  Anselm and Aristotle........................................ 49

**III. Anselm's Dialogue in First Philosophy** ...................... 53
    i.    The Submergence and Emergence
        of the Self........................................................... 55
    ii.   Negativity: The Denial of God's Existence .. 59
    iii.  Truth as Rectitude............................................. 64
    iv.  Comprehension and the Incomprehensible.. 71
    v.   The Supra-Substantial Divine Subject........... 78
    vi.  Anselm's Response to Criticism...................... 81
    vii. Anselm and Descartes...................................... 90

**IV. The Cartesian Refounding of First Philosophy**............ 97
    i.    The Divorce of First
        Philosophy and Theology................................. 98

|     |       |                                                      |     |
| --- | ----- | ---------------------------------------------------- | --- |
|     | ii.   | Negativity: The Methodic Doubt                       | 104 |
|     | iii.  | The Being Beyond Doubt                               | 111 |
|     | iv.   | Addressing the Self Alone                            | 117 |
|     | v.    | The Supra-Substantial Human Subject                  | 128 |
|     | vi.   | Truth as Certitude                                   | 135 |
|     | vii.  | First Philosophy as the Foundation of Physical Science | 140 |
|     | viii. | Descartes' Response to Criticism                     | 148 |
|     | ix.   | Descartes and Anselm                                 | 157 |

**V. Feuerbach's Reduction of First Philosophy to Anthropology** ............... 165
    i. Religion and the Logic of Subjectivity ........... 167
    ii. Negativity: Theology as Anthropomorphic .. 172
    iii. The Being Beyond God ................................. 179
    iv. From Subjectivity to Intersubjectivity ............ 186
    v. The Inversion of Anselm .............................. 192

**VI. The Historical Travail of First Philosophy** ............... 203
    i. The Removal and Perdurance of Mystery ..... 208
    ii. The Modern Misunderstanding of Anselm ... 217
    iii. The Cartesian Regulative Notion .................. 223
    iv. The "Essence" of Feuerbach .......................... 229
    v. That by which Man is Man ............................. 237
    vi. The Mystery of Evil ...................................... 243

**Epilogue** .............................................................. 255

**Primary Texts and Translations** ....................... 267

**Notes** ................................................................... 271

**Index** .................................................................. 291

# Prologue

In a previous effort, *The Logic of Modernity*, it was argued that the developmental unity of modern philosophical thought—underlying positions that oppose each other in a dynamic co-operation—is a transmission and articulation of the theoretical content of medieval Christianity. This argument required a synthesis of the major ethical, epistemological, and metaphysical implication of the "new science" of the sixteenth and seventeenth centuries. The purpose, however, was not simply to provide another history of modern philosophy but, rather, to begin a philosophical reflection on the meaning of the present age.[1]

This is also the purpose of the present work: together with its predecessor, it constitutes a propaedeutic for a more fully developed philosophical reflection on the meaning of the present age. *God and Subjectivity* is a specification of the thesis defended in the previous effort: it focuses on fewer philosophers; it provides a more detailed textual analysis; it is concerned exclusively with metaphysics; and the theoretical content of medieval Christianity which it examines is that presented by St. Anselm of Canterbury. It is offered, however, in such a way that a reading of the earlier monograph is not prerequisite. Although the earlier provides a context for the later work, each can be read and judged on its own merits.

The present work is a report on first philosophy as a history—the history of the concept of being. This history is the *Geschichte*, the travail, the anguish, the "what-happened-to" of the concept of being. This book is a *Historie*, a biography of the life of the concept of being—or at least that portion of the life of the concept that is a global event, namely, the transformation of substance into subject. More specifically, as a report on the history of the concept of being, *God and Subjectivity* is a reflection on what mediates between the ancient founding and modern refounding of first philosophy. In essence it is about St. Anselm as a metaphysician—his meditation on and dialogue in first philosophy.

The burden of the ancient founding of first philosophy is the analysis of being in terms of what is actual in nature, the *thing* in its real-ization. The being that manifests itself in being*s*—*qua* being—is never an hypostatized being, for being means an occurrence inherent in particular and individual things as an immanent principle of determination. The nature which accounts for particularization, although it is dis-concealed in man, exists independently of man's faculty of thinking or even his desire to think. The substance disclosed in the founding of first philosophy is never, as such, the particular being of the knowing agent—of man as a subject. Existence never becomes a problem in this founding: the existence of the "this" is in no way problematic since it is simply given, simply "there." The only problem is the "why" of formal causality and the "wherefore" of final causality. Substance can be visible in particular sensible things only because, in its pure actuality, it is the "final form"—the pure universality of thinking which thinks itself.

This founding is the work of Aristotle. The key to this founding is his analysis of the identity of being and intelligibility in terms of the actualizing universality which particularizes the *ob-ject* which exists by nature. The point of Aristotle's founding of first philosophy is that those who follow him will answer the call to reflect on the being that manifests itself in being*s* and, in this way, reenact and perpetuate the birth of the concept of being.

But the counterpoint to this point in the early modern refounding of first philosophy by Descartes is that those who follow him will never again need to engage in first philosophy. First philosophy is now seen to have as its goal the turning of the human subject to the tasks of modern mathematical physics. The key to the Cartesian refounding of first philosophy is the analysis of the identity of being and intelligibility in terms of the possibility inherent in the particular human *sub-ject* which is not, as such, given by nature and can, therefore, be the master or lord of nature. The actualization and positivity of what is by nature are superseded by the negativity and potentiality of what is human and particular. The modern refounding places man *between* God and nothingness rather than *within* nature.

The burden of the Cartesian refounding of first philosophy, then, is the analysis of being in terms of the finite or human subject, a *self* with infinite aspirations. This ontological reification of the grammatical first person implies that it is only as a system of body and self, as a composite whole, as a being among the beings of nature, that I am subject to error and that "my" infirmity must be acknowledged. But this infirmity is not really mine—not really a part of my pure "partless" essence, of my "ego," which in itself is not really a being among the beings of nature. Because of this, I am able, in the modern physical sciences, to be the master and possessor of nature—even that corporeal nature with which I am so intimately connected. First philosophy is now a quest for certainty, for an indubitable existence which is more truly *mine* than the ordinary life which I lead within the confines of what nature makes accessible to me.

But contrary to its own claim, the early modern refounding of first philosophy is not an absolutely new beginning. The midpoint between the point and counterpoint of the history of the determination of the concept of being is the ontological precondition for the dynamics of modern philosophical subjectivity. This midpoint is St. Anselm's analysis of the identity of being and intelligibility in terms of the notion of being as a predicate of a divine but particular subject of being—a subject which is absolutely other than nature. The midpoint in this history of the concept of being—equidistant, so to speak, from the ancient founding and the modern refounding of first philosophy—is the presentation of being *qua* being as the actuality of a creative substance which transcends form as such—a supreme, supranatural, particular "something" or "aliquid."

This Anselmian transformation of the Aristotelian founding of first philosophy required a shift from a real-ization immanent in nature to an actuality which transcends nature. For all the fundamentality of the distinction between God and the world, in Anselm's first philosophy, God cannot be seen to be established by that distinction. For all the fundamentality of the inseparability of God and world, in Aristotle's first philosophy, divinity must be seen as established by the distinction between itself and non-divine things in this world. Whereas Aristotle's God is always a first substance within the world, the God whom Anselm addresses is a supra-substantial existent, a supranatural "aliquid" by whom all other existents—which might not have existed at all—can exist.

The meaning of substance is now approached by Anselm in virtue of a causality and good which are not *of* this world of realized forms and which transcend form as such. Substantiality is now hypostatized as a primal subject of being completely other than this world. The being of the particular, i.e., existence, is now eminently problematical; and the existence of a multiplicity of good things requires one particular thing that is not only supremely great or "summe magnum" but is that which human thinking cannot think beyond.

Central, then, to the life of the concept of being is the midpoint constituted by Anselm's transformation of the ancient beginning of the history of the concept of being. This transformation required a radical alteration of language, including the kind of language that Aristotle used. We see this most clearly in the contrast *between* Aristotle's careful attempt to delineate, and be faithful to, the ordinary, everyday, but not arbitrary usage of words *and* Anselm's equally careful attempt to articulate the difference between the ordinary, everyday usage of language and the special signification that would have to apply to the God that is the object of Christian faith—a faith which Anselm makes an *object* for reason.

It is precisely Anselm's alteration of the language of first philosophy—especially his addressing God as an absolutely unique something, a particular being that is at once the pure actuality of being, an absolute particularity that is not of this world—which is at the center of the dynamics of philosophical subjectivity in the modern world. In effect, the desire which Aristotle saw as characteristic of all the movements of nature—a desire for a perfection immanent in nature—had been transformed by Anselm into a desire of the self, of my mind, of "mens mea," for existence in a perfection which transcends nature. And this transformation had become a *given* in Descartes' reification of the grammatical first person, in Descartes' attempt to refound first philosophy.

The outcome, however, of the early modern refounding of first philosophy is late-modern atheism which attempts to analyze being in terms of the complete rejection of the identity of being and intelligibility. Here, in Feuerbach's efforts to reduce first philosophy to anthropology, is found the negation of first philosophy itself: the divine particular being is now conceived as an alienation of the excellences of the human subject. Feuerbach saw that modern philosophy is a negation of the claims of theology—a negation which is itself based upon theology. For him the only resolution of this "paradox" was to show that the anti-theological "theology" of modernity was really reducible to anthropology, to a kind of "devout atheism" which teaches us that only existence in time and space is true existence, that the revelation of God is only the self-unfolding of the human subject, and that God himself is really the omnipotence of human feeling without regard to anything else. Feuerbach claims to have uncovered and explained the mystery of the object of Christian faith: God is the essence of the human subject of being treated objectively, i.e., man's seeing his own essence as outside of himself.

But if, indeed, there is a history for first philosophy, a history which *is* first philosophy, a life of its own for the concept of being, it is that of an arduous development of language about *to be*. Any purportedly atheistic outcome of this history—because of its assumption of all values into negativity and its absorption of negativity into all values—presupposes that the transformation of the ancient founding first occurred when thought first encountered a positive significance for negativity in first philosophy. The late-modern atheistic outcome (in Feuerbach) may be nothing more than an attempt to turn this first encounter (in Anselm) against itself.

In Anselm's dialectic, the lived atheism of the "fool" (the denial of his "heart") can only be a kind of perverted imitation of the belief of the believer when that belief is lived, i.e., when the heart and understanding are congruent. Throughout Feuerbach's anthropological first philosophy, this Anselmian dialectic of what is *split* in the atheist as an imitation of what is *united* in the believer reappears but precisely as inverted. It is now the unlived theism of the believer—i.e., the theological and, therefore, merely conceptual antithesis of God and man—which is a perverted imitation of the lived atheism of the believer himself, that is, the omnipotence of human feeling or the human heart made into a "God" by the human imagination. It is thus Feuerbach's contention that God must exist in the human understanding *alone* if, in fact, God is to be conceived as existing independently of the human understanding. But this is nothing but an inversion of Anselm's claim that God must exist independently of the human understanding if, in fact, God is to exist in the human understanding *at all*. The "essence" of Feuerbach's attempt to bring the history of the concept of being to an atheistic conclusion is precisely his inversion of the primacy of belief over unbelief in Anselm's first philosophy.

If our biography of the life of the concept of being, of the development of the destiny or fate of talk about being, is to be faithful to that development, must it not respond to the call for a thoughtful return to the transformation of the ancient founding of first philosophy, a return to the midpoint in the history of language about being *qua* being? Reflection on this transformation, after all, would seem to be a highly desirable, if not necessary, preliminary to a consideration of the significance of the sedimentation of modern philosophical subjectivity into the regions of common sense or ordinary experience in our own time.[2] Reflection on this midpoint, furthermore, is what is needed if we are to elucidate the significance of the ancient founding of first philosophy. This founding constitutes the first step that any philosophy must repeat and reenact; but when modern philosophy returns to this founding, it does so by virtue of an understanding provided by medieval Scholasticism[3] which, in turn, had its beginning in St. Anselm.

At the center of an endeavor to report on the history of the concept of being, then, stands a thoughtful return to Anselm's contribution to first philosophy. And in such thoughtfulness, would we not be compelled to raise the question of whether or not the late-modern negation of metaphysics is the final word? Whether or not modern self-confidence or self-assertiveness is empty without confidence in God?[4] In the final analysis, the decisive question for the future of philosophy is whether or not philosophy itself—in its speculative and (not merely) critical integrity—can be done any longer in an intellectual milieu where the ontological claim presupposed by belief in the existence of the God of infinite wisdom and power—the God of Abraham, Isaac, and Jacob—is no longer taken seriously.

A book which takes such considerations as its purview will be making a large claim. It will be more than just an interpretation of St. Anselm's so-called Ontological Argument, since it will endeavor to place that argument in the context not only of Anselm's *Proslogion* as a whole but his *Monologion* as well—both his dialogue in first philosophy and his meditation on first philosophy. Furthermore, it will attempt to place both of these works within the context of the history of first philosophy as the development of the concept of being, that is, the founding of first philosophy in Aristotle's *Metaphysics*, its refounding in Descartes' *Meditations Concerning First Philosophy*, and its reduction to anthropology in Feuerbach's *The Essence of Christianity*.

But the problem inherent in making such a large claim is to be solved by focusing on a more modest claim. What makes Anselm such a unique and important moment in the life of the concept of being, it will be argued, is not simply the so-called Ontological Argument but an insight that runs throughout his writing—although frequently submerged in other considerations—and that finds its most incisive expression in that argument. The more modest claim, underlying the report on the history of the concept of being presented in this book, is to uncover this genuinely metaphysical insight and to elucidate the range of its influence and ultimately its possible bearing on the future of philosophy.

What is new in Anselm is not the articulation as such of the basic doctrinal deposit of Christianity. That articulation was close to having been accomplished by the time of Anselm. Rather, his most fundamental and truly metaphysical insight amounts to eliciting a decisive *philosophical* implication of the Christian mysteries of Creation "ex nihilo," the Incarnation, and the Trinity—an implication which would, in turn, prove decisive for the modern invention or, in its own estimation, "discovery" of subjectivity.

Prior to Anselm, the problem of first philosophy had remained the problem of the being that is manifested in being*s*, the oneness that pervades the manyness of the particulars of nature. Being *qua* being was an entelechy or substantiality which endures as permanent throughout change—in a single order of nature where understanding and the thing-understood are inseparably conjoined—and which accounts for whatever significance can be disclosed in the particular entities of nature. But for Anselm, the problem of being *qua* being is precisely the problem of being as an attribute of a preeminently particular subject, viz, God, who would exist even if there were no being of nature and who provides the very power to *exist* of the human knower. Anselm thus departs from the prior notion of a single order of nature where understanding and the thing-understood are inseparably conjoined. Anselm makes explicit, seemingly for the first time, a split between what is *in* the human understanding and what is *in* the order of things.[5] This means that for Anselm the identity of being and intelligibility is no longer a *given* in the order of nature but is a *condition* for the possibility of nature—a condition found in the unique, supranatural, divine subject of being. This new metaphysical way of addressing the Parmenidean identity of being and intelligibility will be preconditional for any subsequent (modern) attempt to present the human self, or what Anselm called "mens mea," as a radical subject which cannot think its own nonexistence.

The being of God had been of the utmost significance for ancient as well as for medieval philosophy. But what makes Anselm so important in this regard is that he intimately connects the being of God with the idea of God in the human knower. Faith had been of primary significance for prior medieval philosophy, but what makes Anselm so important here is that he makes faith an *object* for a reflection that is no less metaphysical than it is theological. Anselm introduces a certain distance between faith and reason (not to be found, for example, in St. Augustine) and thereby makes faith an object for reason. On the one hand, the Aristotelian identification of first philosophy with theology is present in Anselm as it had not been in any prior medieval thinker. But, on the other hand, the interpretation of first philosophy which concentrates on a substance which is more than a substance—a substance which is a subject—functions in Anselm as it does in no subsequent thinker until the time of Descartes.

In one sense, it might be said that Anselm is an anomaly in medieval philosophical speculation: the thread that never gets pulled by subsequent medieval philosophers—with the lone exception, perhaps, of Duns Scotus—but which is pulled only later by Descartes, in founding the logic of philosophical subjectivity, and by Hegel[6] and Feuerbach in systematizing that logic and attempting to draw it to a close. Anselm's insight in first philosophy is germinal but lies fallow, by and large, for hundreds of years before it finds its proper conditions for germination—conditions which are turned up and cultivated by Descartes and brought to the most ironical of "fruitions" by Feuerbach. And yet to say this is not to imply that Anselm's insight is fully grasped by modern philosophy. But even, and perhaps especially, when it is misperceived, this insight is decisive for the logic of modern philosophical subjectivity.

But in another sense, much as Aristotle might be said to be the most Greek of Greek philosophers,[7] Anselm might be said to be the most medieval of medieval philosophers. Coming out of the monastic tradition in medieval culture, Anselm is a consummation of a tradition issuing from St. Augustine—a voice for something that will be less and less audible as the Scholasticism of the universities assumes the dominant position in medieval culture. And yet, Anselm is no less a founder of medieval Scholasticism itself, a point of transition to the culture of the university in the Middle Ages. Carved out of the monastic tradition, Anselm's contribution is a peculiar emphasis on the thinkability of God as the precondition for the existence of thought in man. The nature of language about God is a precondition for the intelligibility of language itself.

It is precisely Anselm's insight into human thought's being grasped by something that it itself cannot grasp which is the basis of what he calls the "cogitantis inspectio" or the act by which thinking looks into itself in man. It is precisely this "cogitantis inspectio"—now called "mentis inspectio" by Descartes—which is appropriated in the Cartesian refounding of first philosophy. The Anselmian notion of the act by which thinking looks into itself is now confined in the modern world to the human subject alone—an *ego* held to exist beyond the being of nature and which would exist even if there were no being of nature. In this, the Cartesian *ego* is modeled on the Anselmian *God*. Anselm's ascent to the God that grasps human thought but which human thought itself cannot grasp is the paradigm for Descartes' descent into the *ego cogitans* that grasps—and is grasped by—itself.

In this way, Anselm's contribution to first philosophy might be spoken of as a "recessive gene"—a peculiar flowering of that part of the history of the concept of being found in medieval speculation—which finds its organic material in the dynamics of modern philosophical subjectivity. But it can also be argued that the recessive gene here is the very source of the material of the dynamics of modern philosophical subjectivity. Anselm, as a neglected spokesman for first philosophy, even, and especially, when he is misunderstood by modern philosophers, is at the center of the storm that constitutes the historical transition of metaphysical thought from substance to subject. In the very middle of the historical travail of the concept of being stands the "quiet eye" of Anselm's notion of being *qua* being

This would seem to suggest that the modern philosophical quest for certitude—which is of the greatest consequence for the contemporary renunciation of that quest—finds its condition in the medieval attempt to understand the intelligibility of faith—what Anselm called "ratione fidei." The Cartesian notion of truth as certainty finds its metaphysical precondition in the Anselmian notion of truth as rectitude. And whatever truth is to be found in—or whatever ontological ground is to be uncovered for—the philosophical subjectivity which is at the center of modern philosophy is, in the final analysis, a transmission and articulation of the "germ" of the theoretical content of Christianity in the Middle Ages.[8]

Feuerbach's assertion that only existence in time and space is true existence has at this point in time become a commonplace. Existence, in our contemporary intellectual milieu, *is* in and of *this world* and in and of *temporality*. What may yet turn out to be the astounding outcome of the history of the concept of being, however, is that in being left with this-worldliness and temporality alone, we are being left with precisely that which should not be *there* if being *qua* being is *only* human subjectivity as the horizon in time of this world. Could it be that the one remaining mystery in a demystified and de-anthropomorphized world is that of evil, of the nothingness which we reserve a place for in our subjectivity?

Anselm had spoken of evil as a nothingness which is treated or spoken of as if it were something—a "quasi aliquid." But he confessed his ignorance of what this nothingness is—"quid sit." The problem of evil was thus seen to be insoluble within the confines of the very Creation "ex nihilo" which first raised evil into a problem. This problem runs steadily, though as the least visible thread, through the travail of the concept of being. Could it be that we today are now in the position to see the "problem" of evil as more than a problem—as the inverse reflection of the mystery of a God who is the absolutely unique something, the absolutely unique "aliquid" who freely created the world "out of" nothingness? Could it be that we today are in a historically and philosophically unique position to ponder the relation between that which is spoken of *as if* it were something and that which *is* something absolutely unique?

St. John of the Cross once remarked that the purer the light, the more it blinds the eye of the owl.[9] So also might we account for the metaphysical "blind spot" in the eye of the Owl of Minerva in its contemporary habitat. In the nine-hundred years since St. Anselm's transformation of the concept of being, the light of reason, what Descartes called the "lumen naturale," has become progressively purer, as man has progressively removed mystery from the natural world—so pure that what is now seen is darkness. But if there still remains the mystery of man as the stand-in, the placeholder, for this darkness or nothingness—"Der Mensch ist der Platzhalter des Nichts"[10]—then we may have here the thread which, if tugged upon, will enable us to raise again, but in a new way, the question of the existence of God which Anselm first raised in the context of first philosophy—the question of the existence of *something* that is reducible to no other thing, neither a component of this world nor the totality of this world. If so, it would seem that the *Geschichte*, the travail, of the concept of being is not yet over; and any report on the life of the concept, at this point in time, must remain incomplete. It is with this sobering realization that we must begin—and end—the report on the life of the concept which follows.

# God and Subjectivity

# I

# The Aristotelian Founding of First Philosophy

Martin Heidegger's report on the history of the concept of being begins with the distinction between "whatness" (das Was-Sein) and "thatness" (das Dass-Sein), that is, it begins with a "judgment" about being which is no mere "doctrine" of metaphysical thinking but which discloses an "event" in the history of being as metaphysics. It is Aristotle who first brings this distinction and judgment to their essential ground by bringing the notion of being as emergence (Aufgang) and dis-concealment (Entbergung) into the formulation of presence in the sense of enduring. But, in understanding what is permanent and present as something which is somehow at rest, Aristotle conceives rest as that which preserves the completion of what is moved. In its primary sense, presence, for Aristotle, is the persisting of something which persists of itself—the substance of the individual thing. Aristotle makes explicit, for the first time, the individual as the actual: being *qua* being is the enduring of what is realized in the individual thing.[1]

### i. Essence as Substance

Aristotle accounts for the origin of first philosophy by claiming that those of his predecessors who posited "the forms," although they have not explicitly introduced the notion of essence, have come closest to this notion, for they perceived the forms as something like the essential nature of all other things. Yet they failed to see the problem in what they posited. For how can the forms, if they are the substances of things, abide in separation from these things? Aristotle thus judges his predecessors to have spoken "falteringly" in first philosophy, and, in announcing this philosophy as the science which includes everything, he first requires a distinguishing of the several senses in which things are said *to be* in ordinary discourse.²

The faltering efforts of Aristotle's predecessors have something to do with the fact that, although first philosophy deals with the most obvious principles, the human mind in respect to these principles is in a situation somewhat like that of bats in daylight. Although it is the familiar that is intelligible, the principles which are most true (because they cause all other things to be true) are "dark" to human understanding. This means that human understanding cannot simultaneously seek for knowledge *and* for the method of procuring it; nor can there be demonstration of everything. In effect, the term "being" is used in several senses, but it must have reference to one idea and definite nature; it is not merely a common "epithet." Because of this, first philosophy can be said to be the science which studies being *qua* being and the properties inherent in it by virtue of its own nature—a science which attempts to grasp the first causes of being *qua* being (ὂν ᾗ ὄν).³

The diverse senses of being, then, require that being always have reference to one principle, and this one principle is substance (οὐσία). Thus, it is of substances that the first philosopher must seek the first principles and causes, not by way of the exercises of dialectic but by understanding (γνωριστική). This understanding proceeds from a principle at once most familiar and most certain, namely, that it is not possible for the same attribute to be at once predicated and not predicated of the same thing in the same relation. This most certain of all principles is not itself demonstrable, since all demonstration presupposes it as a necessary and ultimate "opinion."⁴

Not only, then, is there a primary signification among the diverse significations of "being," but this signification as such is a definite meaning pertaining to both *to be* and *not to be*. The very existence of what is accidental implies a predication about some substrate (ὑποκειμένου) in order that the predication itself not proceed to infinity. The accidental presupposes a signification for the necessary, for what cannot be otherwise, and it is from this sense that all other senses of the necessary are derived. But this means that the necessary in its primary and proper sense is the simple, for it cannot *be* on more than one condition. This, in turn, would entail that those things are truly united whose concept (in which the essence is thought) cannot be separated either in time or in place; and of these, such as are substances are most truly one. Thus the one is seen to be the starting point of what is knowable in respect to each particular thing. Consequently, insofar as we are addressing absolute being as distinguished from accidental being, we are dealing with two senses of substance: first, the ultimate substrate which cannot be further predicated of something else, and second, whatever has an individual and separate existence, that is, the shape and form of each individual thing (ἑκάστου). Insofar as we are addressing accidental being, we are dealing with the definition of potency (δυνάμεως) in the primary sense, namely, a principle which produces change but which is in something external to that in which the change takes place.[5]

Since being as accidental cannot be the object of first or primary philosophy, this philosophy differs from all other sciences in that these sciences focus on some existent thing or class of things and give no account of the essence (τί ἐστιν), whereas first philosophy endeavors to find the principles and causes of the things which are *qua* being. In being concerned with what *is* primarily, not with what is in a qualified sense, first philosophy is concerned with the primary sense of being, that sense which denotes the "what," that is, substance. In this way, the most fundamental of all questions, the one raised long ago by Aristotle's predecessors, and the one which will always be raised, namely, "What is being?" (τί τὸ ὄν), is none other than the question "What is substance?". Among the four principal significations of "substance," namely, the essence, the universal, the genus, and the substrate, the last one is that of which the others are predicated, while it is not itself predicated of anything else. However, if the substrate is to be taken as the first sense of substance, it must be said that it is not matter alone but the form united to the matter which is most properly substance. Insofar as the formula for essence is that which defines the term for what is defined but does not contain that term, it can be said that the primary signification of essence is substance, since the "what it is" is said unqualifiedly of substance and only qualifiedly of all else. But this is to say that each individual thing is one and the same with its essence, for to have knowledge of the individual is precisely to have knowledge of its essence. In fact, essence as such really means nothing more than "substance without matter."[6]

In this way, the completed whole of the individual thing is to be distinguished from that which generated it by virtue of its matter; but its form (being indivisible) is identical with the form of that which generated it. However, the individual thing in its concrete particularity has no definition, but can only be apprehended by the formula of the universal. It is precisely the fact that particular sensible substances contain matter—which can be said both to be and not to be—that accounts for their indefinableness. Nonetheless, the universal never exists as separate apart from its particulars, and so no universal term by itself can be a substance. Far from being a component or element of an individual thing, substance is a principle which accounts for *this* matter's being one thing and *that* matter's being another. Always it is the givenness of the thing, the nature of the thing, which determines the rightness of the thought or the language about the thought.

The sense, then, in which being is substance is precisely the same as the sense in which being is unity, for in "one man" nothing more is predicated than in "man"; but to be one is always to be an individual thing.[7] In founding first philosophy, Aristotle has made explicit the individual thing as the actual.

### ii. Divine Substance

It is, however, the real-ization of the singular thing, the inseparability of substance and that of which it is substance, which requires—for Aristotle—that not everything, that is, not every substance, can exist unseparated from singular things. For if it were the case that all substances existed only in and as individual or particular things, it would follow that every substance would be sensible. This would mean—unless one were willing to concede that sense perception as such is knowledge—that there could be no knowledge of anything: nothing would be intelligible. For first philosophy to be a science of absolutely first principles, that is, for first philosophy to be wisdom, this philosophy, consequently, must be in search of a peculiar meaning of substance, one which exists apart from and independently of other substances and has no connection with sensible things. The very fact that nearly all of his predecessors sought for such a peculiar meaning of substance suggests to Aristotle that it would seem natural that such a meaning exists. For how can there be any order in the universe unless there is some meaning of substance which is *in* the universe—a meaning which is eternal, separate ($\chi\omega\rho\iota\sigma\tau o\hat{\upsilon}$), and permanent?

What is somewhat perplexing, however, is that all sciences treat of universals and not particulars, and yet substances are always found as particularized universals. But, in the case of the peculiar meaning of substance sought after by first philosophy, substance is something separable from sensible things. This perplexity is removed by recognizing that although substance as such is not a universal, the science which constitutes first philosophy is concerned with being *qua* being universally and not with some part of being. First philosophy, although it investigates substance as such (substance being in some way inherent in the individual thing), does not investigate particular things as such, that is, individual things in so far as each of them has some definite attribute, but studies that which *is*, in so far as each particular thing *is*. The concern of this science with universality is thus a concern with a principle inherent in particular things. And this principle, about which we cannot make a mistake and which is most familiar and most certain, is that the same thing cannot at the same time both be and not be. But unless this principle finds its operation in a Being that is separate from sensible things and not characterized by the movement of sensible things, then its immanence in sensible things makes no sense. In this way, first philosophy, as the highest science (whose province is the attributes which belong to being *qua* being), turns out to be theology, as distinguished from mathematics and physics.[8]

Whereas, then, physics deals with things containing a source of motion in themselves, and mathematics deals with permanent things but with things which cannot exist separately, first philosophy or theology deals with that which exists separately and is immovable. And if there is such a substance in this world of (natural) things, here certainly must be the divine, the first and most fundamental principle (ἀρχή) of which first philosophy is in search. As theology, first philosophy would have to be the highest of the speculative sciences because, in effect, it would be dealing with the most important aspect of reality. And yet such a substance would not be infinite, for the infinite (τὸ ἄπειρον) has no actual existence since, if it did, any part of it would itself be infinite.

But if first philosophy is ultimately concerned with a substance that is divine, it is nonetheless concerned with an operation that contains its own generative principle, that is, a substance which belongs to nature, for nature is a generative principle in the thing itself. If all substances cannot be perishable, since otherwise all reality would be perishable, and since everything that is moved, while it moves, is something intermediate, there must be something which moves without being moved and which is both actual (ἐνέργεια) and a substance. This substance which moves without being moved is such that it is the object of desire (τὸ ὀρεκτόν) and the object of thought. As unmoved and actual, it causes motion insofar as it is an object of love, whereas all other things cause motion because they themselves are in motion.

Such, then, is the first principle upon which depend the heavens and the natural world, and its life is like the best which human beings enjoy only for a brief time. Of this Being it can be said that since thinking in itself is concerned with that which is in itself best, thinking in the highest sense is concerned with that which is in the highest sense best. In this Being, then, thought thinks itself through participation in the object of thought.* Thought and the object of thought are the same because that which is the object of thought (i.e., essence) is thinking itself. Moreover, since the actualization of thought is life, and this Being is actual (and in no way potential), the essence of this Being is life "most good and eternal." Therefore, life and a continuous (eternal) existence belong to the divine, for that is what the God (ὁ θεός) is. There is, Aristotle concludes, some substance which has its being in the world and is eternal, immovable, and separate from sensible things.[9]

This substance, moreover, cannot have finite magnitude, for it is impartible and indivisible, nor can it have infinite magnitude, for there is no such thing. Given the impassive and unalterable nature of this Being, Aristotle can say of the traditional myths, to the extent that they presuppose that the divine pervades the whole of nature, and to the extent that the gods of which they speak can be regarded as "primary substances," that they ought to be regarded as "inspired sayings." For the nature of this divine substance (which is most truly substance) is that Mind thinks itself (if it is that which is best), and its thinking is a "thinking of thinking."° Since thought and the object of thought do not differ in this Being—for this Being contains no matter—it follows that the act of thinking in this Being will be identical with the object of thought. And much as the human mind can be said to exist in a certain space of time, so also the absolute self-thought of this Being can be said to exist throughout all eternity. As to the question of how the world can be said to contain this supreme good—whether as something separate from and independent of its parts or as the orderly arrangement of its parts—Aristotle answers that it is probably in both senses, much as the efficiency of an army consists partly in its order and partly in the general. But just as the efficiency of the army consists chiefly in the general (for he does not depend upon the army's order, but that order depends upon him), so also the world

---

\* αὑτὸν δὲ νοεῖ ὁ νοῦς κατὰ μετάληψιν τοῦ νοητοῦ

° ἡ νόησις νοήσεως νόησις

contains its supreme good *principally* as something separate from and independent of its parts.

In securing first philosophy as theology, Aristotle claims to have overcome the difficulty inherent in the Platonic theory of the forms, namely, that the proponents of this theory treat the forms as universal substances but also as separable and particular. The problem is that, on the Platonic view, universals and particulars are practically the same kind of thing. For Aristotle, although it is clear that in one sense knowledge is universal, it is also clear that in another sense it is not.[10] Substance as he sees it is not so much a universal but rather inheres in particular sensible things. But it can do this only because substance as purely actual exists apart from sensible things as the pure universality of a thinking which thinks itself.

### iii. First Philosophy as Theology

Joseph Owens, in his classic study of Aristotle's first philosophy, notes how being *qua* being, for Aristotle, becomes identifiable with a being separate from sensible substance, and how amid the diverse senses of being, which Aristotle presents, he himself does not appear conscious of a fundamental inconsistency among these diverse senses. The thing known is never as such the terminus of a process in which a change in the nature of the thing has occurred by virtue of the knowing process. The thing known is always prior to conceptualization and verbalization. Because of this, it is always the formal cause—which contains the ultimate meaning of all other causes—which is most knowable. Aristotle's starting point, namely, the being of individual things, is never absent throughout his first philosophy, but the question from start to finish is precisely how these individual things can be known in their particularity as one and the same with themselves. Always the principle of what makes these things knowable and what makes them permanent has to be located in these sensible things themselves. This principle is substance, for it is in reference to substance that all other things are being. Being *qua* being is seen to be identical with substance, for substance alone contains in itself the nature of being.

But substance must in some way extend itself to all other beings, if being *qua* being is to have its primary meaning in substance and if, in having this primary meaning, it is to be regarded as an entity which is not abstract. Being *qua* being is thus determinate, definite, although the question for Aristotle is precisely how this determinate entity can be universal in regard to all other beings. What enables it to be universal in this regard is its priority to all else—priority in the sense in which the divine, the immobile and eternal, is prior to what moves and is moved, while at the same time being *in* visible and sensible things as their first principle. If, then, primary being, that is, substance, is the being which comes to expression in every other instance of being, Aristotle's move in first philosophy to a substance separate from sensible substances is precisely a response to studying all beings in so far as they are being, that is, a response to contemplation of the divine in things sensible or visible to man. Theology is what a first philosophy, which attempts to grasp the nature of the being of individual things, will have to be.[11]

In singling out substrate as the primary sense of substance, Aristotle is, in effect, singling out the form as that through which the matter is substance, much as he isolates substance as that through which the accidents can be said *to be*. Form is thus seen to be both the cause of the unity which characterizes the singular or individual thing and the ground of the definition of universals. In a sense, the form—in being the cause of both the individual unity of the singular thing and the universality of the definition which applies to the genus or species to which the individual thing belongs—is neither singular nor universal. But this form is no longer a Platonic form or idea but is visible to the human mind in sensible things alone, that is, in things which by their nature are changeable. In this way, the form (which is unchangeable) must be prior to sensible individuals while at the same time being within them and identical with them. While it cannot be a universal, the form has to be the basis of the determinate identity of each singular thing which is signified by the universal. While it cannot be a particular, the form has to be the cause of the unity which Aristotle associates with the individual, sensible thing. It is, then, Owens argues, the coincidence of universality and particularity that we find in the forms of sensible things. It is one and the same form which is actually individual and potentially universal, and this is what is involved in the meaning of form as act, for Aristotle.

But it is precisely the way in which things are known without undergoing any change in themselves which suggests to Aristotle the notion of a separated substance which is desired without undergoing any change in itself—that is, the notion of an unmoved mover. Furthermore, Aristotle assumes that if this Being must be the very perfection of form itself, without any matter, then this Being must be pure mind, for a form which is not as such the form of a matter would have to be pure mind—mind dependent on no other thing. And so, this divine substance must be a knowing of itself, wherein (unlike all other substances) the know*ing* rather than the know*able*ness is the "divine" aspect. Thus, whereas the good of the universe would seem to be found in both its inherent order and the separate entity which serves as the desired object for all moved things, it is in the separate entity that this good primarily abides and in the inherent order that it abides in a secondary way.[12]

If, then, for Aristotle, there are as many different things signified by "to be" as there are ways of using this term, but the primary signification is substance, of which alone it can be said that it *is* a being rather than merely that it is *of* a being,[13] it also follows that this primary being itself (substance) has primary and secondary significations. The primary signification is the form in sensible things, a form which, in turn, in *its* primary signification is seen to be the pure act of the divine Being. As the act or ενεργεια found in sensible things, form is necessary and unchangeable and the basis of universality. But when found separate from matter, it is purely actual in such a way that it is a pure knowing, a perfection of knowledge as pure form without matter, that is, a knowing of knowing or thinking of thinking. Sensible things, existing as singular and particular (and, therefore, as corruptible), cannot be or attain this divinity, but this divinity is seen in the perpetuity of the species to which these singular things belong. Ultimately, although singular things have inherent in them being as such, being in its primary signification, that is, substance, they themselves—in and by themselves —do not matter when compared to the perpetuity of their species and the divinity of which their species are mobile imitations. Effectively substance pertains to material things because the forms of these things are capable of sharing more or less in the perpetuity of the divine. All other substances are capable of being, of enduring in being, to the degree that they imitate the perdurance, the self-contained permanence, of the separate divine substance.

In the final analysis, *to be* means to endure, to perdure, to be present as permanent, not to change. Sensible, individual things have this primary sense of *to be* operative within them, but they themselves (insofar as they are particular) are not this *to be*. And when we call these sensible things by their own proper names, we are expressing their "proper" nature, namely, to have the principle of the permanence of being within them while not as such *being* that principle. But when we call them "being" in the primary sense, we are thereby expressing not their proper nature, but the nature of the divine of which they are an imitation or μίμησις and in relation to which they are a *desire*. Much as what is contemplated in the statue of a man is not the statue but the man of which it is a statue, so also what is contemplated in the individual, sensible things in the world is the divinity immanent in this world—the being of the primary unmoved mover and of thought thinking itself.

The absence of a (positive) notion of infinity and of a (negative) notion of contingency for the world in the Aristotelian first philosophy only serves to confirm all of this. For there is no primary sense of being which in some way is not form or reducible to form and (therefore) finite. There can be no primary signification of being which transcends form, not to mention an act of "existence" which is irreducible to form, or an absolute act of creation of form as such.[14] First philosophy, here, finds its focus in the realization of form in nature, in a nature populated by individual, sensible things which are imitations of and desires for a divine perfection which, although it completely transcends matter, is nonetheless immanent in nature.

The unity of Aristotle's first philosophy which emerges in Owens' exposition and interpretation is also manifest in that of Giovanni Reale. The sensible individuals which lie at the starting point of Aristotelian first philosophy, as Reale notes, are the objects of experience. But experience is constituted by sensations, and here we never attain a knowledge of the "why." It is in art or τέχνη that we first meet this knowledge of the "why." But, whereas art always aims at production, science (ἐπιστήμη) is purely theoretical or ordered to the contemplation of truth. As the supreme science, first philosophy makes explicit the first principles of all other sciences and, therefore, of all beings, but in such a way that the mystery of the being of these beings is not dispelled but more fully disclosed. But the being of these beings is not something universal in all things, nor is it a genus gathering up diverse species (as it seems to be in Plato). Whether we are talking about the being of privation, or the being of qualities, or the being of generation, we are talking about the being of substance deprived of something, or of substance qualified by something, or of substance generating or producing. And this implies that the highest science, which deals with substance as such, must be said to be theological in order to distinguish it from the science of physics *after* which it is said to come. In starting with sensible substances and in remaining fixed in its gaze on sensible substances, first philosophy opens into (and discloses itself to be) theology.*

---

* In effect, if the question of what is being *qua* being turns out to be the question of what is substance, this latter question can only be answered satisfactorily upon answering the question of what substances actually exist. In answering this question, in turn, by alluding to sensible substances, we see a unity in which the matter and the form constitute one same thing, the matter being the thing in potency and the form being the thing in act—but always the selfsame thing. This means that sensible substance does not exhaust the answer to the question of what substances exist, since the priority of act would have to entail a sequence of actualizations in which one actualization always comes before another temporally, until we reach the act of the unchanging and eternal prime mover. The question of what substances there are, there-

The world disclosed by this first philosophy, then, is something like a three-tiered, autonomous, organic entity. The lowest and most inferior, but most immediate level is composed of sensible and perishable substances constituted by form (εἶδος) and matter (and, therefore, by act and potency). Here the potentiality and destructibility of these substances, these individual or particular things, issue from the presence of matter (ὕλη) which, as such, is an irrational substrate for reality. On the second level are sensible but incorruptible or eternal substances, the occupants of the heavens, which, in their perpetual circular motion, have their own peculiar matter that enables them to be in potency only in regard to certain aspects of their being. These substances reflect the eternal nature of the universe, an eternity that is somehow shared with matter. On the third and highest tier are the unmoved movers and among them the prime mover, pure form, substance without matter (and, therefore, pure act—but a pure act which does not transcend the world of which it is the desired perfection, a perfection, in the end, immanent in nature). Because of the existence of the second level, astronomy is seen to be the science which is closest to that of first philosophy since both have as their object substances which are eternal. On the other hand, astronomy is closer to physics than it is to first philosophy since, like physics, it has as its object substances which are sensible and mobile. Only first philosophy, as theology, has as its object the eternal, unmoved, suprasensible substance of nature.

In the final analysis, then, as Reale sees it, theology is no mere postscript to Aristotle's first philosophy but is the ultimate and complete sense of that philosophy. There would be no first philosophy were there no primary substance, no separate divine substance existing apart from sensible substances; physics or, rather, astronomy would be the highest science.[15]

---

fore, can only be answered in such a way that first philosophy is seen to be theology.

### iv. The Being of Beings

The interpretation of Aristotle's first philosophy provided by Werner Marx fills out the interpretations of Owens and Reale and returns us to our initial allusion to Heidegger's perception of that philosophy in terms of the individual as the actual and the actual as the enduring.

The world that frames the Aristotelian first philosophy is one in which being is readily manifested in nature—in which, to use Heideggerian terminology, "the Being of beings in its *difference* from beings"[16] becomes clear in and to man at the highest reach of his engagement in science. Man is the gathering point of the truth of this Being *of* beings, that is, the point where, as Marx suggests, the first truths are dis-concealed. This self-disclosure of reality to the contemplating mind of man is possible because there is a nature (φύσις) by virtue of which being*s*, that is, particular things, are said to have particular nature*s*. The being that runs through beings, being *qua* being, is never an hypostatized being, for being means an occurrence inherent in particular and individual things as an immanent principle of determination. And the nature which accounts for particularization, though it is dis-concealed in man, exists independently of man's faculty of thinking or even his desire to think. The substance disclosed in man's highest science is never as such the particular being of the knowing agent (of man as a subject). What we have, instead, is that man, in contemplating being *qua* being, in trying to bespeak the nature running through particular natures, discovers that only the nature of substance is accessible to him. The Aristotelian philosopher, in directing his attention to the many substances in the world, sees the diverse ways by which these substances "substantiate" themselves. These diverse ways are simply moments of "the one pregiven unity of substantiality" articulated (by man) *as* the prime unmoved mover and thought thinking itself.[17]

In this way, the philosopher knows being primarily as a substantiality that is in and for itself and from which the subsistence of all else is derived. This substantiality is the Being for which the individual thing, the matter-form unity, strives. This striving, in fact, is precisely what makes it a "this." But if being speaks through man, that is, man is the point where its dis-concealment occurs (although *what* is disclosed is higher than man), the language that man speaks, in its constitution as a striving for absolute permanence, never quite reaches the "this." All the categories of language, as man speaks it, are universal and designate a "such" but not a "this." And yet, in first philosophy, man, as that being in which being discloses itself, directs his attention to the power that empowers, the act that enacts, in all of nature—a substantiality that is neither strictly a "this" nor strictly a "such" but can only be spoken of in terms of "such," in terms of universal categories. Thus, man speaks of substantiality as determining the diverse ways *to be* of the many beings of nature, beings in which potency is silently present in act, and act is present "absently," so to speak, (by its being an ever-not-yet) in potency. In all of this, the substantiality of substances, the being of beings, the reality of the real is never touched by predicates, for certainly this substantiality cannot be a predicate of anything, no more than it could be the "this" that it actuates—or any "this" for that matter. It can best be articulated as the divine permanence which broods over all of nature, as an immanent completion in nature, which all of nature strives for: the perfection of all of nature's movement, the perfect rest toward which all movement is a striving. And in this way, *existence* never becomes a problem for Aristotle; the existence of the "this" is in no way problematic, since it is simply given, simply "there." The only problem is its "why"; only the "why" leads the philosopher to wonder, leads man to philosophy.

But this "why," in first philosophy, is not the "why" of everyday questioning which seeks for the efficient cause of things, but the "why" that strives to dis-conceal what constituted this particular being, this individual, to be this actual individual. It is the "why" of formal causality, but ultimately a formal causality which seeks to disclose the "wherefore," the final cause or, better yet, the "final form" for the good of which all particular things are what they are. In this way, man can speak of being *qua* being; the substantiality of substances is seen as an end (τέλος). Substance *qua* end, Marx suggests, is for Aristotle the "only humanly accessible expression" of being *qua* being. God cannot be among particular individuals, among beings whose form can only be intelligible by reference to matter, among beings whose act must entail potency. Rather, the substantiality of God, substantiality *qua* substantiality, can only be spoken of, albeit imperfectly, as pure form, pure act, that is, thought thinking itself, the actuality of mind (νοῦς).[18]

Aristotelian first philosophy, in starting with the contemplation of the sensible individual, the composite unity of matter and form, that is, the concrete whole, sees this individual as a living endeavor to realize the perfection of form, the perfection of mind which is God. This perfection of form must exist as separate from all sensible substances, but it is "visible," so to speak, among the sensible substances to which man has access in the universe. And this is suggested by the very etymology of the primary word in Aristotle's first philosophy, namely, οὐσία, which appears to be formed from ὤν, the participial form of εἰμί which means primarily "to be."[19] Here we have hinted at the "to be" of beings, the "to be" which is the realization of the particular individual, which is to be identified with the individual as actual, but which can be so identified only because what makes this individual actual is a striving for the absolute "to be" of the permanence that is the "nature" of all of nature and which man can speak of as "the God."

Aristotle can be said to be the founder of first philosophy, then, because he makes explicit for the first time the individual as that which is actual, and that which is actual as the enduring, which, when bespoken, amount to the language of theology. For the individual as actual is a striving for the enduring of being that *is* God. What unifies the diverse senses of being is the notion of being *qua* being which is identified with substance; and what unifies the diverse senses of substance (namely, that which is capable of existing independently, the essential characteristics, the concrete particular, a center for change, a logical subject, and a substratum) is the notion of being as the lasting or permanence of the actual—being present to itself, i.e., being as the permanent presence for which all beings are a striving. In this lies the founding event of first philosophy, the initiation of the history of the concept of being. The Aristotelian notion of substance, then, must set the course for the history of first philosophy. But in setting the course for this history, this notion must, ineluctably, be transformed by and in the very process of that history. The question of being *qua* being is launched on a course that will turn out to be a "travail"; and the answer which Aristotle gave—which even for him could not remain unquestioned—will prove to be a deepening of the question.

### v. Aristotle and Anselm

Werner Marx and Heidegger clearly portray the primary place in Aristotle of the individual as that which is actual; and Owens and Reale clearly portray the primary place of theology in Aristotle. But Reale and Marx do not spell out the implications of what they portray for medieval thought and, therefore, do not seem to recognize fully its crucial role in Aristotle himself. And, whereas Owens and Heidegger do see the implications of what they portray for medieval thought in general, they do not dwell on its implications for St. Anselm in particular.

The history of the concept of being entails a transformation of the notion of being as the lasting or permanence of the actual being, i.e., a transformation of the notion of substance. This transformation has a history in both Christianity's appropriation of first philosophy and first philosophy's appropriation of Christianity. In this reciprocal appropriation it becomes clear that even when there is hesitation in applying the term "substance" to God, no other category can be found which is more appropriate, for there really can be no possibility of approaching the being of God as a quality, quantity, or relation. Instead, what we find is the adoption of the term "substance" and a complex transformation of the meaning of that term largely in terms of two traditions that are inextricably intertwined.

The first tradition is negative theology or the "via negativa" in which the divine mystery elicits an emphasis on the negative character of all language about God which would assimilate him to the natural world and the categories of ordinary human discourse. The second tradition is more pedagogically oriented, a "paideia," which attempts to make the divine "substance" accessible to men and which dwells on what can reasonably be expected of men in their relation *to it*. In a sense, these two traditions reflect, respectively, the biblical attributes of the divine justice and the divine mercy, and together they constitute the dialectics of transcendence and immanence, faith and reason. These dialectics find their highest embodiment in Scholasticism where the "via negativa" and "paideia" become a remarkable unity. At the heart of this embodiment is the appropriation and transfiguration of Aristotelian first philosophy. In this appropriation and transfiguration, Aristotelian substance serves to ground the claim that although man is related to God (in a way that he could never be in Aristotelian first philosophy), God is nonetheless not circumscribed by man's relation to him but exists in and of himself. In the process of justifying this claim, however, the notion of substance must be transformed precisely because the God in question is no longer a divinity arrived at in the context of popular belief in the gods. Far from being a God who is denoted by a process in which the gods are reflected on and then all claimants to divinity are eliminated except one, this is a God who is absolutely unique, no part of nature, no aspect of the reality of the world, no immanent perfection of nature. And this means that the name "deus" has to be used with a different logic than "θεὸs," even though the older usage is not entirely lost.[20]

The impact that this new logic has for the history of the concept of being is suggested by Heidegger. The nature of the distinction between "whatness" and "thatness" changes, i.e., the character of *act* in the founding of first philosophy changes into actua*lity*. When being has been transformed into actuality, it is now being*s* that are seen to be real. The concept of being changes from an ἐνέργεια which is immanent in nature to an "actualitas" which is more-than-natural. It is this change which affords to being*s* as a whole that unique status which the representation of the biblical-

Christian belief in Creation can appropriate for itself in order to secure a kind of metaphysical justification (Rechtfertigung).

Actuality, however, now becomes a causality which manifests itself in its purity in that Being which fulfills the *essence* of being in the highest sense because it is that Being which can never "not be"—that Being which when theologically thought is called "God." The greatest being is pure real-ization (Verwirklichung), forever fulfilled, pure act ("actus purus"), which is the greatest good. The goodness of this Being is the cause of all other causes.[21]

This transformation of an ἐνέργεια immanent in nature into an "actualitas" which transcends nature—this transformation of substance in terms of a causality and good which are not *of* this world of realized forms (and which transcend form as such)—means the appearance (in the history of the concept of being) of a unique, particular substance, an hypostatized substantiality, which is a primal subject of being completely other than this world. And this transformation finds its first explicitly metaphysical embodiment at the beginning of that unification of the "via negativa" and "paideia" known as Scholasticism. St. Anselm's first philosophy is this beginning and embodiment, for it is nothing less than the notion of being *qua* being operative in Anselm's thought which unifies his Ontological Argument and indicates his implicit transformation of Aristotelian first philosophy. It is within Anselm's reliance on the notion of God (and God alone) as the subject of being (who is entirely one and the same with himself with no dissimilarity to himself as a result of having parts)[22] that we find the metaphysical transformation of an act resident in nature to an actuality dependent in no way on its being realized in nature.

In the sense that Aristotle saw an act in all natural entities—a drive toward achieving their own proper end—he perceived this endeavor toward permanence as an imitation (to the extent that the limitations of matter permitted) of the one pure form or perfection of the end or τέλος whose "effortless activity" is unimpeded by any matter. Yet he found the basis for this inference to a self-moving principle in a fact of man's experience of nature, namely, desire.[23] It is Anselm's radical recasting of this desire, his resituating it in terms of an actuality which is uncontingent (as distinguished from the contingency of *all* of nature) which signals his transformation of the Aristotelian first philosophy. As such, this transformation is continuous with the Aristotelian identification of first philosophy with theology. There is and can be no decisive break with this founding in the first philosophy of Anselm: there can be no new beginning for first philosophy in Anselm. Yet, underneath his continuity with the Aristotelian founding are palpably discontinuous elements that will constitute the ground for the modern effort to effect a complete break with the founding.

But this means that the historical travail of first philosophy from the substantiality of nature in Aristotle to the more-than-natural subjectivity of man in Descartes is not unmediated. If Cartesian first philosophy is a radical break with the Aristotelian founding of that philosophy, it cannot be a complete break with the Anselmian transformation of that founding. Anselm both transforms the Aristotelian founding and provides what will prove to be the ground of Descartes' refounding of first philosophy.

Perhaps Anselm's contention that it is "negligence" for the Christian believer to make no effort to understand what he believes[*] prompted Dante to place Anselm in paradise among the privileged ministers of the divine gift of reason.[°] Anselm has been called the "father" of Scholasticism[**] and the first purveyor of a "Christian rationalism."[∞24] This is certainly not to be construed as denying that Anselm stands in a long tradition going back to Boethius in the sixth century. Yet by transforming the Aristotelian founding of first philosophy, Anselm provides what will prove to be the ground of Descartes' refounding of first philosophy. The scope of

---

[*] See Anselm's *Cur Deus Homo*, Book I, ch. 1.

[°] See Canto XII of Dante's *Paradiso*.

[**] By M. Grabmann, *Die Geschichte der scholastischen Methode* (Freiburg, 1909), Vol. I, p. 58.

[∞] By H. Bouchitté, *Le rationalisme chrétien de saint Anselme* (Paris, 1842).

Anselm's provision of what will prove to be the ground of Descartes' efforts can be detected in Anselm's *dialogue* in first philosophy—the *Proslogion*. The scope of Anselm's transformation of Aristotle's founding of first philosophy can be discovered in Anselm's *meditation* on first philosophy and its method—the *Monologion*.

## II

# Anselm's Meditation on First Philosophy

In his *De Grammatico*, St. Anselm gives an example of his distinction between appellation and signification: the term "literate" is predicated (appellativum) of man and not of literacy but it signifies (significativum) literacy and not man.[1] So also, we might suggest, the term "existent," for Anselm, is predicated or said of God and not of existence but it signifies existence and not God. Being, in other words, is what can be said (or what must be predicated) of God, but it does not as such signify God. Being is proposed as the predicate of an absolutely unique and supra-natural "something" and no longer simply as substance or the presence of the permanent to itself in nature.

The Aristotelian notion of substance, however, as the permanence of the actual present to itself (the notion of the particular "this" as a striving, a desire) lives on in Anselm, no longer in the context of the Aristotelian notion of an uncreated nature ($\varphi\acute{v}\sigma\iota\varsigma$) but in the context of a nature that is created ("natura") out of nothing. This new context for first philosophy is spelled out in Anselm's meditation on first philosophy, his *Monologion*. In this meditation the founding of the science which examines being *qua* being is both secured in order to be transformed and transformed in order to be made more secure. The science itself is now shown to have a history that is decisive for the science; for, given Anselm's transformation of the founding of first philosophy, Aristotle—although his name be never mentioned—cannot be said to have spoken "falteringly."

## i. The Being Among Beings

In his preface to the *Monologion*, Anselm indicates that he writes this work—from the viewpoint of a man "disputing and investigating" in "solitary thought"—as a sample of meditation on the divine essence at the behest of certain of his brethren who urged him to commit to writing something of what he had given them in conversational discourse. In order that what Scripture says should not be argued on its own authority, Anselm will attempt to make faith an *object* for the "clarity of truth" and the "necessity of reason."\* Central to this work is Anselm's use of "substance" which follows the terminology of the Greek Fathers who spoke of three "substances" and one "person" in the Trinity. But he notes that this was said in the same faith as the Latin Fathers who spoke of "three persons in one substance," for the former designate by "substance" that quality of God which the Latin tradition designates by "person." An Aristotelian term, central to Aristotle's first philosophy, will be central to that of Anselm, but the transformation of the signification of this term is already intimated.

The meditation proper begins by considering a being among beings, namely, that Being which is "best," "greatest," and "supreme" among all beings. But Anselm initiates this consideration by alluding to the man who is ignorant of this Being either through not hearing or not believing. Such a man would hold, despite his lack of knowledge, that if he could convince himself of this Being's nature, it would have to be by "reason alone." Even were his powers of mind quite ordinary, it would be natural for such a man to turn the "eye" of his mind to the consideration of that cause by which the things he estimates to be good are good, and from here he would be led rationally to the truths of which he is ignorant in an irrational way. Although the conclusion he would reach might not

---

\* His attempt is inspired by the charity of his brethren, for it is precisely their having made copies of this work that has consigned it to a long remembrance. For those who might be tempted to view the ideas of this work as "too novel," Anselm asks that they judge it in the light of St. Augustine's *De Trinitate*. But this is the only reference he makes to a prior authority.

be entirely necessary, it would be reached as if it were necessary, i.e., it would appear necessary for the time being. And this is precisely the way in which Anselm proposes any argument in this meditation for which no greater authority than the argument itself can be adduced. Anselm cannot assume the perspective of unbelief in the nonbeliever but he can assume the perspective of reason in the nonbeliever who reasons, for this is the same perspective of reason as that in the believer who reasons. The nonbeliever is just as much committed to making his unbelief an object of reason as the believer is committed to making his belief an object of reason.\* As to whether these objects could exist on the same level, Anselm does not as yet say, but the reason is the same, even when the powers of mind differ.²

This reason is inevitably drawn to the conclusion that, among the diverse goods we experience by the senses or discern by the mind, there is some one thing which is good in itself and by comparison with which all other goods can be said to be more or less good. This highest good is alone good through itself and, as such, is "supremely good." In order to be supremely good, this particular being among beings must be great through itself, not in the sense of "spatial magnitude" but in the sense of greatness as applied to something like wisdom, namely, the greater it is, the better or more worthy it is. Unlike Aristotle for whom the existence of the "this" is unproblematic but is simply given as "there"—the focus of first philosophy being the "why," the formal causality operative in the "this"—the existence of the "this" is supremely problematic for Anselm. The existence of a multiplicity of good things requires an accounting for their existence in terms of one particular thing that is "supremely great."

The being of the particular—existence—is now problematic for first philosophy. There must be a certain nature through which whatever else, that *seems* to exist, exists. Everything that is said to

---

\* Anselm remarks in ch. 3, Book I of his *Cur Deus Homo* that while the nonbeliever seeks "arguments of reason" because he does not believe, and while the believer seeks these argument precisely because he does believe, nevertheless what both are seeking is "one and the same."

exist must exist through some thing since nothing exists through *no* thing. Thus, what is said to exist must either be referred to some one thing (unum aliquid) through which it is, or it must exist separately through itself, or it must exist mutually with other things. The last possibility, however, is an "irrational thought." How can anything exist through a being on which it confers existence? The second possibility implies some power or property of existing through itself, a power which cannot be shared by more than one particular thing, since whatever exists through itself exists in the greatest degree of all things. It follows, then, that there can only be some one particular thing, the "unum aliquid" of the first possibility, of which essence or substance is properly said, namely, that particular being which of all beings is best, greatest, and highest.[3]

But this means that the many particular things, whose existence (and not merely unity) is problematic in first philosophy, are not all contained by an "equality of dignity," but among them are things characterized by an inequality of degree. If the distinction of degrees (graduum distinctio) among these particular things were infinite, we would have to conclude that they would not be limited by any bounds. Since this conclusion is unwarranted, reason "persuades" us that there is a nature among them which has no superior. This particular nature (aliqua natura) is so superior to other natures that there is none, by comparison, with which it could be ranked as inferior. If "nature" here is understood in the sense of "essence," this superior nature would be the essence of these other natures. The problematical character of the existence of particular things, then, can only be resolved if among all these existing beings there is a certain nature, substance, or essence which is through itself good and great, and "through itself is that which it is," and through which exists whatever is truly good or great or whatever is something at all. This Being derives existence from itself while other beings derive existence from it.

But how is existence through and from itself able to be understood? Certainly the same signification does not belong to being in that which exists through itself as belongs to being in those things which exist through another, for whatever exists through another exists through some "other aid" as if through an "instrument," and it is always in some sense posterior. But the "highest nature," since it cannot exist through another or be posterior to anything, is not able to be created either by itself or by another. But if it cannot come into being by any creative agency, this supreme nature would seem to be either nothing at all or, if it is something, to derive its existence from nothing. Anselm's personal meditation on first philosophy has brought him to a fundamental objection to his train of thought. If this train of thought is to have a "more established strength" which comes from leaving no ambiguity, such that even slower minds can grasp it, it is incumbent upon Anselm to pass over no objection that occurs to him in his private disputation. It is incumbent upon him, in other words, to attempt to weave a proof (probationem contexere) for the falsity and absurdity of the propositions that the supreme nature is nothing and that the supreme nature exists through nothing.

Since, in the first place, he argues, this supreme nature, this essence, cannot exist prior to itself, it follows that in no way can it exist through itself out of nothing, for to have derived its existence (exstitisse) from nothing would mean that it could not be the highest of all things, the supreme nature. It is, then, not even understandable that some thing (or even nothing) preceded this "supreme substance" which cannot be understood to have come to exist even from its own "matter." Much as there is light (lux), the act of lighting (lucet), and the quality of being light (lucens), so also in the highest substance there is essence (essentia), existence (esse), and the quality or predicate of being (ens). And as with light, these three are one and the same particular thing. The supreme substance can no more *be* nothing than light can be nothing.[4]

If, then, the supreme substance were nothing, the whole number of those things[*] which we call "natura" would also be nothing. Whatever exists in this whole would have to exist through another, (and this means ultimately) through a supreme substance which is

---

[*] rerum earum universitate

other than this whole. Far from being nothing or having proceeded from nothing, this "supreme essence" is the only "something" which cannot not be something, which cannot be tinged with nothingness. On the contrary, it is this supreme essence which produced all other things by itself out of nothing. The diversity of composite things, of sensible forms informing matter, that Aristotle addressed in his first philosophy, is now addressed by Anselm as fitly diversified, as form*ed* by the supreme essence out of nothing. "Nothing" in this context is to be construed as not-something, so that the supreme essence is really a creative essence, a creative substance (creatrice substantia) who creates all other things, but creates them "not from anything," in such a way that what before was nothing is now something and is to be truly esteemed as something.

What accounts for the existence of the particular things of nature, then, is the actuality of the existence of a creative substance beyond nature. It is this existence which transcends form itself for Anselm. Yet, for all this, Anselm still maintains the Aristotelian term "form" as a model or likeness in the reason of the supreme nature. This "form" of created things is a kind of expression or "locutio" of these created things in the divine reason itself. But this divine expression is not the same as the ordinary human conception of words which signify objects, but is rather a keen vision of thinking (acies cogitationis) of objects destined to exist. This divine vision of the mind is not a sensible utilization of sensible signs, nor is it even an insensible thinking of those signs which are sensible when used outwardly, but it is rather an expression of the things themselves which are destined to exist. It is this sense of expression which is the proper and principal signification of the word "locutio," and this is the expression which is proper to the creative essence (creatrix essentia). Whatever exists other than this essence cannot be anything except that it be something entirely through the "locutio" of this essence, through its innermost expression. It is through *some one being*, through its "creative presiding essence" and its "preserving presence," that all other beings exist. Where this Being is not, nothing is, so that it both supports and surpasses, encloses and permeates, all other beings. In all things and through all things, this Being is that something "from which and through which and in which all other things exist."[5]

### ii. Substance as Essence

In effect, then, being *qua* being, although still addressed by Anselm as substance, requires a shift in the meaning of Aristotelian substance, a shift from what can be said of the substantiality of the Being that runs through beings *to* what can be substantially (substantialiter) said of *that* Being whose existence is the existence through which all else exists. Being *qua* being is now *a* being among beings rather than the being that is permanent in being*s*. In presenting being *qua* being as a being among beings, however, Anselm does not intend to present this being among beings as a member of the class of beings whose existence is derived, as should be clear from what has been said in the first section of this chapter. On the contrary, this being is *among* beings only to the extent that it is absolutely unique in its existence: it is among beings in such a way that it need not have been among beings. In other words, it could, had it chosen, have been the only being. In shifting "substance" from the Aristotelian signification of the permanence of the Being that all beings strive for *to* the new signification of what can be permanently or absolutely said about that *one* and only being that is among beings in such a way that it need not have been among beings, Anselm has established his focus for the transformation of the Aristotelian founding of first philosophy.

The question, as Anselm sees it, is what can be substantially said (or absolutely predicated) of this unique being among beings as distinguished from what can be accidentally said (or relatively predicated) of this unique being. None of the words which we use to designate things created from nothing could be worthily said of the creative substance of all things. These words would be said relatively of this supreme substance, and so they would not, as such, signify its substance. To speak, then, of this unique substance as the highest of all things, or as greater than all things which have been created by it, or to use any other relative term that can be said of it, is not to designate its "natural essence." For if none of the things ever existed in relation to which it is called "supreme" or "greater," it could not be understood (intelligeretur) as "summa" or "maior," yet it would not, on this account, be less good, nor would it be less in its "essential greatness." In effect, the supreme substance is able to be conceived as not supreme in this sense: it would be no greater or lesser were it not the highest of all beings (summa omnium), i.e., if it were the *only* being in existence, than if it were the highest of all beings, that is, if it were a being among beings. If this substance would be none the greater or lesser if it had not created than it is in having created, then it follows that the term "supreme" does not describe its essence—an essence which is in every way greater and better than "whatever is not what it itself is."

From the fact, then, that this essence is able to be understood as not supreme—even though it *is* supreme by virtue of having created—it would follow that to be supreme is, in general, not inherently *better* than not to be supreme, and that not to be supreme, in general, is not inherently better than to be supreme. Whether this essence were or were not supreme, it would still be that than which there is nothing better at all[*]—that which is *better* than all things which are not what it is.[°] For if there were nothing other than it, it

---

[*] qua penitus nihil est melius

[°] To the extent that we can relatively predicate "summa" of this "essentia," we presuppose that this essence is not any one of those things to which something, which they themselves are not, is superior. But we also presuppose that this essence would be something to which everything, which is not what it is, is inferior. Thus, since it is better to be living, wise, powerful, true, just, blessed, and eternal than it is to be the opposite of all these attributes, we predicate them absolutely or substantially of this essence. But if this essence cannot be just except through itself, then it is clear that this essence is itself "justness," and so also with the other attributes that are predicated absolutely. All of these attributes show not merely of "what kind or how great," but they show what this essence is (quid sit). Yet, in being so many goods, this essence is "simple," for its being is a single good signified by many names (pluribus nominibus significatum), and any one of these goods is the same as all of these goods whether taken together or singularly. In this sense, the "essentia," which is said by relative predication to be "summa," is not anything in such a way that it is not this same thing in another way or according to an-

would be no better than if there were something other than it (as, in fact, happens to be the case).[6]

Furthermore, in being a being among beings which need not have been a being among beings but which could have been the only being in existence, this essence cannot be said in any way to have had a beginning: neither through nor from nothing, neither through nor from another, and not even through or from itself. For whatever begins to exist, begins to exist from or through something and can by no means be the same as that from or through which it begins to exist. Thus, not only its eternity but also its truth is discovered to be that which is without beginning and (therefore) without end, for were truth to have either a beginning or end, it would be true that truth did not exist before it began and it would be true that truth will not exist after it shall have ended. What applies to truth and eternity must, however, apply to all the other attributes that are absolutely predicated of this essence since this essence is simple and one. This "essentia" is without beginning or end: no thing could exist before this essence and no thing could exist after it.

But this would seem to entail that this essence succeeds a nothingness which somehow precedes it. And if this follows, then whatever in his meditation on first philosophy that Anselm has made firm by the "ramparts" of necessary truth is "necessarily unsettled," demolished, by empty nothingness (inane nihilum). Anselm attempts to overcome this threat to his meditation on first philosophy by distinguishing between two senses of "nihil," viz., a time before (priusquam) the supreme essence when there was *nothing*, and the sense in which there is *not anything* before (ante) the supreme essence. It is this second sense of nothingness which makes coherent and consistent the putting-together of all the elements of his prior meditation. In this second sense, when properly distinguished from the first, it can be said that neither something nor nothing (in

---

other consideration. Yet, whatever it is "essentially," or what can be said of it by absolute predication, is all of what it itself is.

the first sense) either preceded or will follow the supreme essence.[7]

But if it can be said that there was not anything before this "essentia," and if it cannot be said that there was a time before this essence when there was nothing, then the eternity of this essence must be an absolute timelessness and not as such a time without beginning and end (an infinitely divisible time, as Aristotle seems to conceive of time[*]). Thus the duration of the existing (existendi diuturnitas) of this essence would be to have no place or time, that is, not to be compelled to submit to "the law of place or time" in any way. This would have to be the case in order for this essence's power—which, like all the other attributes absolutely predicated of it, is nothing different from its essence—to contain under itself all those things which it created. But here again the "secret murmur of contradiction" lurks, for if it cannot be the case that this "essentia" exists merely at *some* place and time, and if it is not the case that it exists "nowhere and never," then it must be the case that it exists "everywhere and always." It would thus seem to be subject to place and time.

This seeming contradiction, however, can be dispelled by realizing that, when we quite properly say that this supreme essence is simultaneously present in all things and in each place and time, although the form of our expression (prolatio) here is the same as that which we apply to local or temporal natures because of the accustomed usage of language (loquendi consuetudinem), nonetheless, what is to be understood is quite different from this accustomed usage. The intended sense is that the "summa essentia" is present *to* (not contained *by*) all places and times, i.e., it exists *with* (rather than strictly *in*) place and time. Although it can properly be said (proprie dicitur) to exist *in* no place or time, it can be understood in a way unique to itself to be *in* every place or time, in the sense that whatever beings other than it which exist are sustained by its presence, for otherwise whatever else that exists would "fall into nothingness." It has not taken to itself temporal and spatial

---

[*] See Aristotle's *Physics*, Book VI, 6, 237b, 20.

distinctions, and it is in no way subject to the fleeting present (labile praesens) in which we live; thus it can be said to exist nowhere and never but only in the sense of a *where* that excludes other "wheres" and an *ever* that excludes other "evers." Yet, it can also be said of this Being that has deigned to be among other beings that it is *as if* it suffered change; in this sense it can be said to exist as the highest of all essences everywhere and always. In these different understandings there is nonetheless a "consistent truth," for this is the "essentia" which need not be among other beings but which has freely chosen to be among other beings, i.e., to create other beings.[8]

In sum, then, since—for Anselm, as for Boethius before him—it is the same for this essence to live as it is to exist, it possesses interminable life as a perfect whole at once, for its eternity, unlike the fleeting present in which we live, is never unlike itself. All of this would be true whether this essence were the only being that existed or a being among beings. But in having chosen to be a being among beings, this "essentia" seems to partake of (what Aristotle would call) "accident," since, as Anselm says, the fact that it is greater than all other natures and that it is dissimilar to them seems, in its case, to be an accident (videatur accidere). Yet, in taking upon itself such an accident, its substance undergoes no variation. In this way, although the supreme nature in its simplicity has never undergone accidents which effect mutation in itself, yet it does not disdain on occasion to express itself in terms of accidents which are in no way inconsistent with its "supreme unchangeableness." Its essence can never be variable but is always and in every way substantially identical with itself (eadem substantialiter), and it is never in any way different from itself, even accidentally.

Thus it can be said that the sense in which this supreme essence is substantial is such that it is *beyond every substance** and it is uniquely (singulariter) whatever it is. Though every substance is susceptible of change by accident, the unchanging wholeness (immutabilis sinceritas) of this essence does not have accessible to

---

\* sit extra omnem substantiam

it admixture or mutation in any way. It cannot, then, be properly called "substance" unless it is called substance with respect to essence,* since it is beyond and above every substance. In being supra-substantial, it has from itself, without the aid of any other being, whatever existence it has, and it is what it is singularly and apart from its fellowship (consortio) with its creatures. From this it follows that whatever name it has in common with other beings, a "different signification" must be understood in its absolutely unique case.

Yet, the supra-substantiality of this absolutely unique "essentia," which has no "universal essence" in common with other beings, does not warrant our refusal to call it "substance." Since it not only most certainly exists but exists as the highest of all beings, and since the essence of anything is usually called its substance, we can conclude that if anything worthy can be said of it, we should not be prevented from calling it "substance." But in calling it this, we would have to speak of it not as bodily and divisible but as an indivisible (i.e., individual) spiritual substance—an "individuus spiritus." This is the Being with other beings who is in its essence the substance beyond substances, the supra-substantial spirit which exists in so "marvelously singular" and so "singularly marvelous" a way. This is an absolutely unique being (solus sit) for which there is no class of which it could be a member—no genus, no species, no nature ($\varphi\acute{v}\sigma\iota\varsigma$)° operative in sensible substances in which it is, by any *necessitation* of its essence, immanent. All other beings which appear to be comparable to it are not really so, for this spirit alone exists simply and perfectly and absolutely. Only this "individuus spiritus" does not fail now to be what it was or will be at any time, but whatever it is, it is no more than once and yet interminably.[9]

Since all other beings have come from non-existence to existence and would seem destined to return from existence to non-existence, it can be maintained that they are almost non-existent, that they scarcely exist (vix esse). But this absolutely singular, hu-

---

* nisi dicatur substantia pro essentia
° See pp. 14, 23 above.

manly unutterable spirit, this "ineffabilis spiritus," can be said to be that which alone exists, in comparison to which created things do not exist, at least according to the kind of reasoning offered by Anselm at this point. Yet, created things are not wholly non-existent because, through this spirit that alone exists absolutely, they have been made something from nothing. This "creator spiritus" does not, like the God of Aristotle, require the world in order to be. Its divinity does not require the being of the non-divine over against it. The existence of beings in the world is not something that is simply "there" or pregiven but is entirely gratuitous on the part of that single something which exists absolutely.

If whatever has been created by this "creator spiritus" was created by its expression, and if this expression or "locutio" is nothing else than what this spirit itself is, then it is impossible that this expression is "confined" among created beings. Everything created was created through this expression, but this "locutio" itself could not truly be created by itself. The expression by which this spirit creates cannot be a member of the class of the things it creates because that expression is the very intelligence of this spirit by which it understands all things. The expressing of this spirit is the same as its understanding since, unlike man, this spirit never fails to say what it understands; and since this spirit is indivisible, its expression must be "consubstantial" with itself. This means that its "locutio" does not consist of many words but is the one word (unum verbum) through which all things were made.[10]

### iii. Created and Uncreated Essence

The word itself which is consubstantial with this supreme spirit, being that through which all things are made, is that through which all things are said (dicuntur): all things other than this "summus spiritus" are thus spoken into being out of nothing. The act of existing (existendi) of created beings is an imitation of the word of supreme truth which is subject neither to gain nor to loss, in the sense that each created being exists so much more and is so much more excellent the more it is like that being which exists supremely and is supremely great. Thus, some natures *exist more or less* than others; existence among created beings is a matter of degrees. Created essences will exist in a greater degree the more like they are to that uncreated essence which exists in a certain unique way (singulari modo) of its own. In this fashion, the word itself of this uncreated essence, through which all other beings were created, does not exist as the likeness (similitudinem) of these created beings but exists as their true and simple essence. Each of these created beings does not exist as itself a "simple and absolute essence" but only as an imitation of that true essence, that "verbum," which does not exist as more or less true and which does not exist in terms of any likeness to created things. Every created nature is thus seen to have a higher degree of essence and dignity the more it approaches the word of this uncreated spirit.

This spirit, which is as supreme as it is eternal, is, like the Aristotelian God, "eternally mindful of itself." But, unlike the Aristotelian deity, if this spirit understands itself eternally, then it expresses or says itself (se dicit) eternally; and if it expresses itself eternally, its word is co-eternal with it. This means that, unlike the Aristotelian divinity which can only be the perfection of final causality if there is a world in which that perfection can be immanent, the word of this spirit must be coeternal with this spirit, whether this word be thought of in connection with other existing things or it be thought of in connection with no other existent essences.* Whether or not this spirit creates, whether or not there is a world, this spirit still utters itself. But it is by one word that this expressive spirit utters itself and what it creates. The word by which it utters itself and the word by which it utters the created world are of one substance, for even if nothing but that supreme spirit ever existed,° reason would still testify to the "necessity of the existence" of that word by which this spirit utters itself and which does not exist as other than what this spirit itself is. And the reason that compels here is that of the human mind (mens humana)

---

\* nulla alia existente essentia

° si nihil umquam aliud esset nisi summus ille spiritus

which, for Anselm, is his own mind (mens mea) in silent disputation with and by itself.[11]

In fact, when the "mens humana" comes to understand itself in its thinking, the image of itself is born in its thought, or, better yet, its own thought is the very image of its own existence,[*] in its own likeness, as if it were formed from its impression. And the more truly the human mind expresses the likeness of an object in its own thinking, the more truly can it be said to think the object itself. Thus, when this mind understands itself in thinking, it has "with itself its own image born of itself," its own thought in likeness to itself. But it cannot, unless by reason alone, separate itself from its own image, an image which is its word. And so also, the "supreme wisdom" understands itself by expressing or uttering itself and thus begets a likeness of itself which is consubstantial with itself—its own word. But this word, by which what is created is uttered, is not, like the word of the human mind, the likeness of the creature but is, rather, the creature's "principal essence." Unlike the word of the "mens humana," which expresses things in the world by a word corresponding to things in this world, the word by which this world is created does not correspond to this world. In no way does this uncreated word belong to the created world even when this word is expressive of the created world. The word of the human mind, however, which is expressive of itself and of the created world, does not belong *only* to itself (as does the word of the uncreated spirit) but also belongs to the created world of which it is a part.

What is to be marveled at here is that the one and only word of the supreme spirit (to be distinguished from the one word and yet many words of the human mind) can be expressive of both uncreated and created being, i.e., of creative (creans) and created (creata) essence, for when this "summus spiritus" utters itself, it utters all things which were created. Both before they were created and now that they have been created, these things are always in this creative spirit not what they are in themselves but what they are in this spirit. For in themselves they are changeable beings created

---

[*] ipsam cogitationem sui esse suam imaginem

according to the immutable reason of the "creative essence," but what they are in this creative spirit is such that they find their "primal essence" and the very truth of their act of existing (veritas existendi) in the existence of this spirit. But what is even more marvelous is that the "creans essentia" need not have expressed any created beings in expressing itself and would remain no more or less expressive had it not expressed any created being in expressing itself. To marvel at this is to realize that how this spirit utters itself or even how it knows the things that were created by it is unable to be comprehended by human knowledge.* Because created substances in themselves exist by virtue of their own essence, they exist more truly than they exist in human knowledge wherein they exist by virtue of their likeness. But they exist even more truly in the word or intelligence of the creative spirit (wherein is had the beginning of all created things) than they do in themselves.[12]

But if the word of the supreme essence is consubstantial with that essence, so that both always hold an indivisible unity, they nonetheless admit of an "unspeakable plurality," for this word derives existence from that essence of which it is the word. Thus, in the very midst of their unity, supreme being comes from supreme being (summum de summo), so that it is one and the same being which is from one and the same being. This being most truly begets (gignat) itself and is most truly begotten (gignatum) of itself, so that in this "supreme unity" is seen to exist a marvelous "plurality" which is as humanly unutterable as it is rationally unavoidable. In this unyielding hiddenness (impenetrabile secretum), so opposite are the relations of the word and that of which it is the word that the one never receives the property of the other; and yet so harmonized are they in nature that the one always has the essence of the other. In this way, the relation of the word to that of which it is the word has a perfect likeness to the offspring of a parent, and the relation of parent and offspring can be ascribed to no beings as fittingly as it can be applied to the supreme spirit and its word. Since the first and principal cause of offspring is in the father, if the one

---

* ab humana scientia comprehendi non posse

## Anselm's Meditation on First Philosophy

is most truly parent and the other is most truly offspring, it follows that the one is most truly father and the other is most truly son, but in such a way that the perfectly supreme essence is at once the father and the son, while the son subsists through himself and yet has existence (habeat esse) from the father.[13] Whereas the relation of father and son to the created world is that of production, their relation to each other is that of generation.

The significance of Anselm's remark in his preface to this meditation on first philosophy now becomes clear. What the Greek Fathers of the Church understood by "substantia," the Latin Fathers understood by "persona," and Anselm's transformation of Aristotle's notion of substance now becomes clear. The *what* of the divine substance is precisely a *who,* and since the substance of the person is transmitted in generation but not in production, the substance of the divine person is transmitted in the generation of his son but not in his production of the world. The substantiality of the things of nature is not a partaking of a divine substantiality which can *be* only to the extent that it can be immanent in nature. Instead, the substantiality of natural things is a created product, an artifact of a divine person who does not need to be immanent in nature.

### iv. First Philosophy as Trinitarian Theology

To the extent that substance can be spoken of in regard to the divine being, the meaning of substance is seen to be the meaning of person. This *substantia qua persona* requires that the true word is the "intelligence of the Father," that is, the perfect intelligence which conceives the entire perfection of the substance of the Father in the Divine Trinity. The Son is thus no imperfect imitation but rather the whole truth, the "integra veritas," of the very essence of the Father, since he is not other than what the Father is. In this, the Son is the intelligence of intelligence, the "knowledge of knowledge, the wisdom of wisdom, the truth of truth." Furthermore, since it can be seen in the human mind that the word of this mind is born of memory, and were this mind capable of always thinking of itself, its word would be always born of memory, it can be said of the supreme wisdom, which always utters itself, that in the unending or eternal memory of itself in the Trinity its coeternal Word is born. Unlike the word of the "mens humana," the Word of the supreme wisdom *is* itself its own memory. The Son is memory born of memory, wisdom born of wisdom, while the Father is memory and wisdom born of none. The Son is the memory of memory, the "memoria memoriae," the memory that remembers the Father who *is* memory.

But if Father relates to Son as memory relates to the "memory of memory"—that is, the relationship is asymmetrical (the Son cannot be memory born of none or Father in relation to the Father, and the Father cannot be memory born of memory or Son in relation to the Son)—then a symmetrical relation, a relation which they have in common, must obtain if they are to have the same existence (idem esse). This symmetrical relation is the disposition of mutual love (mutui amoris) between the Father and the Son—a disposition which Anselm finds none more delightful to contemplate in the supreme spirit. This supreme spirit loves itself *because* it remembers and understands itself, since no thing is loved without remembrance or intelligence. Because what is loved or what loves in the Father and in the Son is entirely the same, it follows necessarily that each loves himself and the other with an "equal love." And if the "summus spiritus" loves himself as much as he remembers and understands himself, and if he remembers and understands himself as much as his essence exists (since otherwise this essence would not be able to exist), it follows that his love is as much as he himself is. Father and Son and the love of both exist as one supreme essence, and it can be said that Father and Son equally "send forth" so great a good—a love which proceeds singularly (a singulo) from each and simultaneously (simul) from both—not as two wholes but as one and the same whole.[14]

Since this love "proceeds" from the Son no differently than it proceeds from the Father, it cannot, in the usage of common discourse (communis locutionis), be spoken of as "unbegotten" or "begotten." Only this love of both is neither begotten nor unbegotten because it is neither son nor offspring, and so it may be called the "spiritus" of Father and Son, for in a sense they "breathe" ("spirant") their love not by parting from it but by existing through it. If there is any need that this indescribable way of breathing—this spiration—be accorded a proper name (proprii nominis),* it would have to be the name "Spirit" which designates the mutual participation (communio) of Father and Son, their very "substance."[15]

It is this name—insofar as it suggests substance *qua* person, *substantia qua spiritus*—which leads Anselm to the conclusion that Father and Son and the Spirit of both exist in each other with such an "equality," that no one of them exceeds the other, that no one of them exists without the other. Yet each one taken singly is the "summa essentia." Each taken singly is everything that is inherent in the existence (inesse) of that essence. Although the Father alone is the begetter who speaks, the Son alone the begotten who is spoken, and the Spirit alone what proceeds equally from both, "each utters himself and the other two."

This would seem to suggest that there are as many words in this "summa essentia" as there are speakers and beings who are spoken. This would be the conclusion to be drawn, were the human mind the model for what is to be said about the supreme essence, for in the human mind there are as many words in its thinking as there are objects thought. But we must remember that in the human mind, the word which corresponds to the object thought is not born of that object itself, but is born of some likeness or image of that object which is in the memory; whereas in the "summus spiritus" the Word is born of its object (that is, the Father) itself, with the result that the uttering or speaking (dicere) is one with the thinking (cogitando). But if to know and to understand are not different from *to speak* in the supreme spirit, then it follows that there are not many beings that are expressed but only one essence, and thus there are not many words but only one Word.

---

* Aquinas, in speaking of the procession of love (per modum amoris) in the Trinity indicates that it has no proper name (non habet proprium nomen).

Yet there is something that elicits the wonder endemic to first philosophy here, something that Anselm finds unexplainable, namely, that this one Word, through which each of the persons expresses himself and the others equally, cannot be said to be the word of all three but can only be said to be the word of one of these persons, for it is had by him alone for whom it has existence by being born. What is to be marveled at is the inexplicable plurality in what must be the absolute unity of the supreme essence. And this finds its reflection in what is to be marveled at in the human mind, Anselm's own mind (mens mea), for in the case of this mind *to say* is not identical with *to think*. This is a mind which requires many words. And yet there is an inexplicable unity underlying this plurality, for as Anselm notes (prefiguring his approach in his dialogue in first philosophy) there is a certain expression (locutio) of the human mind which is not other than the act by which thinking looks into itself (cogitantis inspectio) in this mind.[16]

Anselm's meditation on first philosophy is thus confronted with what is inexplicable to the human mind, for the hiddenness of so sublime a matter transcends every keen vision of the human understanding,[*] and for this reason the attempt to explain *how* the divine unity can yet be a plurality would best be refrained from. Anselm's meditation has been an inquiry into what must be an incomprehensible matter to the human mind, and yet it has been an inquiry in which reasoning has brought him to the recognition that what he has sought to know most certainly exists (certissime esse). In this way, the "mens humana" by reason has been able to address what it cannot explain and has thus shown that what it cannot explain is worthy of belief (credendum sit)—worthy of a certainty which is peculiar to faith (fidei certitudinem).

In the end, that which exists completely beyond everything which exists in the world would have to be incomprehensible and unutterable for a mind which exists in that world, and yet that mind can "rationally comprehend" that the supreme wisdom exists as beyond comprehension—"incomprehensibile esse"—in relation to that mind.

---

[*] sublimis rei secretum transcendere omnem intellectus aciem humani

The human mind, in other words, is able to make explicit by reason *how* the supreme wisdom is beyond the reach of the many words this mind utilizes. The "summa essentia" is so beyond every other nature that whenever anything is said about it in words which are common to these other natures, the sense of these words is in no way common to these other natures.

But this ability to make explicit the very incomprehensibility of that Being which is a being among beings but which *could* have been the only being (because it is as such completely beyond and other than any other being) would seem to threaten the integrity of Anselm's entire meditation on first philosophy. For if the common and familiarly used sense of words is alien to that Being, then whatever Anselm has reasoned to as pertaining to it does not pertain to it. Could everything said in his meditation be but an example of speaking about things which he does not properly express as they are in themselves, as if he were speaking in figurative representations (aenigmata) or gazing into a darkened glass (speculo)? Yet, even were this so, reason lies behind his use of "aenigmata," and he can come to see something of the things he seeks to see in themselves. For he utters and yet does not utter, he sees and yet does not see what he seeks to utter and to see. He fails to utter and to see what he seeks by virtue of that which is "proper" to what he seeks, but he utters and sees what he seeks by virtue of that which is "other than" what he seeks. In this way, although the "summus spiritus" remains ineffable because it has not been expressed in this meditation according to what is proper to its own essence, yet because it has in some way been designated negatively through what is other than it, nothing disproves the truth attained in this meditation, even though what the mind attempts to achieve by means of shadowy signification (tenuem significationem) is not sufficient to unveil the unique depth of that Being through which all things were made from nothing and preserved from nothing (servantur a nihilo). If it is incapable of being made known through the many words at the disposal of the human mind, nonetheless what can be "estimated" of its intrinsic worth in a figurative representation by the teaching of reason (ratione docente) is not false.[17]

It is through the human rational mind that the knowledge (cognoscendum) of this supreme essence can be most nearly approached, since this searching mind (mentem indagantam) is aided by the very creative essence of which it is in search and is thus enabled "to rise" to the investigation of this essence. In effect, the more eagerly the "mens humana" stretches forth (intendit) to learn of itself (se discendum), the more effectively does it rise to the conception of the creative essence. And the more the human mind neglects to direct its attention to itself, the more it descends from contemplation of that essence. This is so because the human mind itself is the darkened mirror and image of that creative essence. The human mind can be most aptly said to be, as it were, the "mirror" of itself in which it contemplates the image of that which it is not able to see "face to face." It is, in other words, the power of remembering (reminisci) and understanding (intelligere) and loving (amare) the best and greatest of all beings which makes the human mind the image of the Creator, the very image of the Father and Son and Spirit of both.

In this way, Anselm brings into a unity the two traditions of medieval Christian thinking, viz., the "via negativa" and "paideia," for the supreme essence is seen to be knowable by—in its very unknowableness for—the human mind. In contemplating itself in its very search to comprehend the incomprehensible, the human mind is raised to some kind of contemplation *of* what is incomprehensible to it *by* what is incomprehensible to it, because *what* is incomprehensible to it is really a *who*, a substance beyond all substance*s*, a *substantia qua spiritus*, a *substantia qua persona*, who has nonetheless chosen to be among substance*s*. The incomprehensibility of divine substance can now become an object of knowledge for first philosophy in the sense (and to the extent) that this substance is a person who *freely* communicates himself to the searching human mind and *not* simply an *object* to be contemplated by that mind. And since the image of this Being beyond beings who has chosen to be a being among beings is impressed through a

## Anselm's Meditation on First Philosophy

"natural potency" on the human mind, that mind is meant to be eager for nothing so much as for the expression of this image. Since, furthermore, what is within the scope of the powers of the human mind ought to prevail in the human will (voluntate), the eagerness to express this image must proceed through willing. Human being was thus created in order that it might love the supreme essence above all good things, but it is not able to love this essence unless it is eager to remember and understand this essence.[18]

But if human being can come to love this essence, then it can come at some time to live in "true blessedness." And if human being can come to love this essence "without end," if it can always be eager to love the supreme life (summam vitam), then it can "never have its life withdrawn from it." The human soul would thus be truly "secure" from death itself.* If the very support of love (amoris fulcimentum) is as it is declared to be in this meditation, then what shall this supreme goodness, this "summa bonitas," return to the being which loves and desires (and hopes for from) it except itself?[19]

### v. The Being Beyond Beings

But whoever, in the first place, is not able to believe, according to Anselm, is not able either to love or to hope, for it is by believing

---

* The human soul, then, to the extent that it can devote itself entirely and without end to the love of "supreme blessedness," shall enjoy that blessedness in the sense that what it now sees through a darkened glass and through figurative representation, it shall then see "face to face." And just as this soul, to this extent, will then experience an unchanging sufficiency (immutabilem sufficientiam), so also the human soul which disdains to love the supreme essence shall experience an inconsolable want (inconsolabilem indigentiam). But whether it loves or despises that which it was created to love, the human soul's existence must be immortal. And whether it is to enjoy unending sufficiency or to suffer unending want, no human being is unjustly deprived of that good for which it was created by the supremely just and good Creator. Nor ought any human being despair of being able to reach that which it reaches for, for "eagerness to exert oneself" in this regard is as "useful" to man as the "hope of attainment" is necessary.

in the "summam essentiam" that the human soul reaches out for it. The most fitting way to signify this "striving for" the supreme essence, consequently, is to say "believing in" this essence. For in saying that he "believes in" this essence, man shows both that, through the faith which he professes, he strives for or reaches out to this essence and that he believes those things which pertain to his intended aim. For neither the man who does not believe what pertains to striving for this essence nor the man who does not strive toward this essence can be said to believe *in* it. It would thus be appropriate to say that rather than being merely a striving *toward*, belief is a striving to exist (tendendum esse) in the "summam essentiam."

The singularity and unity of the theological virtues (faith, hope, and charity) are thus the image in the human soul of the singularity and unity of the Father, Son, and Spirit in the triune supreme essence. Much as the Son is of the Father, and the Spirit is of both the Father and the Son, and the Father is of none, while the Father, Son, and Spirit are *of* one supreme essence, so also hope is in regard to what can be believed, and love is in regard to both what can be believed and hoped for, and belief or faith finds nothing other for its object than the "summam essentiam." But the belief that Anselm addresses is an operative faith (operosa fides) because it is not simply an assent of the human mind but an effort of the human will to express the image of the supreme essence which exists in the human mind. Because of this, true faith is always a living faith, a "viva fides," which seeks an embodiment of man's will in his action, i.e., an embodiment of "belief *in* that which ought to be believed" in the life of love (vitam delectionis). In this, it is to be distinguished from "dead faith" which merely intellectually assents, which merely believes *that* which ought to be believed.[20]

The situation of faith, then, is what ought to be the situation of man: striving to be *in* the supreme essence of which he is the image, but being unable to say in one word (uno nomine) why the Father, Son, and Spirit are three persons, a triune unity (trinam unitatem) in one trinity (unam trinitatem). It is at this point, at the conclusion to his meditation on first philosophy, in the recognition

## Anselm's Meditation on First Philosophy 47

that faith is expressive of what the true nature of man is (namely, to be a seeking to exist *in* the supreme essence by which all things exist and of which the human mind is an image), that Anselm can say that to this supreme triune essence alone, which he has meditated on, the name of God is to be properly assigned.* This name can be alone assigned to a particular substance (aliquam substantiam) which is "valued" as "above" every nature that is not God. The realization is now had that God is not only God but that God is the only God (solus deus) who is (for the many words of man) "unutterably three and one" and, as the only God, is a "supremely wise all-powerfulness" who in no way requires the things of nature in order to exist. In the realization that God in no way requires a relation to the things of nature, while these things require a relation to him if they are to exist, it becomes clear that absolutely no thing in the world can be said to be governed alone by the disordered flow of chance or fate.° The "deus" of Anselm's meditation on first philosophy, unlike the θεὸς (which perdures as the final perfection *in* the world) of Aristotle's founding of first philosophy, *exists* as that "from *whom*, and through whom, and in whom, are all things."[21]

St. Anselm's solitary thinking, pursued in silent meditation, and having for its object that essence which exists in a certain unique manner of its own, has issued in the conception of being *qua* being as a predicate of an absolutely unique *something* or "aliquid" and not (as in Aristotle) as the substance (οὐσία) or thing in its real-ization which is the presence of the permanent to itself in nature.

Aristotle had perceived the primary signification of essence to be substance, conceiving essence as substance without matter, and arguing that the sense in which being is substance is precisely the sense in which being is a unity, and the sense in which being is one is precisely the sense in which it is a particular being in nature. This assertion that the universal is never visible in separation from its particulars, however, required the further assertion that the sub-

---

\* soli summae essentiae proprie nomen dei assignatur
° sola casuum inordinata volubilitate

stantiality of substances is a substance separate from sensible things but which has its being in the world and is eternal and immovable. For Anselm, however, essence is not really reducible to substance; on the contrary, substance, when predicated of the supreme spirit, is seen to be reducible to essence, for this spirit cannot properly be called substance unless it is denominated substance with respect to essence. This spirit is said to be substance without accidents which affect its essence, in the sense that it transcends all substances and is individually or particularly whatever it is. In this way, the supreme essence cannot properly be called a substance except insofar as the term "substance" is used in the same sense or signification as "essence." If, for Aristotle, essence can be said to be substance without matter, then, for Anselm, substance, when referred to the supreme spirit, can be said to be essence without matter.

Whatever names this supreme spirit shares with other beings, a very different signification must be understood in its case, a signification which is nonetheless consistent with the truth that the human mind is its own mirror wherein it contemplates itself as the image of that supreme spirit which it cannot now see "face to face." Being is now seen to be no longer the substantiality of substances that runs through particular beings but, rather, the attribute of a preeminently particular Being, a subject that is not of this world but which is nonetheless a subject which accounts for whatever particular existence is in this world. And the thinking of this subject that is absolutely other than this world is seen to constitute the being of the human mind—the "cogitantis inspectio" or act by which human thinking looks into itself.

The primary thrust, consequently, of Anselm's meditation on first philosophy—of his transformation of the Aristotelian founding of first philosophy—is not simply the intelligibility of the "why," but the addressing of the very intelligibility of particular existents in the world—the "that" of beings. It is the addressing of a spirit beyond this world which can be said to be substance, but which is not strictly substance because it transcends every substance. To prove that this supra-ουσια is not nothing—and thus that what can finally be called "God" is not nothing[22]—constitutes the primary purpose of Anselm's meditation on first philosophy.

### vi. Anselm and Aristotle

The scope of Anselm's contribution in his meditation—which will be brought to its perfection in his dialogue—is excellently articulated by Robert Sokolowski in a recent work. Anselm unleashes the basic conceptual outlook which allowed for the emergence of universities in the Christian Middle Ages since, in pointing out the peculiarity of the object of Christian faith as an existence that could not be denied by reason, he established the "security of faith before reason."

This was the beginning of something new, since, before Anselm, Christian thinkers treated reason in the context of Christian faith but never really turned reason toward faith, never really made faith an *object* for reason. But in Anselm's meditation on first philosophy, faith itself is made the theme to be meditated on, and the unbeliever is confronted with what his denial of faith might mean. This is, in fact, how the meditation proper begins. There is a kind of "distance" established between reason and faith which we do not see in prior Christian thinkers, and there is a definite sense in which reason has prerogatives to make judgments about the meaning of faith.

But in starting something new, Anselm is really transfiguring something old, something older than Christianity. The pagan gods are a part—albeit the most important part—of the world, and for them to be divine there is required the being of what is not divine. Even the one God of Aristotle, as the prime unmoved mover and thought thinking itself, although a considerable advance, since the other claimants among the gods are in a sense seen to be mythic approximations to it, is necessarily an element in the world, and it is equally necessary that there be non-divine things if this God is to be. But Christian faith introduces the notion of a world that might not have existed, and corresponding to this is the notion of God as a Being whose goodness and greatness would be undiminished even if the world had never been. The existence of God as "solitary" is "counter-factual," Sokolowski notes, but it is "meaningful," that is, the mind can conceive it without contradiction. Thus, what Anselm makes explicit as a principle for first philosophy is that the "essentia" of God would be the same as it is in having created the world as it would be if he had never created the world. This creation does not follow as any necessity of God's reason but only from the freedom, that is, the will of God. Creation, in this way, means "more," in the sense that there is more being, that is, being*s*, but it does not mean greater or better existence. Far from being pregiven in its being, the world is a gift with no parallel to the generosity of its giver to be found within the world.[23]

The most fundamental principle, consequently, which can be articulated in Anselm's first philosophy is precisely a distinction which cannot be found in that of Aristotle or in any pagan thought, namely, the absolute, unqualified distinction between what *is* in the world and what God *is*. And yet, *what God is* is even more fundamental than this principle, more fundamental than this distinction, since God makes possible the very distinction itself. But *what God is* can only be approximated by the plurality of human words through what is not-God. This means that what is most fundamental *as such* cannot be articulated by human words in first philosophy, as evidenced in Anselm's consideration of the inexplicability of *triune* unity and *one* trinity. However, what is most fundamental *for man* can be articulated in first philosophy, viz., the absolute otherness of God and the world as the condition for God's being that "from whom, and through whom, and in whom are all things."[*]

For all the fundamentality of the distinction between God and the world, God cannot be seen to be established by the distinction, in Anselm's first philosophy. For all the fundamentality of the inseparability of God and the world, in Aristotle's first philosophy, divinity must be seen as established by the distinction between itself and non-divine things in this world. And this is still reflective of the situation of the pagan gods who are established by the myths

---

* Cf. pp. 47, 28-29 above, 1 Corinthians 8:6, and Hebrews 2:10.

## Anselm's Meditation on First Philosophy

in terms of their difference vis à vis other things in the world. The Christian God, however, is absolutely unique, has no class of which he can be a member, and cannot be (as Aristotle said of the divine) the most important *aspect* of reality. This is reflected in the significance that Anselm sees in the Trinity, for the one essence he addresses could not be addressed in the way he does if God were an essence in the world, a "kind" of being that is there only by virtue of a contrast with other kinds of being. In this way, Sokolowski can suggest that, for Aristotle, the determinateness of being is always seen in the context of the totality of natural things; this determinateness is "the actualization of what can come into prominence within the whole." It is not, as it is in Anselm's first philosophy, being as "actualitas," that is, being as something which is over against being*s* which might not have existed at all. In this sense, there can be no problem of "existing," of "esse," for Aristotle. Whereas Aristotle's God is always a first substance within the world, the God which Anselm addresses is a supra-substantial existent, a supra-natural "aliquid" by which all other existent*s* can exist.

The fundamentality for man, then, of the distinction between God and the world is like no other distinction that man makes,[*] for all other distinctions are made and can only be made within the context of the beings to be found in the world.[24] Actuality as causality can now come into prominence in Anselm's first philosophy because inquiry has shifted from Aristotle's search for a formal (and ultimately final) causality *in* the world to the search for an absolutely unique efficient causality *of* the world as a whole. This shift would require a radical transformation of language, including the kind of language Aristotle used. We see this most clearly in the contrast between Aristotle's careful attempt to delineate and be faithful to the ordinary, everyday, but not arbitrary usage of words and Anselm's equally careful attempt to delineate the difference between the ordinary, everyday usage of language and the special

---

[*] "In this respect," Sokolowski points out parenthetically, "the Christian distinction is analogous to the distinction we gradually come to make between 'me' and 'the world.' "

signification that would have to apply to the God that he attempts to show is not nothing.

This transformation of language is accomplished in the *Monologion*. The desire which Aristotle saw in his *Metaphysics* as characteristic of all the movements of nature—a desire for a finite perfection immanent in nature—has been transformed in Anselm's *Monologion* into a desire of "mens mea" for existence in an infinite perfection which transcends nature. The fruit of this transformation is to be found in the *Proslogion*.

# III

# Anselm's Dialogue in First Philosophy

In the *Proslogion* Anselm no longer engages in a solitary meditation but in a dialogue with God in the form of prayer, thereby *enacting* the mind's being raised to God which was alluded to in his meditation. His reflections on the degrees of being, negativity, particularity, substance, and essence in the *Monologion* are molded into a unity, a unified reflection in the *Proslogion*. The single argument for the existence of God which he presents in the *Proslogion* constitutes the consummation of his first philosophy. This single argument will be found to be not simply a transformation of the Aristotelian founding of first philosophy but it will prove to be the ground of the Cartesian refounding of first philosophy. The unifying thread that gives his entire contribution to first philosophy the range of influence that it will exert for the modern refounding of this philosophy is the insight that being in the highest degree—that is, what alone can account for the problematical existence of things in the world—is possessed only by *that* existence which cannot be conceived not to be.[1]

The *Monologion* had made clear that the human mind requires many words and yet there is an inexplicable unity underlying this plurality, for the very expression of this mind is not other than the "cogitantis inspectio" or act by which its thinking looks into itself. Thus, the more eagerly this mind stretches forth to learn of itself, the more effectively does it rise to the conception of the creative essence itself. In this way, the power of remembering, understanding, and loving this essence makes the human mind the image of the expressive Trinity. His attempt in the *Monologion* to prove that this supra-substantial Trinity is not nothing had enabled him to make faith, as a striving to exist in this Trinity, the theme of reason, and to confront the unbeliever with what his denial of faith might mean, namely, that it is a denial of the very desire of the human mind for existence in a perfection which transcends nature.

It is only in the *Proslogion*, however, that the full significance of the connection between the human mind or "mens mea" and the existence of God is made manifest, for the desire of this mind to exist *in* a perfection which is more-than-natural is at the heart of the single argument for God's existence presented in Anselm's dialogue in first philosophy. C.S. Lewis was not wide of the mark here when he observed that the "dialectic of Desire, faithfully followed, would . . . force you not to propound, but to live through, a sort of ontological proof."[2]

It is precisely this intimate connection between the human mind's desire for God and the supranatural actuality of God—a connection already suggested in the *Monologion* in terms of the connection between what is most fundamental for man (the otherness of God to the world) and what is most fundamental as such (what God *is*) — which will find its embodiment in a single proof for the existence of that which alone can be named "God." And this single proof in the *Proslogion* is nothing less than a metaphysical precondition for the modern invention (or, in its own estimation, discovery) of human subjectivity.

The *Proslogion* engages in an exploration of what the *Monologion* spoke of as the "cogitantis inspectio" or the act by which thinking looks into itself. This exploration presents truth as the distinctive trait of proper understanding in the human mind and will enable Descartes to identify truth with certitude, i.e., with the consciousness within the human *ego* of what is known. Heidegger suggests what we will propose as the connection between Anselm's dialogue in first philosophy and Descartes' refounding of that philosophy. The Creator-God of Christianity, Heidegger says, is the first primal cause (die erste Ursache), that which primarily works in the sense of "effecting," and his effects are the world and man who (within the world) is the true "effector." Because of this, truth (which was, in the Aristotelian founding of first philosophy, a dis-concealment of an "emerging" that was brought into the formulation of permanence, that is, substance) is now (in metaphysics transfigured by Christianity) transformed into the distinctive trait of the divine and human understanding. It only remains for the modern refounding of metaphysics to transfigure this ultimate essence of truth into certainty (Gewissheit). In this modern refounding, the only knowledge that is seen to be valid is that knowledge which simultaneously knows itself (and what it knows as such) and in this knowledge is "certain of itself." Certainty thus becomes the consciousness, conscious of itself, of what is known, the authoritative mode of knowledge, that is, the "truth."[3]

What mediates the ancient founding of first philosophy—insofar as this founding involves the notion of truth as a dis-concealment of the permanence of the being of nature—and the modern refounding of that philosophy—insofar as that refounding involves the notion of truth as certainty, that is, as the human subject's consciousness of itself in being conscious of what is known—is precisely the notion of truth as a rightness of the understanding, a rightness that can exist in the human understanding to the extent that this understanding has its source in God. This notion of truth as a distinctive trait of understanding, as a rectitude of understanding,[4] lies beneath the *Proslogion's* argument for the existence of that which cannot be conceived not to exist—an existence which will be predicated of God and which (although it cannot itself signify God) will be signified by the name "God."

### i. The Submergence and Emergence of the Self

In the preface to his dialogue in first philosophy, Anselm indicates that after having published what he took to be a sample of meditation on the intelligibility of faith (ratione fidei) which joined together into a sequence many arguments, he sought whether he might discover a single argument—"unum argumentum." What he sought was an argument that would require no other and would suffice by itself for proving that God truly exists, that he is the "summum bonum" who is in need of nothing else but whom all other beings "need" is order to exist and to exist as good (bene sint), and who *is* "whatever we believe about the divine substance."

In seeking a single argument, which in its self-sufficiency would be reflective of the very self-sufficiency and absolute singularity of the Being whose existence it sought to prove, Anselm realized that, although at times it seemed that he nearly grasped what he sought, at other times it entirely eluded his keen mental vision (mentis aciem), so that he was close to "despairing" of his quest as something impossible. But when he had reached the point where he had decided to put aside entirely his search, he found that the idea he was in search of, even though he was now unwilling, began to force itself upon him more and more "importunately." Finally, one day, worn out in his resistance, and in the midst of the conflict of his thoughts, there offered itself the very idea which he had despaired of finding, and he eagerly embraced* this idea (cogitationem) which in his anxiety he had repelled.[5]

One cannot help being struck, as is evident from the style of Anselm's Latin, with the detail of his report on the genesis of his dialogue and with his free use of the first person. Neither of these is to be found in Aristotle, and both, in conjunction with the absence of references (other than scriptural) to prior, longstanding authorities, seem to be something very nearly new in Anselm's own time. Anselm's most private thoughts are made public—something entirely new when compared to ancient philosophers. Even Anselm's contemporary, his biographer Eadmer, reflects the nov-

---

* Judging that what he "rejoiced to discover," were it written, would give pleasure to some who would read it, he wrote his dialogue from the personal viewpoint of one attempting to raise his mind to the contemplation of God (sub persona conantis erigere mentem suam ad contemplandum deum) and seeking to understand what he believes (intelligere credit). It was at this point that he decided to give to his already published meditation the title "An Example of Meditation on the Intelligibility of Faith" and to his as yet unpublished dialogue the title "Faith Seeking Understanding." After both works had been copied many times, under these titles, he was urged by many to affix his name (nomen meum) to these works. And that this might be done more fitly he changed their titles, calling the first *Monologion*, i.e., soliloquy (soliloquium), and the second *Proslogion*, i.e., an address (alloquium).

elty of Anselm's approach and chooses to do something which previous biographers did not do—to pay the most careful attention to the most private conversation and thoughts of Anselm and, in effect, to make them public.[6] Of course, there is precedent in the *Soliloquies* of St. Augustine and certain passages in his *Confessions*; but Anselm's uniqueness consists in transposing this precedent into the realm of first philosophy, thereby making his work here the precedent for Descartes. Yet, the distance between him and Descartes may begin to be sensed by alluding to his indication that he was *urged* by his brethren to affix his name to this work. But it is also to be noted that while Anselm indicates that he published his meditation at the behest of his brethren at the monastery of Bec, he makes no such indication for his dialogue but, on the contrary, discloses his *own* desire to publish it. The subtle interplay which we see in Anselm's works between the submergence and emergence of his own self might be said to reflect the unique interplay between spirituality (or the desire for sanctity) and the life of learning which Anselm brought to its realization at the monastery of Bec (even though Anselm was already Archbishop of Canterbury when he composed the *Proslogion*).[7] But, once again, if there is precedent for what emerges in Anselm's dialogue, his use of precedent is unprecedented; for his dialectic of the submergence and emergence of his own person is effected in the context of a properly metaphysical endeavor—first philosophy. Modern philosophical subjectivity is not yet present in his first philosophy, but that its condition is, is already intimated in the opening lines of his dialogue.

In the opening chapter of his dialogue, entitled "The Waking [Excitatio] of the Mind for the Contemplation of God," the submergence of his self seems to be conditional for its emergence. Anselm exhorts "little man" to flee for a "little while" from his occupations, to hide for a time from his "tumultuous thoughts," so that he might abandon himself to (and rest for a short time in) God by entering into the "chamber"* of his own mind. In this chamber

---

\* Anselm alludes here to Matthew 6: 6, "intra in cubiculum tuum."

everything except God and those things which can aid him in seeking God will be excluded.

Anselm now begins his dialogue (in prayer) with God, asking God how he can seek (quaerat) and find (inveniat) him. He gives thanks that God has created him in his own image, so that he may remember (memor), think (cogitem) and love (amem) God. But this image is so effaced and worn away by "vices," so obscured by the "smoke of sins," that it is not able to do what it has been made to do unless God "renews" and "re-forms" it. Certainly Anselm does not attempt to "penetrate" God's depth (altitudinem tuam) since in no way can his understanding be compared with that depth. But Anselm does desire to understand in some degree God's truth—a truth which his heart (cor meum) believes and loves. In sum, Anselm believes in order that he may understand, for unless he believed he should not understand.* He does *not* seek to understand in order that he may believe.[8]

Long before Anselm, St. Augustine° had attempted to conjoin the language of the heart and the language peculiar to philosophy.[9] But what is peculiar to the opening chapter of Anselm's dialogue in first philosophy is that the language of the heart and of faith have now become an *object* for philosophy. The desire of the human heart for existence *in* an existence not of this world and the faith which seeks understanding have, in Anselm, become the *theme* to

---

\* credo ut intelligam . . . nisi credidero, non intelligam

° What Anselm says here parallels Book XV, ii, 2 of St. Augustine's *De Trinitate*. In this passage, Augustine attempts to justify the investigation of the incomprehensible, arguing that the investigator has come to *know* something in this investigation if he manages to know *how far* what he seeks exceeds comprehension. In "comprehending the incomprehensibility" of what he seeks, he is urged to go on seeking as long as he is constantly made better by the search after "so great a good—both sought that it may be found, and found that it may be sought." In this sense, Augustine suggests, faith is said to seek, and understanding is said to find (fides quaerit, intellectus invenit). This, of course, becomes, in Anselm, "fides quaerens intellectum" or "faith seeking understanding." Like Augustine, Anselm renders Isaiah 7: 9 as "Unless you believe, you shall not understand." But this passage, as it appears in the Vulgate, actually concludes with the words "non permanebitis," i.e., "you shall not persevere."

be investigated by reason, by first philosophy. And this reason is the reason of Anselm's own mind—of "mens mea." The self of Anselm which is submerged before the immensity of the God whom it seeks turns out to be the self which emerges before this God to ask of him a measure of understanding of divine being commensurate with the existence of that self. The desire for a finite perfection immanent in nature (found in Aristotle's first philosophy) is now the desire of the human heart (in its particularity) for the infinite, for that which transcends nature. And yet, what the *mind* of Anselm seeks is a *finite* comprehension of this infinity, a comprehension which fits his condition as a seeker of wisdom, as one who is seeking understanding—as a *philosopher*.

## ii. Negativity: The Denial of God's Existence

The human heart that "spoke" in chapter one becomes an "object" for the human mind which now, in chapter two, addresses God but only as Anselm's "Lord" (domine). Anselm asks of his Lord that he give understanding to faith (fidei intellectum) so far as his Lord knows it to be advantageous (expedire). What is to be understood here is that this Lord is *as* we believe and that he is *what* we believe. We believe him to exist as *something* than which nothing greater is able to be thought.* But is there no thing of such a nature since "the fool [insipiens] has said in his heart: there is no God"? Anselm quotes here from the opening of the thirteenth and fifty-second psalms in the Vulgate. The remainder of the first verse of the thirteenth psalm says, "They are corrupt, and in their eagerness they do abominable things: there is not one who does good, not even one." The second verse describes the Lord as looking down from heaven over the "sons of men" to see if there is anyone who understands or seeks after God (requirens Deum). And the third verse responds by saying that all have gone astray (declinaverunt) and at the same time have been made useless (inutiles): there is not one who does good, "not even one."[10]

---

\* credimus te esse aliquid quo nihil maius cogitari possit

In the sense of the Vulgate—which would seem to be the sense that Anselm has in mind, given his frequent references to the psalms—the man who says there is no God, the "fool" or "insipiens," is one who neither understands nor seeks after God but is eager, instead, not for what is good but for what is evil—one who has become useless for other men. This would seem to suggest no "ordinary" atheist and might even be construed as consistent with one who says with his mouth that there is a God. The "insipiens" would seem to be the biblical blasphemer who, by his actions and convictions (which may even be hidden from himself), "denies" God's existence. What seems to be significant here is that Anselm addresses God only as "Lord," whereas the fool or blasphemer utters (at least in his heart) the name "God": "non est deus." The name uttered and the denial evinced in the heart of the fool would seem to pertain to a person, not at all to a universal or class concept, not to mention the impersonal νοῦς of the Aristotelian God. It has been pointed out that the appearance of the fool as a blasphemer, a hater of God, whose denial in deed of the existence of God might even be compatible with a theoretical acceptance of this existence, has its parallel in the everyday phenomenon of hatred and betrayal. There is a sense in which the betrayer proves the existence of the betrayed "by the very structure of infidelity."[11] But if this is the case, the fool is necessary to Anselm's argument, not because his lived nonbelief is something completely apart from the believer, but because, in some degree, the believer, in the imperfection of his *lived* faith (and, therefore, hope and love), still shares in the lived denial of the fool.[12]

This same fool, Anselm reflects, when he hears of that which is spoken, viz., "something than which nothing greater is able to be thought," understands what he hears. And what he understands is *in* his understanding (in intellectu), even if he does not understand it to exist (esse). For it is one thing for something to exist in the understanding and another to understand that "something exists." The fool, then, can be said to think *that* God does not exist but without thinking as such *of* God as not existing.[13] His thinking *that* God does not exist—his saying in his heart—is a willed or lived denial of God's existence that is quite compatible with an admission that God "exists" as a *thing* in his understanding; and this willed denial would seem to be a thinking *that* God does not exist which "cohabits" with a thinking *of* God's existence in his understanding.

Anselm gives the example of a painter who, when he preconceives (praecogitat) what he will execute, has what he will execute in his understanding but does not yet understand it to exist because he has not yet made it. But when he has painted it, he both has it in his understanding and he understands it to exist.[14] The situation of the fool, then, would seem to be similar to that of an incomplete human creative process in which the existence of the artifact is thought but the artifact is never understood to exist. Such an incomplete creative process would be peculiar to man, since in the divine creative process, as Anselm has examined it in his meditation, the very thinking of the existence of the artifact would be identical with the understanding of the artifact to exist. Furthermore, given the fallen condition of man which Anselm has addressed, the situation of the fool might also be said to be peculiar to man—that is, what man says in his heart could be at odds with what he thinks in his understanding. If the fool is the extreme case of this split, the split itself is not completely foreign to the believer, and once again the importance of the fool's denial of God's existence for Anselm's argument becomes clear.

Even the fool, then, Anselm continues, is convinced that "something than which nothing greater is able to be thought" exists in his understanding since he understands this phrase when he hears it, and whatever is understood is *in* the understanding. But certainly "that than which a greater cannot be thought"[*] is not able to exist in the understanding alone. For even if it is only in the understanding, it is able to be *thought* to exist *also* in reality (in re) which is greater (maius). If, therefore, "that than which a greater is *not able* to be thought" is in the understanding alone, then it is "that than which a greater *is able* to be thought." Since this cannot be the case, we must conclude "without a doubt" that there exists

---

[*] id quo maius cogitari nequit

something than which a greater cannot be thought (cogitari non valet) both in the understanding and in reality.

In effect, Anselm has argued that if "that than which a greater cannot be thought" could be thought not to exist in reality, then *it itself* could be thought to be greater since it could be thought to be something which *cannot* be thought not to exist in reality.[15] The principle here would seem to be that a nonexistence which is inconceivable has to be "greater" than a nonexistence which is conceivable.[16] Thus, a nonexistence which is inconceivable would have to attach to the idea of that than which a greater cannot be thought. It is not only the case that the fool's heart or will is in conflict with his understanding (in this, the believer is like the fool) but it is also the case that the fool's understanding is at odds with itself, for this understanding conflates a nonexistence which is inconceivable with a nonexistence which is conceivable. And here the situation of the fool is seen to be very different from that of the believer. Though they be alike in having the same sin and the same reason (and the same object for their sin and reason), they are different in that the objects of their will and reason exist on different levels. For the believer recognizes by his reason that in the case of "that than which a greater cannot be thought," it either really exists or what is really thought is something less, some "ordinary, humanly comprehensible, *mere* concept."[17] Although having the same object, the affirmation of the believer and the denial of the "insipiens" do not proceed on the same plane. In conceding the intramental existence of the object of his denial, the fool tacitly concedes the inferiority of the plane on which his denial operates.[18]

But if the lived denial of God's existence is shown to be productive of an essentially inferior plane on which the reason of the "insipiens" meets its *object* (viz., the existence of that which he denies in his heart or with his will), it is by no means obvious that the formulation that Anselm uses is an expression of the lived affirmation of God's existence. "Something than which nothing greater is able to be thought" is not the formulation that a lived faith, a "viva fides," would propose, for there is a certain cerebral ring to it. It seems to be completely useless outside the context of the argument

in which it is proposed. In fact, it seems to have a definite history*
outside the context of Christian faith that Anselm makes a theme
of reason in this dialogue.[19] Anselm's originality here does not
consist in the formula which stands at the center of his argument
but rather in the way in which he makes this formula function in
the argument as a whole. Moreover, the fact that Anselm does not
at this point speak of the formula as the idea of *God* would seem to
suggest that he himself was well aware that the formula, as such,
was not the object of lived Christian faith. Anselm, in other words,
has yet to show that this formula (although it cannot itself signify
God) portrays something that can be signified by the name "God."
Anselm, that is, has yet to show that what this formula signifies is
consistent with all the predicates which can be ascribed to the God
of Christian faith.[20]

In this way, it is his view of God (still to be presented in this dialogue) which will elucidate the rudiments of the so-called Ontological Argument presented in this chapter. Already implied in his meditation is his view of God as the very Word from which man's "locutio" or expression is derived—as the source of the words for existence which are spoken by the human mind. What has yet to be made explicit in his dialogue is how the thinking of what is signified by the formula he uses in this chapter can be expressive of that

---

\* In the first place, there is Boethius who tries to prove in his *De Consolatione Philosophiae* that God can be shown to be good by the common conception of human minds, for since nothing better than God could be found out by thinking (nam cum nihil Deo melius excogitari queat), who could doubt that that than which nothing is better is good (id, quo melius nihil est, bonum esse). Anselm, of course, uses the term "greater" (maius) rather than "better" (melius), but even here there is precedent. In his *Quaestiones Naturales*, Seneca, in answer to the question, "What is God?", answers: that than which nothing greater is able to be found out by thinking (qua nihil maius excogitari potest). In using the term "maius," however, he seems to be addressing the spatial magnitude of the totality. Even when there is an explicit reference to the context of Christian faith, the formulation does not seem to be offered as one which is decisive for that faith. Thus, Augustine in his *Confessions* remarks that no mind has ever been or ever will be able to think of something (cogitare aliquid) which is better (melius) than God who is the highest and best good (summum est optimum bonum). All of these formulations in all of these thinkers seem to occupy a peripheral place.

innermost Word which makes manifest the very nature of human speech itself, grounded as it is in an interior word.[21] But even with the bare formula—"aliquid quo nihil maius cogitari possit"—which is something purely formal and purely negative, something which is not expressive as such of the lived affirmation of faith, Anselm has already indicated the shape of the consummation of his efforts in first philosophy. For he has suggested, by his use of this formula, that nothing above what the name of the Christian God signifies can be thought. He has intimated that this name, even when reflected on in first philosophy, is the name of a person, a "nomen personae." In doing this, he has more deeply addressed the making comprehensible of the incomprehensibility of something, an "aliquid," which is not *there* in the way that any other thing is there, but exists in its own absolutely unique manner—the impossibility of the nonexistence of which he has set forth in this chapter.[22]

### iii. Truth as Rectitude

Chapter three of Anselm's dialogue in first philosophy addresses the conclusion of chapter two by making explicit the positive significance of negativity implicit in chapter two, for the theme of chapter three is that which is not able to be thought not to exist.[*] The claim which the "insipiens" makes by his lived or willed denial, namely, the necessity of the nonexistence of God, cannot really have existence in his understanding, for something than which nothing greater is able to be thought so truly (sic vere) *is* that it is not able to be thought "not to exist." Something is able to be thought to exist which is not able to be thought not to exist, and this is greater than that which is able to be thought not to exist. If it were the case that that than which a greater *cannot* (nequit) be thought were able to be thought not to exist, then that thing than which a greater cannot be thought would *not be* that than which a greater cannot be thought. But this is not "consistent."[23]

---

[*] quod non possit cogitari non esse

It is, then, the impossibility of the nonexistence of *that* which the "mens humana," i.e., the mind of both the fool and the believer, cannot think beyond (as indicated by Anselm's use of "nequit") which entails that this particular something, this "aliquid," truly exists. It is not only the claim of the believer's understanding (which he seeks to embody in his will and actions) but the willed claim which the "insipiens" has said in his heart (that he fails to think in his understanding) which presupposes the impossibility of the nonexistence of that "aliquid" which is the object of both claims. The human mind, then, whether it be "insipiens" or "credens," and though it be a valid measure of possibility, is itself measured by the pure actuality of an "aliquid" which this mind is not able to regard as merely possible. Since this actuality would truly have to exist, it would have to be the truth itself which is the object sought for by the "mens humana" of both the fool and the believer.

It is thus Anselm's notion of truth as a characteristic of understanding, an uprightness or rectitude of understanding, which underlies his making explicit the positive significance of negativity in this chapter. For it is now clear that for Anselm the only place where the universal is to be found is in the human mind as a valid measure of possibility, not in the forms which inform the particular things of nature.[24] In his *De Veritate*, Anselm indicates that truth is not able to be understood as other than "rectitudo," other than an uprightness, a correctness, a fittingness of existence. Truth, therefore, is not only a characteristic of the understanding as such, but is to be found in action, i.e., in willing. Truth is something that is *done* or not done by the signification of propositions, by propositions which signify either something willed or something understood or something both willed and understood. Thus, in the fundamental sense of truth as rectitude, the sentence "It is day" *does* the truth (veritatem facit) when it signifies the existence of day, independently of whether, at the moment, it is or is not day. In this way, truth can be in a materially false sentence (falsa oratione) to the extent that, in order for the sentence to be judged false, it would have to contain the truth by which it is judged false. In this sense, the sentence must perform the truth by which it can be judged true or false as a description of things. Rather than being a disclosure of the permanence of being both immanent in and imitated by the particular things of nature, truth in its most fundamental sense is an uprightness or correctness by which understanding thinks and the will conforms to what rightly exists—what should exist if the sheer problematical existence of particular things is to make sense at all.

Because of this there is a truth of deeds as well as a truth of propositions articulated by the understanding. As an example, Anselm suggests the situation of a man who is confronted by edible and poisonous herbs but does not know how to tell them apart. With him is someone whose ability to distinguish between the two he does not doubt. Suppose, Anselm suggests, this companion points to one kind as edible but then proceeds to eat the other kind. Which is to be more believed: his word or his action? Of course, he would be "saying (diceret) more by his deed (opere) than by his word (verbo) which herbs were edible. Anselm's use of "diceret" here suggests that the truth fundamental to both willing and understanding is a word, an interior word present to both the heart or the will and the understanding. The fact that the fool can say in his heart what cannot be in his understanding means that he presupposes a fundamental truth (viz., the impossibility of the nonexistence of God) in witnessing to this nonexistence in his deeds. If it is the case, in other words, that whatever exists (by the very fact that it is) *says* (dicit) that it ought to exist (debere esse), there must be something of which it cannot be said by the understanding that it ought not to exist. Only by the will could it be said of this something that it does not exist, that is, that it ought not to exist.

But what distinguishes the truth in the will and the truth in the understanding is that the rightness of existence which is either willed or not willed is a "rectitudo" comprehended only by the mind (mente sola), i.e., the understanding as reflexive. If justice can be said to be a "rectitude of the will" preserved for its own sake, then just men can properly be called "upright of heart"* ("recti corde").[25]

---

\* Psalm 31:11 (Vulgate)

The fool, then, is a man devoid of an upright heart and thus is a man capable of saying by his will what he cannot say in his understanding. His actions bespeak what he is saying inwardly by his will, and so we trust his actions here more than what he speaks with his mouth. But the fact that the rightness is only comprehensible by the reflexive understanding leads us to realize that he cannot bespeak a "rectitudo" for what he says by his will or in his heart. The only rightness that is bespoken by the fool is that bespoken by means of his understanding, namely, "deus," to which the will alone, in its peculiar posture of treating the impossible as if it were possible, can add "non est."

It is this "deus," the God of Christian faith, which Anselm can now identify with that than which a greater is not able to be thought:* "And you are this [hoc es tu], O Lord, our God." Anselm now addresses his Lord as God. So truly, therefore, does God exist that he is not able to be thought not to exist. In effect, the formula of chapter two is now seen to be related to the Lord of faith who is the God that the believer both thinks and strives to will and the "insipiens" thinks but denies with his will. The desire for the infinite is ineluctably present, then, in both the believer and the fool, i.e., present in the human mind, the reflexive understanding of *human* being. This desire is seen to be not so much what the human mind *has* as what it *is*. This mind cannot entirely appropriate for itself the object of its desire, but this object (no less than the desire itself) is somehow present[26] to this mind which in the fool, no less than in the believer, is a striving to be a "thinking in God" as preconditional for a "thinking about God."[27]

It follows, then, Anselm says, that it is appropriate that God is not able to be thought not to exist, for if some mind was able to think of something better (aliquid melius) than God, the creature would rise above and judge the Creator. But this is palpably absurd because whatever else there is except God alone is able to be thought not to exist. Here Anselm has shown why the formula used in chapter two can be said to be signified by the predicates of

---

* id quo maius cogitari non potest

the God of Christian faith, namely, because that than which a greater is not able to be thought (which could not be understood not to exist in reality) could only refer to an "aliquid" that (in being supreme as a being among beings) *need not have been* a being among beings (and, therefore, need not have been in relation to anything other than itself). The formula of chapter two is thus seen to refer to the Creator of the world who is not necessitated by his essence to be such a Creator—who does not need a world in order to be God. And this is precisely the God that Christian faith presents, the God who by definition is an "infinite exception," and who, therefore, can be the only real content for the universally presupposed (but particular) subject of all true predicates that is *negatively* addressed as that which could *not* conceivably be surpassed by anything else.[28] Since the formula of chapter two could not be understood in regard to any item or collection of items in the world (or even the world itself), it can only be understood in regard to the God upon whom the Christian believer is utterly reliant.[29]

God alone, then, of all things most truly exists, and of all things he has existence (habes esse) in the greatest degree. Whatever else is, *is* not so truly as God, and so has existence in a lesser degree. Anselm's argument, then, has attempted to show not only that the existence of all things except God is unthinkable without God's existence but that the very non-existence of God is entirely unthinkable in any circumstance[30]—even in the materially false but possible circumstance which the human mind or reflexive understanding can conceive, namely, the very non-existence of the world.

In thinking the non-existence of the world, the human mind would be left with "nothing," but a nothingness which would admit of being understood. But this nothingness would not be *in* its reflexive understanding, since this "nothing" would merely signify the removal of something and would not posit anything in the understanding. The human mind would be left with a "nothing" which is spoken of "as if" it were something (quasi aliquid), but it would not be capable of understanding this nothingness as if it were something or an "aliquid" beyond God. Its very capacity to understand nothingness as if it were something would presuppose its incapacity to think the non-existence of (God as) the something or "aliquid" that would exist even if there were nothing else that exists. Why then, Anselm asks, has the fool said in his heart that there is no God, that God, so to speak, is "nothing," if it is so abundantly clear to the rational mind that God exists in the highest degree of all things? Why, Anselm answers somewhat redundantly, unless he is foolish (stultus) and a fool.[31] Yet the redundancy would seem to be unavoidable, for the understanding cannot account for the split between itself and the will, a split which is instanced par excellence in the fool precisely because it is a breach endemic to human being in consequence of its fallen condition. In the end, the problem of the "insipiens" is not primarily his understanding's being at odds with itself but rather his understanding's being at odds with his will. The problem is ultimately that of evil, and this problem Anselm has yet to address in his dialogue.

Nonetheless, in chapter four, Anselm attempts to spell out a deeper significance in his redundant answer. Why is there, in the first place, a problem in the fool's saying in his heart what he is not able to think (cogitare), or how could he not think what he said in his heart? The problem arises only because there must be a sense in which to say in the heart and to think are the same. And so there must be a sense in which the fool truly both thought (because he said in his heart) and did not say in his heart (because he was not able to think). The "insipiens" *truly thought* that God does not exist—insofar as he thought the term "God" as referring to an *object* signified by the term—because he spoke by his will or heart of God as nonexistent. Yet, he *truly did not say in his heart* or by his will that God is nonexistent because he could not think the very entity, the "aliquid," which God is, as nonexistent.*[32]

---

\* In one way a thing is thought (cogitatur res) when the vocalized word (vox) signifying it is thought. In another way a thing is thought when the very entity (id ipsum) which the thing is, is understood (intelligitur). In the first way, when the "vox," which is taken to signify God, is thought, God is able to be thought not to exist. But in the second way, when the very entity that God is, is understood, God is not able to be thought not to exist. No one, understanding what God is, is able to think that God does not exist, even when he says these words in his heart, for God is that than which a greater is

To the extent, then, that the human will or heart can, by its actions, will the nonexistence of God, i.e., to the extent that man can act as if God did not exist, then man can think that God does not exist, but what he is thinking here is the term "God" as signifying an object, a being among the other beings whose nonexistence he can conceive, i.e., the possibility of whose nonexistence he can conceive. In effect he is thinking God *only* as a being among beings and *not* as a being who need not have been a being among beings; he is thinking God as a being who needs some other being in order to exist. But to the extent that man thinks God as the very person or subject of existence or absolutely unique "aliquid" who would exist even if there were no world (no beings for him to be among)—i.e., to the extent that man thinks God as the subject of which nonexistence could in no way be a predicate and not merely as an object to which a thought in the human mind refers—to this extent, the human will is incapable of willing, the human heart is incapable of saying, the human being is incapable of acting in terms of the nonexistence of God. Man, in other words, can only think the nonexistence of God if he thinks of God as an object of one of his ideas, an object in some way like the objects of the rest of his ideas. He can only think the nonexistence of God if he implicitly conceives of God as a creature, as a being in some way immanent (by necessity) in this world. And he can only will God's nonexistence ("say in his heart" that God does not exist) if he acts as if all that existed were this world of natural entities. In the end, what man *thinks* when he thinks God is either a creature or is some kind of participation in the self-knowing of God.[33] And in the final analysis what he *wills* is either *a* world "as if" it were uncreated or *the* world in its truth—the world created out of nothing.

And so, in what would appear to be a signal that the basic thrust of his single and self-sufficing argument has now been displayed,

---

not able to be thought, and whoever understands this well also understands that this same Being so exists that not even in thinking can it not exist. Therefore, he who thinks (in the sense of understanding) the very peculiarity of the entity that God is, cannot think him not to exist (nequit eum non esse cogitare).

Anselm gives thanks to the God to whom he has spoken in this dialogue. The raising of the "mens humana" to God could only have been an act, a gift, of God, but the gift has shown the human mind (and that necessarily means "mens mea") to be the image of the God who raises it to himself. In no way is this mind divine or possessed of a divine part. It is human and only human; otherwise it would have no need of being raised to God by God. For this particular mind, which is purely human and always "mens mea," to think and to say in the heart are the same to the extent that they *ought* to be the same. The "ought" here suggests that the very nature of the "mens humana" is a striving to be *in* that existence that it ought to be in—a striving to be raised to that which can exist in its understanding but which does not *only* exist in its understanding. What Anselm is thankful for is precisely this illumination that his mind is in a fundamental sense not circumscribed by itself, not fully contained by itself. The sense here, however, is not merely that of Aristotle (viz., the human mind as a part of nature which depends upon the rest of nature in order to gather its truth), but is the more important, fundamental, and astounding sense that what the mind strives for is somehow thought by it as that innermost Word which is at the bottom of its particularity but which is there only by virtue of that Word's existing completely beyond its comprehension. Reason is no less a gift than faith: the former being an illumination of the latter. What Anselm previously believed through God's gift, he can now understand by God's illumination. And the gift of reason[*]—not to mention the gift by which reason is raised to God—is such that even if (like the "insipiens") he did not want to believe that God exists, he would not be able to understand what he would want to deny.[34]

### iv. Comprehension and the Incomprehensible

Having presented the structure of his single and self-sufficing argument, Anselm must now spell out its implications. What does

---

[*] See p. 20 above.

the argument entail for what can be said about what God is? By virtue of addressing God here as the God who is Lord, the answer seems quite clear: the highest of all beings who "alone exists through himself" and who "made everything else from nothing." The basic thrust of his single argument in this dialogue has not addressed God in this positive way as the highest of all beings. But here in chapter five Anselm attempts to draw a connection between what the argument has established (that "that than which nothing greater can be thought" truly and "most truly exists") and what would have to pertain to this Being as Lord (viz., his being the "summum omnium" and "Creator ex nihilo") in the view of Christian faith. If God were not Lord (i.e., the highest of all beings and the Creator of all other beings out of nothing) there would be *less* being than what is able to be thought. There would be only one being rather than many beings, yet God would be no greater or lesser were he not Lord. If God had not created the world, it would be possible to think of "less" being in the sense of fewer beings, but God himself would be no lesser were he not Lord, nor would he be any greater were he, in having created the world, Lord. We can think the situation of there being less being if there were no world, but we cannot think the situation of God's being less if there were no world. We can think the situation of there being more being if there is a world, but we cannot think the situation of God's being more if there is a world. The logic of "more or less" cannot be applied to God but only to the world. But when it is properly applied to the world we realize that since there is a world—that is, since there is not less being than we can think—then God would have to be its Creator and the highest of all beings, for otherwise nothing would be good without a highest good through whose creative act every good exists.

God would have to be whatever it is better to be than not to be. It would not be better in and for God, however, to be the highest good (among several goods) and to be "Creator ex nihilo," but it would be "better" for the world that there be a highest good and a "Creator ex nihilo." And, in fact, what is "better" for the world is seen to be what is *necessary* to account for the problematical existence of particular things in the world. What would be better absolutely, however, would be to be just rather than unjust, veracious rather than a deceiver, blessed rather than unblessed, all-powerful rather than not all-powerful.[35] And these attributes would have to be had by God in being that than which nothing greater can be conceived. In sum, it is in relation to us that God would have to be the highest good and the Creator of the world "ex nihilo" and not in relation to himself; whereas it is in relation to himself that he would have to be just, truthful, blessed, and omnipotent[*] (and not, as such, in terms of his relation to us). The basic thrust of the Ontological Argument, in other words, cannot establish the impossibility of the non-existence of God's Creation "ex nihilo," but this Creation is the only satisfactory account for the problematical existence of things in the world. Although this Creation is not a direct conclusion of the Ontological Argument (since it would not be necessary from God's viewpoint, and the argument is precisely the attempt on the part of the human mind to be raised into some kind of participation in the self-knowledge or viewpoint of God), it might be said to be a corollary of that argument, since, given the argument's conclusion, the human mind would not exist unless God had created it.[36]

What had enabled Anselm to claim that to say in his heart is the same as to think (i.e., that to will and to think are the same in the sense that they *ought* to be the same) was his notion of a fundamental truth or rectitude underlying both willing and thinking-as-understanding, that is, a fundamental word underlying both willing and understanding in human being. But this fundamental "verbum"

---

[*] If God is everything which it is better to be than not to be, however, his omnipotence, as Anselm indicates in chapter seven, must be consistent with his *not* being able to do everything, such as, e.g., "deceiving" or making the true into the false. These deceptions must really be understood as an "impotence" through "power" because the more anyone has these deceptive "powers," the more "adversity and perversity have power over him." God, then, is truly omnipotent because he is capable of nothing through impotence, and nothing is able to have power over against him. Creation "ex nihilo" would be a fitting expression of such omnipotence, but it would hardly be necessitated by such omnipotence.

is subject in man to the expression of many words, and so the heart or will is capable of being at odds with the understanding—a situation fundamental to man in his fallen condition but which finds its "highest" instantiation in the "insipiens." The biblical fool attempts to will the world as uncreated, i.e., he attempts to act in this world as if this world contained the source of its own intelligibility. To this extent he can say in his heart that there is no God who is completely other than the world, while at the same time thinking that which (as other than the world) nothing greater can be conceived. The thought underlying his will is the nonexistence of God, i.e., the thought of God as identifiable with (or containable by) the world—the thought of God as merely a creature. But the thought underlying his understanding is the true idea of God as that than which nothing greater can be conceived, that is, as that which cannot be anything in or of this world. The truth or rectitude that is in his understanding is not in his will. Because justice is a rectitude of the will, an uprightness of the heart, the "insipiens" brings the injustice to be found among men to its most poignant expression: he attempts to order his life as if both the conclusion and the corollary of the Ontological Argument could not obtain. Interestingly enough, justice, as the rectitude of the will, is precisely one of those attributes that the biblical God would have to possess and *be* in himself. But it is involved in a kind of biblical dialectic with God's mercy. And this dialectic may underlie the very grandeur of Anselm's effort to bring into a unity the medieval Christian traditions of the "via negativa" and "paideia," that is, traditions which dealt, respectively (but never entirely apart from each other) with what God is in himself and what he is in relation to man.

In keeping with this dialectic, Anselm, in chapter eight of his dialogue, asks how God can be both "merciful" and "passionless." He answers that when God looks at us in our misery, *we* feel (nos sentimus) the effect of his mercy but he does not feel what we feel. Therefore, God can be said to be merciful because he saves the miserable and pardons sins, but he can also be said to be not merciful since he does not experience any feeling of compassion for the miserable. But how, Anselm asks in chapter nine, can the all-just and supremely just Being "spare the wicked" and yet justly have mercy (iuste misereatur) on the wicked. Confronting the problem of evil here, which the existence of the "insipiens" raises, Anselm answers this question with another question. Is it because God's goodness is incomprehensible to man that the answer to this question is "concealed" in the "inaccessible light" in which God dwells?[*] For truly, it can be said that in the most profound (altissimo) and hidden (secretissimo) dwelling place of God's goodness is concealed the "fount from which the stream of his mercy flows." Though God is all-and-supremely-just, he is also "beneficent" even to the wicked precisely because he is all-and-supremely (totus summe) good.[37]

Although the fount from which God's mercy flows is incomprehensible to man, Anselm attempts to comprehend the nature of that incomprehensibility. If we look at God's goodness in relation to man, there is a sense in which God would be less good if he were beneficent to none of the wicked, for one who is good to both good and wicked men would be "better" than one who is good only to good men, and one who is good to the wicked by both punishing and sparing them would be better than one who only punishes them. From this admittedly human point of view, God would be merciful because he is all good and supremely good. But man can only "discern" where the river of God's mercy flows, that is, he can only investigate this mercy in terms of its effects in the world, but he cannot perceive the hidden fount from which this river is born. He can see that it is from the "plenitude" of God's goodness that God is gracious with those who sin, but in the depths of this goodness is hidden from man the reason for this graciousness. All that man can know is that God "willed" to do this, and he is left to wonder at this will.

If God is the "immeasurable goodness" which exceeds all understanding, Anselm can only ask that the mercy which flows from (profluit) God flow into (influat in) him. If it is difficult to understand how God's mercy is "not apart from" his justice, it is,

---

[*] "lucem inhabitat inaccessibilem" (1 Timothy 6:16).

nonetheless, necessary to believe that it is in no way opposed to that justice. For if God is merciful because he is supremely good, and he is not "summe bonus" unless he is "supremely just," then he is merciful because he is supremely just. All that Anselm can do is to ask God's help that he may *understand* what he says here.[*] Is it the case that because it is just for God to be so good he cannot be understood to be better? Is it the case that God "works so powerfully" that he is not able to be thought to be "more powerful"? But from man's perspective as the recipient of God's goodness, this would not be the case if God were good in relation to man "only by retribution" and "not by sparing," and if God made good only those not yet good and not also the wicked.[°][38]

It would not be the case, however, that God is so just that he cannot be thought to be more just if he only returned good to good men but did not permit evil to be returned to the wicked. For those whom he wills to be punished, it is not just to be saved; and for those whom he wills to spare, it is not just to be damned, since that alone is just that he wills, and that is not just which he does not will. But if God is good even in sparing, it would be possible for him who is supremely just to will "good for the wicked." In all of this, however, man is unable to comprehend why among those who are wicked, God saves some rather than others through his supreme goodness and damns some rather than others through his supreme justice. But what man does know by reason is that certainly whatever God is, he is not through another but through his own self. God is the very life (ipsa vita) by which he lives (qua

---

[*] ut intelligam quod dico

[°] But from man's very human and this-worldly perspective, what is more just than that the good should receive good things (boni bona) and the wicked evil things (mali mala)! From this perspective, man would conclude that when God punishes the wicked it is just because it agrees (convenit) with their merits. But when God spares them it must also be just, not because of their merits, but because it is compatible (condecens) with God's goodness. Yet the reason for this is hidden from the human perspective. In this way there is no inconsistency between (the Vulgate) Psalms 24:10, where "all the ways of the Lord" are said to be "mercy and truth," and 144:17, where the Lord is said to be "just in all his ways."

vivis), the very wisdom by which he is wise, the very goodness by which he is good to both good and bad men. For God—but, it would seem, *only* for God—there is *no* problem of evil, since a problem exceeds the capacity of the investigator to the extent that it is a problem, and for God there is nothing (i.e., *no thing*) which is greater than what he is.

Because of this, Anselm says in chapter thirteen of his dialogue that no place or time "confines" God of whom it can be said that he is everywhere and always, that he is uniquely "uncircumscribed" and eternal. This means that there is a sense, as Anselm indicates in chapter fourteen, in which God is both seen and not seen by those seeking him. Anselm can say in regard to his single argument in this dialogue that he seems to have found God with such certain truth (certa veritate) and with such true certitude (vera certitudine). But if he has truly discovered God, why is it that his soul does not feel (sentit) God? Has it *not* found that which it has found to be the light and the truth? But how did it understand this unless by seeing the light and the truth? Is it that it saw both truth and light and yet did not see God because it saw God only "somewhat" but did not see him as he is? Anselm strives to see more than he has seen, but he sees nothing "beyond" what he has seen except "darkness." The "eye" of his soul is both darkened (tenebratur) by its own infirmity and dazzled (reverberatur) by God's splendor, obscured by its own smallness and overwhelmed by God's immensity, restricted by its own narrowness (angustia) and overcome by God's fullness (amplitudine). For how boundless is God who in one glance (uno intuitu) sees whatever has been made and how it was made from nothingness. The purity, simplicity, splendor, and certitude of this one glance is clearly more than can be understood by a creature.

It is thus in chapter fifteen that Anselm draws out the most important implication of his "unum argumentum." God is not only that than which a greater cannot be thought but he is something greater than can be thought.* For since something of this kind is

---

\* quiddam maius quam cogitari possit

able to be thought to exist, if God is not this very thing, then something greater than God is able to be thought, and this cannot be the case.[39] The ultimate implication of the single and self-sufficing argument of his dialogue is that "that than which nothing greater can be thought" *is*, as such, something greater than can be thought. And the very fact that the mind can think this identity means that God *is* this very identity.

In the end, the human mind thinks the existence of that whose essence is beyond its capacity to think. The "mens humana" in its own negative way comprehends the necessary existence of that which is incomprehensible to it. The reflexive understanding of man is grasped or comprehended by something that it cannot grasp or comprehend. And yet this understanding can comprehend *its being grasped by something that it cannot grasp*.

### v. The Supra-Substantial Divine Subject

The "lux inaccessibilis" in which God dwells cannot be penetrated by anything other than God which would be able, so to speak, to "look over" God. Anselm can say that he does not see this light because it is "too much" for him, and yet, whatever he sees, he sees through this light, much as the weakened eye sees what it sees by the light of the sun but is unable to look at the sun itself. Human understanding, i.e., Anselm's understanding (intellectus meus), cannot grasp this inaccessible light, nor can the "eye" of his soul suffer itself to be turned toward (intendere) this light for too long. This light is "as far" from Anselm as he is "near" to it. It is as "far removed" from his vision (conspectu me) as he is "present" to its vision. This light is within him and around him and yet he does not feel it, for it is nonetheless still "hidden" to his soul which turns (versatur) in its darkness and misery. Although God has given to created things in their own "sensible mode" those qualities which he himself has in his own "ineffable mode," the senses of Anselm's soul have been hardened, dulled, and obstructed by the "ancient weariness of sin." And so, once more, disturbance, sorrow, and mourning stand in the way of Anselm's

## Anselm's Dialogue in First Philosophy

seeking "joy" and "gladness." Having striven "to ascend" to the "lucem dei" or light of God, Anselm has only "fallen back" into his own darkness—a falling, however, which had occurred before his mother conceived him, for all men fell in the first man in whom they all sinned.*

As a result of this primal human fall which Anselm can say perdures in his own falling, all men lost that which, when they will to seek it, they do not know it, and when they seek it they do not find it, and when they find it, it is not what they seek.° The condition of the "insipiens," then, of willing what he does not understand and of understanding what he does not will is still, in some fundamental sense, the condition of Anselm—the very condition of human being. And in response to this, Anselm can only ask that God free him from himself *for* God. In the realization that the most important implication of his single argument in this dialogue is that the human mind is grasped and touched by something that it itself cannot grasp and touch, and in the sadness that has returned to him after the joy of having found this argument, Anselm summons for one last time all of his understanding (toto intellectu) in order to consider the light that this realization might shed on the significance of his argument.[40]

In doing this, Anselm is thrown back on the question that he already raised, viz., what God is—not what is this "what" that God is but what is this "who" that God is. But now "substantia" seems to be put aside completely, and Anselm rephrases the question: What shall his heart (cor meum) understand God to be?

Anselm now strives to examine the truth, the word, that underlies both his heart or his will and his understanding. Assuredly, God is every "true good," and these are many, but Anselm's "narrowed understanding" is not able "to see them all simultaneously in one glance," so as "to delight in all at once." Whatever is joined of parts is not entirely one but is in a certain way other (diversum) than itself. But all of this would have to be foreign

---

\* See Psalm 50:7 (Vulgate) and Romans 5:12.

° Cf. p. 58 above.

(aliena) to God than whom nothing better is able to be thought.\*
God must be so much one and the same with himself that in nothing is he dissimilar with himself. He must be "unity itself" not even divisible by the understanding. His eternity, therefore, is always a "whole," which means that it is completely timeless (extra omne tempus), so that nothing can contain it but it contains all things. In being before (ante) and beyond (ultra) all things, God "makes full" and embraces (complecteris) all things. All other things are in no way able to exist without him, but in no way would he be any the less were they to return into nothingness.° He alone is always "present" at that point which any given thing has not yet reached, and his timeless eternity contains "the very ages of time" insofar as he exists entirely without space.

Whereas everything, Anselm says in chapter twenty-two of his dialogue, in the world—insofar as it is one thing in the whole and another in its parts, and insofar as it always has something mutable in it—is "not entirely what it is," God alone is fully what he is and who he is. The world itself began from non-existence (non esse) and "is able to be thought not to exist"; and so everything in the world does not exist "properly and absolutely." God alone is what he is entirely because whatever he is, he is "wholly and always." He alone exists as present in such a way that he is entirely sufficient to himself, wanting nothing but being that which "all things want" if they are to be and *to be well*. He is so simple, in fact, that there cannot be born of him an other than what he is. Nor can there proceed from his supreme simplicity an other than that from which it proceeds. God, in other words, is "trinitas," i.e., tri-unity, in which whatever each person is "singly," this is the whole trinity simultaneously. Each person here is not other than the "supremely simple unity" and "the supremely unified simplicity" which cannot be multiplied. As triune, God is that one thing necessary\*\* which contains the joyfulness (iucunditatem) of all things good.[41]

---

\* quo nihil melius cogitari potest. Cf. p. 30 above.
° nullo modo minus es ... etiam si illa redeunt in nihilum.
\*\* "unum est necessarium," Luke 10:42

Anselm thus returns in his dialogue to where he started—to the joy which he seeks in the midst of the desolation of his condition, that of fallen man. The more obvious product of his attempt to understand the God which faith seeks has been his singular attempt in this dialogue to prove (probare) the existence of that God. The less obvious product—the one which he seemed to grasp but also to have lost hold of—is joy and "delight."[42]

If the salvation that has been accomplished, he says, is joyful, how joyful is the salvation which accomplishes all salvation. To desire this simple good, which is entirely good, is enough (satis) for man—is the "unum necessarium." For how greatly would be the rejoicing of the human heart, this "needy heart," if it loved God with its entirety! Although the whole heart and soul of man do not suffice for the grandeur of this love (dignitati dilectionis) and for the fullness of this joy (plenitudini gaudii), Anselm can now, in chapter twenty-six of his dialogue, claim that he has discovered a joy which is more than full and that lies in the *future* where the whole of that joy will not enter into those who rejoice but they will enter wholly into that joy. Although he is not able to rejoice fully "in this life," he can pray to advance daily in this joy until it comes to fullness, so that here in this life his joy may be great "in hope" and in the next life full "in reality." In this life, meanwhile, his mind can *meditate* on the fullness of this joy, his heart can *love* it, and his soul can *hunger* for it.*[43] With this, Anselm concludes his dialogue in first philosophy, his dialogue with God, his prayer for the understanding which faith seeks.

### vi. Anselm's Response to Criticism

Anselm, in the end, claims to be a philosopher, a seeker and lover of a wisdom which he does not possess. But the wisdom which he seeks is not, as in Aristotle, an impersonal νοῦς which by necessity is immanent in nature, but is a person who completely transcends nature. As this kind of philosopher, Anselm stands over

---

* meditetur ... amet ... esuriat

against the fool whose actions belie this kind of wisdom. But the fool enters Anselm's dialogue with God in such a way that his presence is necessary for the kind of philosophical activity in which Anselm engages. The negativity of the formula that stands at the center of Anselm's single and self-sufficing argument requires the negativity of the lived denial of God's existence.

This, it would seem, is something new, not only when we compare Anselm with Aristotle's founding of first philosophy, but when we compare him with prior Christian theology and philosophy as well. A positive significance for *both* infinity and negativity would seem to be articulated for the first time in first philosophy. The lived affirmation of a supranatural, infinite measure for all of nature is made an object for reason but only to the extent that the lived denial of this measure is also made an object for reason. The lived denial is seen to be a perverted imitation of the lived affirmation of faith to the extent that the reflexive understanding (underlying both the lived denial and affirmation) cannot deny the existence of the subject of being (God) that is affirmed in faith. But the lived denial that is incarnate in the "insipiens" lives on within Anselm (by virtue of his sinfulness) to be struggled with by Anselm the philosopher—the seeker of wisdom, the seeker of God. In this way, the philosopher is involved in a struggle with himself that does not seem to have any precedent in ancient philosophy and certainly not in the Aristotelian founding of first philosophy. In fact, the very *self* of the philosopher is now precisely what is at issue, just as Anselm's personal authorship is what is stylistically at issue. And although the inspiration in this regard is quite distinctly Augustinian (as can be seen in the *Confessions*), the molding of this inspiration into a single argument and the way in which reason makes faith an object for itself in this argument is something *new*—a decisive event in the history of first philosophy—to the extent that the self of the philosophical investigator is now matter for metaphysical speculation.

The self who believes and the self who denies are now the material for metaphysical speculation. The fact that in the *Proslogion* Anselm is carrying on a dialogue with God (and not a meditation by himself or a dialogue with the "insipiens") is the clue here. The self of the believer and the self of the biblical fool are the *objects* of philosophical speculation. God is investigated but only insofar as the investigator speaks *to* him. Moreover, the self of the believer, the "mens mea" of Anselm, is made such an object only to the extent that the self of the biblical fool is made such an object. And so, Anselm himself has appended to the *Proslogion* a reply to it by one who speaks on behalf of the fool (pro insipiente), namely, the monk Gaunilo.

Gaunilo's reply, in the first place, interprets the negative formula of Anselm's dialogue as if it read positively. Gaunilo speaks of this formula as that which is greater than all those things that are able to be thought.* He claims that this formula is not thought by one who knows (novit) what is signified by the spoken words (voce significari), i.e., it is not thought in terms of the thing signified or as true in thought alone. Rather, it is thought in terms of a movement of his soul (animi motum) whereby he strives to apprehend the signification of the words heard by him. Since from this one cannot conclude in any way that the thing signified by the formula exists also in reality, Gaunilo claims that Anselm's argument has not "indubitably proven" what it has set out to prove. It would first have to be proven that this something which is greater than everything else truly exists somewhere in reality, for then only would the fact that it is greater than everything else make it evident that it also "subsists" in itself.

It must first, then, be conclusively proved, Gaunilo remarks, that there *is* "some higher being" that is greater and better than all things.° Furthermore, his own knowledge of his own existence,

---

\* illud omnibus quae cogitari possint maius

° To illustrate his point, Gaunilo offers the example of what some according to the fable have called a "lost" island which is superior to all other lands inhabited by men by virtue of the abundance to be found there. But suppose someone were to say that you could no more doubt that this island (which is held to be superior to all others) truly exists somewhere in reality than you could doubt that it exists in your understanding. Suppose the reason given here is that it is more excellent (praestantius) to exist in the understanding and in reality than it is to exist in the understanding alone, and so it is neces-

Gaunilo suggests, is an instructive parallel. He knows most certainly that he exists, but he also knows, nonetheless, that he could not exist (posse non esse). What he does not know is whether he can think of himself as not existing *while* he knows most certainly that he exists. If he is able, then why can't he do the same thing with anything else he knows with the same certitude, including the idea of the supreme being? On the other hand, if he is not able, then the quality which Anselm attributes to God (namely, that God cannot be thought not to exist) will not be "proper to God." There is, then, a "rightly sensed" element in Anselm's argument, viz., that perhaps the supreme being or "summa res" cannot be *understood* (intelligi) not to exist or even to be able not to exist, but Anselm goes too far when he says that this being cannot be *thought* (cogitari) not to exist. Furthermore, Anselm goes further astray when he infers from our purported incapacity to understand God as something nonexistent that God actually exists. He would need "a more vigorous way of arguing" to establish, in the first place, the actual existence of God.[44]

In his response to Gaunilo's criticism, Anselm makes note of the fact that in speaking on behalf of the fool, Gaunilo himself is not an "insipiens" but a Christian believer (catholicus), and so it will suffice if Anselm addresses his response to the believer. It would seem that Anselm is convinced that he cannot engage in a dialogue with the fool, even though the same reason is present in both the fool and the believer, precisely because the very *subject* of existence, that is, the existence which cannot not exist, which is addressed by that reason, is encountered by the fool and the believer on different levels. In addressing, then, the *believer* who speaks on behalf of the fool, Anselm points out that the "than which a greater is unable to be thought" is not able to be thought to exist except as "without beginning," whereas whatever is able to be thought to ex-

---

sary for this island to exist in reality, for if it did not, any other island existing in reality would be more excellent than it. Such an argument would be absurd unless its proponent first showed that this island truly and indubitably exists and is not merely "something uncertain" in the understanding. So also might the "insipiens" respond to Anselm's argument.

ist but does not actually exist is able to be thought as having a beginning of its existence. Thus, that than which a greater cannot be thought is not able to be thought as existing and yet not exist: if it can be thought to exist then it exists necessarily. But even more fundamentally, if it can be thought of at all then it is necessary that it exists.*

In response to what seems to be Gaunilo's objection—viz., that to be necessitated to think the impossibility of the nonexistence of "that than which a greater is unable to be thought" does not as such entail the impossibility of its nonexistence—Anselm has offered the following analysis of possibility. If, in fact, it is possible that God exists, then, in order to be "that than which a greater is unable to be thought," it would have to be impossible for God not to exist. If, however, it is not possible that God exists (i.e., it is impossible that God exists), then what is called "God" here is not that than which a greater is unable to be thought. If, in other words, the existence of God is possible, then it is necessary. To think the possibility of his existence is to think the impossibility of his nonexistence, and to think the impossibility of his nonexistence would not be possible without the actual impossibility of his nonexistence. But if the existence of God is impossible, then it is impossible to conceive that than which a greater is unable to be thought, and if it is impossible

---

* No one who denies or doubts that there exists something than which a greater cannot be thought denies or doubts that if it were to exist, it would not be able not to exist either "actually" or "in the understanding," for otherwise it would not be that than which a greater is not able to be thought. Since whatever can be thought but is not existent, if it were to exist, would be able not to exist either in actuality or in the understanding, it follows—merely from its being able to be thought—that "that than which a greater cannot be thought" cannot not exist (non potest non esse). But when we suppose that it does not exist (even though it can be thought), we realize that whatever can be thought and does not exist, were it to exist, would not exist as that than which a greater cannot be thought. To argue, furthermore, as Gaunilo does, that because "that than which a greater is not able to be thought" is not completely (non penitus) understood, it cannot be understood at all and cannot exist in the understanding, is much like arguing that one who does not see the purest light of the sun directly does not see the "light of the day" because that light is the "light of the sun."

to conceive this, then there is no nonexistence the impossibility of which can be thought. But if it is impossible to think the nonexistence of anything (even God), then it is possible to think the existence of anything (even God). We are thus left with the aforementioned alternative where God's existence is possible, namely, that if God's existence is possible then it is necessary.

If, Anselm reflects, what is thought is thought by a thought (cogitatione cogitatur), and if what is thought by a thought is thus (insofar as it is thought) *in* thought, it follows that what is understood is understood by the understanding (intellectu intelligitur), and what is understood by the understanding is thus (insofar as it is understood) *in* the understanding. To say that God can be thought, consequently, is to say that he has existence "in cogitatione," and to say that he can be thought in the sense of understanding the peculiar entity that he is (even if this understanding is only partial) is to say that he has existence "in intellectu." If, however, he is said to have existence in the understanding alone, he is nonetheless able to be thought to exist in reality also. But if he can be *thought* to exist in reality but is *said* to exist in the understanding alone, then whoever so thinks him thinks something which is greater (maius) than him. The result would thus be that if "that than which a greater cannot be thought" exists only in the understanding, it *is* that than which a greater can be thought.

It follows, then, that "that than which a greater cannot be thought," if it is in any understanding, does not exist in the understanding alone.[45] To think God (in the sense of understanding what we think) is to think God as existing in reality; but if God does not exist in reality then what we are thinking is not God. And if we cannot think God then we cannot think anything for which it is impossible not to exist. And if we cannot think anything for which it is impossible not to exist, then for everything which we think it is possible to exist. But if for everything which we think it is possible to exist, then there is not anything which we cannot think. There are no limits to the capacity of our thought to think possibilities. But if there is not anything which we cannot think, then God is thinkable. Once again, we are left only with the alternative of the possibility of God's existence; and if God's existence is possible then it is necessary.

Certainly, Anselm reflects, in the case of Gaunilo's own existence, he is able to think of himself as not existing even while he most certainly knows that he exists, since he is able to think of something as not existing while he knows that it exists because he is able to think the one and know the other at the same time. Whatever exists—except "that than which a greater is unable to be thought"—can be thought of as nonexistent even when we know that it does exist. But if we know that something exists, in the sense of not being able to think of it as not existing, then we cannot think of something as not existing if we know that it exists, since we cannot think of it as existing and not existing at the same time. And this is appropriate to God alone.*

Anselm, furthermore, takes care to point out a fundamental confusion in Gaunilo's understanding of his argument. That which is "greater than everything" and that than which a greater *cannot* be thought (cogitari nequit) are not the same thing when it comes to proving the existence in reality of what is spoken about. For what if someone should say that something that is greater than everything which exists itself exists but that this same being can be thought of as not existing, or that something greater than this same being can be thought of even though this something greater does

---

\* This would mean that Gaunilo's example of the lost island is simply not to the point of Anselm's argument. If anyone shall find something existing in reality or in thought alone, Anselm says, except that than which a greater cannot be thought, to which the connection made in the argument can obtain, "I shall find that lost island and give it to that person never more to be lost." It is only that than which a greater cannot be thought which is not able to be thought not to exist, for it alone exists by such "certain reason of truth" that if it were able to be thought not to exist then it would "exist in no way." If anyone says, then, that he thinks this Being as nonexistent, what he thinks is either something than which a greater cannot be thought or he does not think this Being. If he does not think this Being, then he is not thinking that what he does not think does not exist (non cogitat non esse quod non cogitat). But if he does think something than which a greater cannot be thought, and yet says that he thinks this Being as nonexistent, then he would have to be said to think what he is not able to think (cogitat quod cogitari non potest).

not exist? That which is greater than everything, in other words, could admit of having something greater than it thought by virtue of the fact that the impossibility of nonexistence would not attach to our thinking this something greater than all things. "That which is greater than anything," then, would need another argument in order to be effective; but "that than which a greater cannot be thought" would need nothing but itself in order to be effective. That than which nothing greater can be conceived *cannot* refer to anything which is a member of this world; that which is greater than everything else *could* refer to this world as a totality or possibly to one member of this world. To the extent, however, that we know this world to exist, although we can think its nonexistence, we are "not able to understand" that than which a greater is not able to be thought unless as "that which alone is greater than everything."[46] We are not able to understand God in relation to us except as Creator of this world; but we are able to think God as he is in himself as the being that would exist even if there were no world.

Furthermore, the negative formula is to be distinguished from the positive formula because Anselm is concerned to prove what was doubted (dubium probare), and doubting is essentially the mode of negativity which, as Anselm argues, implies the desire for a certitude than which nothing greater can be thought. The impetus behind doubt is thus the force of the negative formula.[47] In fact, Anselm says, it is "not believable" that anyone is able to deny (negare) the existence of "that than which a greater is unable to be thought" (which, when it is heard, is understood to some extent) on the basis of his denying "God"—the "meaning of which" is thought in no way. It was thus to prove against the fool (contra insipientem) that God exists that Anselm proposed the negative formula since the fool would understand this formula in some way.

There is, however, a way in which this formula can be joined with the attributes which faith predicates of God. Rising, by a distinction of degrees, from the less good to that which is more good, we can (by virtue of those things than which something greater can be thought) unite "that than which nothing greater can be thought" to what is spoken of God by faith. This is precisely what Anselm has attempted to do in his dialogue. Just as one is not prevented from saying "ineffable," although what is said to be unutterable is not able to be said, and just as one is able to think of "nonthinkable" although one is not able to think that to which "nonthinkable" refers (or is said of), so also when "that than which nothing greater can be thought" is said, there is no doubt that "what is heard" is able to be thought and understood, even if that thing itself (res illa) cannot be thought or understood. Whoever, therefore, denies that there exists something than which a greater is unable to be thought understands and thinks the "negationem" which he makes; and this denial is not able to be understood or thought without its parts. But one of these parts is "quo maius nihil cogitari potest." Thus, whoever denies the existence of this part of his denial understands and thinks of its existence as "that which is not able not to exist." What is not able not to exist must be greater than what is able not to exist. Since the same thing is not able, at the same time, to be thought and not thought, one who thinks of that than which a greater cannot be thought does not think what is able *not to exist* but what is *not able not to exist*. On this account it is necessary for what he thinks to exist. The very denial of God's existence thus presupposes the existence of something which is affirmed by faith. What is understood in both the fool's denial and the believer's affirmation is the incomprehensibility of that which faith seeks to understand.

In conclusion, Anselm can thus say in response to Gaunilo's criticism of his single self-sufficing argument that, far from being "weak," this argument contains a sufficiently necessary (satis necessaria) argumentation. In fact, "so great a force" does what is signified by this argument contain in itself, that what is spoken of is proved to exist in reality and to exist itself (ipsum esse) as whatever ought to be believed (oportet credere) about the divine substance. For we believe of this divine essence whatever is able to be thought absolutely to be better to exist than not to exist, and something of this kind cannot exist except as that than which something greater is not able to be thought.

Yet, in both "praising" and "blaming" this dialogue, Gaunilo has blamed those parts which seemed to him to be weak "not from a bad will" but from "benevolentia."[48] It is through Gaunilo, in fact, that Anselm can indirectly address the man who said in his heart that there is no God—a man who is now spoken for (although he himself cannot speak) in Anselm's attempt to engage his own mind in a dialogue with a God who speaks, who is the very condition of speech.

### vii. Anselm and Descartes

Anselm's completion of his first philosophy discloses the central notion of first philosophy established by Aristotle—namely, being *qua* being—to be a pure actuality which is a predicate of an absolutely unique subject, a personal triunity, who is in no way by his essence *in* or *of* the world. Insofar as being *qua* being is this "actualitas" beyond nature and beyond form, it is existence itself, that is, an existence which could not be nonexistence. To be, then, in its primary sense, means to exist. But to exist (exsistere) means to step forth, to be manifest. Thus, existence in its absoluteness is that which belongs to this absolutely unique subject, this tri-unitary person who is not in or of this world by virtue of his essence. This absolutely unique subject is completely manifest to himself, and the tri-unity of this subject is the process of this complete self-manifestation.

But in being a subject, a triune being, possessed not only of understanding but of volition as well, this absolutely unique "aliquid" freely wills his actuality as a causality.\* God freely wills to create the world "ex nihilo." Since God's creation of the world is not necessitated, his actuality is neither entirely manifest nor entirely hidden in the world. He is both present and absent—thinkable and unthinkable—in this world. God is conceivable in his inconceivability and comprehensible in his incomprehensibility. For that 'aliquid' *in* and *of* the world that can think God—namely, the hu-

---

\* See pp. 51, 19 above.

man mind—God's nonexistence is as unthinkable as his complete manifestation to himself is incomprehensible. But the impossibility of God's nonexistence and the incomprehensibility of his intelligibility are inseparable in the human mind. In this way, Anselm in his first philosophy has presented the identity of being and intelligibility in an absolutely unique, particular subject which exists beyond any substance or essence in this world—a divine, more-than-natural subject of being than which no greater can be conceived.

Among those who, in Aristotle's judgment, spoke "falteringly," as far as first philosophy was involved, was Parmenides who spoke of being and intelligibility as the same thing. In Parmenides' judgment one would not be able to find thought (τὸ νοεῖν) without the what-is (τοῦ ἐόντος) in relation to which thought is uttered.[49] This Parmenidean identity of being and intelligibility is retrieved by Anselm in his first philosophy and now developed in terms of his presentation of the human mind's participation in the self-knowledge of the absolutely unique, supra-substantial, divine subject of being. The human mind can think this subject, and insofar as it genuinely thinks this subject, it *cannot* think this subject as nonexistent, as nonbeing, as nothing; for the very attempt of the human mind to avoid thinking this subject as existent discloses that it is not really thinking this subject at all in its "avoidance thinking"—not really thinking God. Atheism, therefore, is a will-act, not a mere judgment. This is nothing less than a new metaphysical insight; for Anselm's attempt to find God entailed posing and resolving anew the problem of the identity of being and intelligibility.

This new approach started with the act by which thinking looks into itself, the "cogitantis inspectio," in the human mind which finds the goal that it seeks—the sameness of intelligibility and being—within itself to the extent that it finds itself grasped by something which it cannot grasp. What Anselm discovers in his transformation of Aristotle's founding of first philosophy—a discovery which finds its most distinctive embodiment in the single and self-sufficing argument of his dialogue—is the indissoluble conjunction of God-as-existing and God-as-thought-by-man. When the human mind really grasps being (which occurs when thought attempts to think itself in this mind), it is grasped by God, so that the "attempt to think being of necessity involves thinking God," the subject of being, beyond which thought cannot think. This subject of being is greater than what can be conceived by the human mind, but the being of which it is subject is conceived by the human mind, so that in this way the human mind, as "imago dei," can conceive the inconceivable.[50]

In being finite, in being contained by what cannot be contained, the human mind, in its very particularity as "mens mea," contains as thinkable what it cannot comprehend, namely, the uncontainable. Being *qua* being is now being *qua* an existence which cannot not exist. But this existence which cannot not exist is encountered as intelligible by an existence which *could* not-exist, i.e., the existence which is predicated of the human mind. Necessary being is present to contingent being, even though necessary being does not need contingent being in order to be infinite.[51] The infinite, which the human mind can only approach negatively, is absolutely prior to the finite; and the finite is entirely contingent being.

This means, given Anselm's transformation of Aristotelian first philosophy, that God is not a purely necessary being in the context of other necessary beings. God is in no way a member of a class, not even the greatest member of a class.* "God" is not a class name which belongs to a primary substance that can somehow be singled out from other substances to which we might be tempted to give the name. It is being *qua* the absolute subject of being, being *qua* God, which Anselm has brought into focus in first philosophy.[52]

The human mind, then, can only "think" that God does not exist *without thinking* of God's nonexistence. The human mind cannot think beyond the impossibility of the nonexistence of God. In no way divine or possessed of a divine part, this mind is never circumscribed by itself, never fully contained by itself in its particularity as "mens mea," but is grasped by something which it itself cannot grasp, which it cannot "look over." Yet the human mind can grasp

---

* See pp. 51, 34, 35 above.

the significance of its being grasped by an absolutely unique subject which it cannot grasp. In this sense it is a mind which is near to God, though God be so far beyond it—a mind which both sees and does not see God, a God who is both present to and absent from his creation. The Aristotelian question of the divine substance is now the question of what the human heart can and must understand God to be: a being so one with itself that there cannot be born or proceed from it anything other than what it is—a personal tri-unity.

But if the question of substantiality has become the question of a subject of being beyond all substances, the question of what the human heart must think about the existence of this subject, then we already have the realization, as Heidegger will put it, that God and man, as knowing beings, are (metaphysically considered) "the bearers of truth" and thus constitute the actuality (Wirklichkeit) of knowledge and certainty. In Anselm, in other words, we might say, is to be found the first metaphysical intimation of what Heidegger will call a *peculiar preeminence* (eigentümlicher Vorrang) of humanity within what is actual.[53]

If God, consequently, is the absolutely unique subject of a being which cannot *not be*, of an existence which cannot not exist, of a being which cannot be contingent, then man, insofar as he can think the impossibility of the nonexistence of this subject, is a contingent image of this subject, i.e., a darkened reflection of this subject. The human mind and heart, in other words, in their particularity, are the negative image, the "after-image," so to speak, of this divine subject of being. In being about this divine subject, Anselm's transformation of first philosophy, we can say, proves *also* to be about a contingent subject which has as its essential "property" the inability to conceive the nonexistence of the infinite subject of being. In this way, humanity is seen to have a primacy in the realm of contingent being, i.e., in the realm of "natura," the ensemble of created being—a primacy which it could never have had in the Aristotelian founding of first philosophy.

The testimony to this is implicit in Anselm's treatment of the joy he experienced in discovering his single and self-sufficing argument for the existence of God. His discovery is that the joy, which he sought and seemed to find in discovering this argument, but which he seemed only to lose hold of once more, is a joy to be attained in the future—in that future where the rift between understanding and will that is embodied in the "fool" (who says in his heart what he cannot think in his understanding), but which is ineradicable for man in his fallen condition, shall be overcome in the prospect of man's entering fully *into that joy* which cannot fully enter *into man*. It is this joy, than which nothing greater can be conceived, which cannot exist in the human understanding *alone*; for if it were able to be thought not to exist, it could in no way exist, not even in the understanding. If it were possible for this joy not to exist, it could not be thought and desired by man.

It is precisely man's desire for this joy that involves him in a dialectic of desire, where he attempts to find objects that assuage his thirst for the infinite, but none of which can survive the desire itself. It is precisely this human desire for an unmediated relation to the infinite, for a total and instantaneous vision of the infinite—which cannot be satisfied by anything in the realm of contingent being, by any created being—that makes possible the act by which thinking looks into itself, the "cogitantis inspectio," in man. Man *is* the very desire for the infinity by which whatever is contingent exists. Man is in the world the darkened image of that light which is inaccessible to the world. Man does not simply *have* the idea of God; man *is* the idea of God in the mode of negativity.[54] The joy which man can be said to be a desire-for cannot be found in the world; nonetheless, man's desire is that this joy be *his*. Man is the thing in this world which is (and is *as*) the desire for a joy beyond this world. What God made, in making man, was a desire for God.

What must remain decisive in Anselm's first philosophy, however, is that man is the *darkened* image of infinity, that man in his particularity is a fallen, effaced image of that absolutely unique particular subject of being who is God. Anselm discovers in the end that it is enough for man to be a *seeker* of that joy than which no greater can be conceived. He finds it sufficient to gain a measured, finite comprehension of what this incomprehensibility of God's goodness can mean. In the final analysis, if man is capable of thinking the possibility of the nonexistence of the world, he is, nonetheless, in his particularity, *in*-capable of thinking the *im*-possibility of his own *non*-existence. Only God—and not man—would still exist if there were, in fact, no world. If the world is no longer the horizon of being *qua* being, it is still the horizon of contingent being.

The Ontological Argument, then, as the unifying argument for Anselm's first philosophy is about reason—human reason. This argument maintains the classical, i.e., Aristotelian, notion that reason can reveal what is. But what is new in Anselm is that what *is* and what is central to reason is "that than which nothing greater can be conceived" which amounts to that which is greater than anything that can be comprehended by man. We have a Christian moment (given expression in first philosophy) conjoined to an Aristotelian conception of reason. We are, then, truly at the midpoint in the transition from substance to subject in first philosophy. But we do not yet have radical (Cartesian) subjectivity.

Anselm's first philosophy does not unleash philosophical subjectivity in the modern sense. But it does seem to provide the metaphysical precondition for that (modern) unleashing to the extent that it attempts to find something *in* the human understanding as particular (mens mea) which cannot be *only* in the human understanding. This new metaphysical way of addressing the Parmenidean identity of being and intelligibility will be preconditional for any subsequent attempt to present the human self as a radical Cartesian subject which cannot think its own nonexistence.

Whatever the shape of such later radical human subjectivity will be, however, it cannot be said to constitute the intention that underlies Anselm's treatment of human intentionality in first philosophy. Nonetheless, the calm waters that finally flow forth at the conclusion of Anselm's intellectual struggle with himself in first philosophy are at the center of the historical and stormy transition from Aristotelian substantiality to radical Cartesian subjectivity.

At the "center" of this center stands Anselm's "unum argumentum," the end point of which is precisely the starting point, namely, God as the absolutely unique subject of being. But in returning to where it started, there is a sense in which the argument is *also* about man or ends with man to the extent that the joy man seeks he wants and can never cease to want to be *his own*. In this sense it might almost be said that the Anselmian Argument "reveals man rather than God."[55] In this sense, it can be said that man in his particularity, i.e., the "mens mea," *is* the Ontological Argument for God's existence. And in this sense, it can be said with confidence that Anselm turns up the soil to be cultivated in Descartes' attempt to refound first philosophy.

# IV

# The Cartesian Refounding of First Philosophy

The modern philosophical quest for certitude finds its condition in the medieval attempt to understand the intelligibility of faith. By himself, as Heidegger remarks, man can never be absolutely certain of his salvation, but through "faith" man is essentially established in the attainment of salvation's certainty (Heilsgewissheit). Modern philosophical subjectivity is invented when man, without faith, attempts to do something which previously he would have to renounce without faith, viz., the making certain of his salvation, his "release" from the bondage to death imposed by nature on him as an individual.

To attempt this is to attempt to determine the essence of certainty according to his own self-assurance (Selbstsicherung) and, thus, to bring humanity to "mastery" within what is actual. This is the attempt of man to cultivate and build by himself what is actual as that which has an effect upon him and as that which he effects. This self-certainty (Selbstgewissheit) of modern man attempts "to raise into itself" the truth of Christianity. This is nothing less than a change of the essence of truth from the rectitude (Richtigkeit) of the assertion that is being thought—as it was in the first philosophy of Anselm—to the certainty of representation (Vorstellens).

Yet, the condition of this change is the medieval attempt to understand the intelligibility of faith, for, as Heidegger sees it, it is in this faith that "certainty rules"—a certainty that is sure even in the "uncertainty" of itself or of what it believes in. In faith and its certainty there reigns the "freedom" of man[1] that permits of the Cartesian discovery of modern philosophical subjectivity and the Cartesian effort to refound first philosophy. Neither that self-proclaimed discovery nor this refounding, however, are absolutely new beginnings, despite the claims of their inventor and refounder. For in order to transform Anselm's notion of truth as rectitude into truth as representation—in order to transform the certainty of truth into the "truth" of certainty—Descartes must incorporate the result of Anselm's transformation of the Aristotelian founding of first philosophy.

What in Anselm was a solitary meditation followed by—and brought to its perfection in—a dialogue in which the mind is raised to God will become in Descartes an exclusively solitary meditation. What in Anselm was a dialectic of discourse, hearing, and persons will become in Descartes a dialectic of observation, sight, and objects in conformity with the method of modern science.[2] What in Anselm was the importance of believing in order to understand will become in Descartes the importance of understanding in order to believe.[3] But in all of these transformations the joy of Anselm's discovery of the impossibility of the non-existence of God—which the act by which thinking looks into itself (cogitantis inspectio) in man cannot think beyond—would appear to be the condition for the ebullience of Descartes' invention of the human subject that cannot think beyond the impossibility of its own nonexistence.

### i. The Divorce of First Philosophy and Theology

In dedicating his *Meditationes de Prima Philosophia* to the Faculty of Sacred Theology of the University of Paris, Descartes indicates that he always esteemed the two questions of God and of the human soul to be "first" among those things which ought to be demonstrated by a philosophical rather than theological work. For although it may be enough for the faithful to believe by faith (fide credere) that the human soul is "not destroyed" with the body and that God exists, it does not seem possible for those without faith to be persuaded unless these two things can first be proven by natural reason (ratione naturali).* Even Scripture itself seems to imply that all that is able to be known of God "can be shown" by reasons that we need not seek elsewhere than in our own mind.

The position, in fact, which claims that "human reasons" persuade us that the soul is destroyed with the body and that "faith alone" can hold the contrary, was condemned by the Lateran Council which commanded "Christian philosophers" to refute these arguments. Nothing "more useful," then, in philosophy could be done than to seek sedulously, once and for all, the best of those reasons which have been offered for the existence of God and for distinguishing the human mind from the body, and to set them forth so "exactly and evidently" that it will be settled for posterity that these reasons are demonstrations. Some people have urged Descartes to do this, aware as they are of his practicing a certain method for resolving difficulties in the sciences—a method which is not really new since "nothing is more ancient than truth." All that Descartes has accomplished in this regard is contained in this treatise in the form of the "most certain and evident" demonstrations—demonstrations that Descartes claims no one could find any better. The importance of this matter and the "gloria Dei" on which it bears force Descartes to "speak somewhat more freely" of himself than is customary.[4]

Although aware that his demonstrations here equal or even surpass the certainty and evidence of those in geometry, Descartes indicates that he is also aware that they cannot adequately be perceived by many, partly because they are somewhat lengthy but principally because they require a mind "free" from prejudice that can easily raise itself from attachment (consortio) to the senses. In

---

* Although it is entirely true, Descartes remarks, that the existence of God ought to be believed because it is taught by Sacred Scripture, and Sacred Scripture should be believed because it is held (habentur) by God, this line of argument should not be proposed to "unbelievers" because they would judge it to be "circular." But Descartes notes that theologians affirm that the existence of God is not only able to be proved by natural reason, but can also be inferred from Scripture, and that knowledge of God is so much easier (faciliorem) to acquire than knowledge of many created things, that those without this knowledge are "culpable."

the end, there cannot be as many who are fitted for metaphysical studies as there are for geometry. Because of this, no matter how forceful his reasons (meae rationes), he cannot hope that they will have a great effect (since they are philosophical) unless the Faculty of Sacred Theology takes them under its protection, for this faculty is deferred to not only in "matters of faith" but also in "humana philosophia." Should this faculty amend and approve his work, Descartes does not doubt that in the future all the errors that have been entertained on these two questions will soon be "removed" from the minds of men. This will cause the atheists, who are usually more "arrogant" than they are intellectually endowed (ingeniosi) or learned, to rid themselves of their "spirit of contradiction." Thus there will be no one who calls back into doubt (dubium revocare) the existence of God and the "real distinction" between the human soul and body. It is for this faculty to judge of the "utility" of such belief once it is "well established," for this faculty can see the disorders presently produced by the doubt of this belief.

Having dedicated his work, Descartes now addresses his readers, indicating that the path he follows in regard to the questions of God and of the human mind is so "little traveled" and so remote from common use (usu communi) that he did not find it appropriate to write this work in French which might be read by everyone, in case weaker minds would believe it permissible for them to make the same attempt. Descartes now proceeds to address two objections raised against his *Discourse on Method*, indicating that in the *Meditations* he will attempt to show from the fact that he knows nothing other than a thinking thing (rem cogitantem) to pertain to his own essence (essentiam meam), it follows that there is no other thing which really pertains to it, and he will attempt to show more fully how from the fact alone that he has an idea of something more perfect than himself *in* himself, it follows that this more perfect thing truly exists (revera existere). As to the possible objections of atheists, Descartes asserts that what is said by them against the existence of God depends either on "human characteristics" being ascribed to God or on our minds' arrogating to themselves so much "strength and wisdom" that they attempt to "determine and comprehend" that which God can and ought to do. The claims of the atheist, then, will pose no difficulty if men consider their minds as finite things and God as "incomprehensible and infinite." Having thus duly regarded the "judgments of men," Descartes can now begin to examine the questions of God and the human mind and begin to lay the "foundations" of first philosophy, without expecting any praise from the vulgar or, for that matter, very many readers (lectorum frequentiam). This work can, in fact, only be recommended to those who desire to "meditate seriously" with him, who can detach their minds from their senses and at the same time free themselves of all kinds of prejudice. Of this kind of reader there are very few.[5]

In his synopsis of the six days of meditation which are to follow, Descartes indicates that in the first meditation he will set forth the causes by virtue of which "we are able to doubt" all things—but especially material things—to the extent that we have no foundations for the sciences (scientiarum fundamenta) other than those previously had. In the second meditation *the human mind*, utilizing the "liberty proper" to it, is seen to suppose that those things whose existence it is able to doubt in the slightest are nonexistent but, in doing this, it recognizes that it itself is not able to bring this to pass except that it exists, i.e., it *recognizes that it is absolutely impossible that it itself does not exist*.[*]

In the third meditation, Descartes sets forth his first argument for the existence of God. Here, in his synopsis, he simply alludes to

---

[*] Descartes notes, in passing, that since he aimed to write nothing in this work for which he did not have "accurate demonstration," the order he follows is that used in geometry, viz., to begin by setting forth as premises (praemitterem) all those things upon which the proposition sought after depends before concluding anything in regard to it. He also notes that we can be assured that all the things which we understand "clearly and distinctly" exist as true in the very way in which we understand them. Finally, he notes that body, although generally taken to exist as a substance, seems to exist only as a "configuration of certain members" and as a bringing together of accidents. But the human mind truly does not consist of any accidents but exists as a pure substance (puram esse substantiam).

a comparison with a "very perfect machine," the idea of which is in the mind of some artificer.  Just as the objective handicraft (artificium objectivum) of this idea must have some cause, so also it is impossible that the idea of God which is *in* us should not have God himself as its cause.  In the fourth meditation it is proved that all those things which we clearly and distinctly perceive are true, and it is explained at the same time in what the "reason for falsity" consists.  But in no way, Descartes adds, does he here address sin (peccato), i.e., error committed in the pursuit of "good and evil," but only that error which depends upon judging between the "true and the false."  In sum, it is not his intention to include matters pertaining to faith or to the "conduct of life" but only those truths which are speculative and are known by the light of nature (luminis naturalis) alone.

In the fifth meditation, "corporeal nature" in general is explained, and also a new reason is given by which God's existence is demonstrated.  In the sixth meditation it is proved that the mind is really distinguished from the body and at the same time that the two are so closely joined together that they compose, in a manner of speaking, one thing.  In setting forth the reasons by which we may conclude to the existence of material things, Descartes sees these reasons to be neither as firm nor as evident as those by which we come to a knowledge of our own mind and of God.  In this way, the most certain and evident of all reasons are those which are able to be known by a *human* mode of thinking (humano ingenio).[6]

In this way, in his somewhat extended preparatory remarks for his *Meditations*, Descartes creates a profile of the nature of the shift he effects in the understanding of truth.  Truth, for Anselm, involved some kind of certainty—the certainty of the understanding that faith seeks.  But for Descartes, certainty of representation—in which ideas that are perceived clearly and distinctly are perceived as true, and in which all the things which are understood clearly and distinctly exist as true in the very way in which they are understood—is itself truth.  If in faith seeking understanding, the freedom of man is seen to rule for Anselm, it is now the liberty proper to the human mind which is presented as pure substance, as natural reason, as the light of nature or "lumiere naturelle," as a reason that we need not seek elsewhere than in our own mind, that is uppermost for Descartes.

There now seems to obtain a separation of the things of faith (which are divine) and philosophy (which is human). There is an explicit exclusion of the matter of sin and the things of faith—as well as of the very conduct of life—from the domain of first philosophy. Yet, the belief of faith is addressed in terms of its utility for the human condition. But this utility is seen to lie in first philosophy's demonstration of the two primary premises of faith: the existence of God and the immortality of the soul (although the issue of immortality is changed by Descartes into the issue of the real distinction between the human soul and body). This utility, furthermore, seems to require the overcoming of the spirit of contradiction endemic to atheism. Yet, the cause of atheism seems to be traced to matters—human characteristics asserted of God, and the attempt to comprehend what God can and ought to do—which very well might be laid at the doorstep of theology. First philosophy, in a word, seems to be announced as no longer in any way theology—and this for the first time. The very utility of faith which Descartes would have first philosophy promote seems to require that we understand in order to believe.

Descartes, however, alludes to the glory of God as the object of his work in first philosophy and refers to himself as in the company of Christian philosophers, even though he uses these allusions to justify his speaking so freely of *himself* in his first philosophy. Although not as such theology, Descartes' first philosophy is commended to the protection of theologians without whom, since it is "pure" philosophy, it can hope for no great effect among the majority who find it so difficult to free themselves of all prejudices and detach their minds from their senses. Faith and theology, then, though lying outside Descartes' attempt to provide a new foundation for first philosophy, are nonetheless important for the attempt itself. Faith and theology are important for what Descartes will have to presuppose in his endeavor to prove the impossibility of the nonexistence of the human subject as that which the human subject cannot think beyond. Certainly Descartes' allusion to a parallel between the idea of a most perfect machine and the cause of this idea in its artificer would seem quite distant from the impossibility of the nonexistence of God which man cannot think beyond in Anselm's first philosophy. Yet, it is precisely the act by which thinking looks into itself or the "cogitantis inspectio" in Anselm which first presents what would appear to be preconditional for the new foundations, the new "beginning" which Descartes has announced for first philosophy. If, in fact, first philosophy is announced as no longer theology, it is still required to be very much concerned with God and God's *existence*—with the "esse" or "existendi" which Anselm made the center of first philosophy.

### ii. Negativity: The Methodic Doubt

Descartes entitles his first meditation "Of Those Things which Are Able to be Called Back [revocari] into Doubt." It is now some time, he remarks, since he first discovered how many were the false beliefs he had admitted as true and how doubtful was what he had since constructed (superextruxi) on the basis of these beliefs. For once in his life, he became convinced, he must attempt to rid himself of *all* his beliefs and begin anew to lay the "first foundations" of his opinions if he was to establish something firm and constant in the sciences. So great was this task, however, that he waited until he had attained an age so mature that he could not reasonably expect a later time when he would be more "fitted" for such a task. It is "today," Descartes says, since he has unloosed (exsolvi) his mind from all cares (curis omnibus), and since he has procured a secure leisure for himself, that he shall, at last, seriously and freely address himself to this general subversion (eversione) of his old opinions.\*

---

\* Anselm too, in the opening chapter of his dialogue, had spoken of freeing himself from burdensome cares (onerosas curas) but in order that he would make room, for some short time, for God. But Descartes does not begin with Anselm's awakening of the mind or "excitatio mentis" for the sake of the contemplation of God but rather with a calling back or "revocari" of his former opinions into doubt.

Were his goal that of showing *all* his former opinions to be false, he would perhaps never reach it. Since, then, reason persuades him that he ought to refuse assent no less to things which are not distinctly certain and indubitable than to those which are "manifestly false," it will be sufficient to reject all his opinions if he finds in each of them some reason for doubting. But it would not be necessary for him to examine each opinion singly, for that would be an "infinite" task. Rather, because the undermining of the foundations (suffosis fundamentis) entails the fall of the superstructure (superaedificatum), he need only "assault" the very principles upon which everything he formerly believed "flourished."[7]

For Anselm what can be said about that than which a greater cannot be thought is precisely what truly is—and rightfully *ought* to be—believed about God.* But for Descartes what *happens* to be believed must be subjected to a method or procedure for doubting before it can be pronounced worthy of belief. The point for Descartes is to locate the first principles for all that he has believed in the past and to subject them to this methodic doubt. The point is not to start with belief and to seek understanding but to start with the suspension of belief and to seek an unassailable certainty which might be said to be the principle of worthiness for belief—a principle which, as such, is extrinsic to belief and to what is believed. Belief of any kind cannot be the *terminus a quo* for first philosophy. First philosophy can only begin with the suspension of first principles, i.e., with the subjection to doubt of any claimed first principle. First philosophy begins, for Descartes, by beginning anew *in* himself and in a purportedly presuppositionless state. And the first principles which he finds to be the foundations of all his former beliefs (and which must be subjected to the method of doubt or negativity) are three.

The first of these principles is the veracity of his sense perception. Everything that he has thus far accepted as certain he has learned by the senses or through sensation, but it is now shown him that at times these senses are "deceptive," and it is the more pru-

---

* See pp. 89, 59, 55-56, 46 above.

dent course "not quite to trust" anything by which he has once been deceived. It must be said, however, that, although the senses may deceive him in regard to things "minute" and "remote," there are many instances which he is not able to doubt, such as the fact that he is seated here by the fire. As a man, he is accustomed to sleep at night and to represent in his dreams things very similar to what the insane imagine when awake. Even though what happens in his dreams does not generally appear as clear and distinct as what happens now, he must remind himself that he has been deceived in his dreams by illusions similar to those by which his senses are deceived when he is awake. He must concede, then, that there is no certain indication by which he is able to distinguish his waking from his sleeping state, and his "astonishment" is such that it is almost able to confirm him in the opinion that he now sleeps. The second principle, consequently, which Descartes subjects to methodic doubt is his capacity to distinguish (with logical certainty) at any given moment whether he is awake and fully conscious or asleep and dreaming.

Suppose, then, he assumes that he is now asleep and that all these particular things (particularia ista) he experiences, such as opening his eyes, or shaking his head, are illusions—like "painted representations" which can only be formed in "similitude to true things." He would realize that at least these "general things," such as eyes, head, etc., are not imaginary but truly exist. Even if these "generalia" are imaginary, however, there must be objects more "simple and universal" which truly exist. Though he can doubt his ability to distinguish (with certainty) whether he is now awake or asleep, he cannot doubt that there is a waking state constituted by access to objects more simple and universal than those that he has imagined in sleep. The class of these more simple and universal objects comprises corporeal nature in general, its extension, the figure of extended things, their quantity, magnitude, and number, the place in which they exist, and the time through which they endure. Because of this, Descartes can now speak of those sciences which consider composite things, namely, physics, astronomy, and medicine, as quite doubtful; whereas sciences which consider only

### The Cartesian Refounding of First Philosophy          107

very simple and highly general things, without concerning themselves with whether or not these things are to be found in nature (rerum natura), such as arithmetic and geometry, must contain something of what is certain and indubitable.

Unlike Aristotle for whom astronomy is the science that is closest to first philosophy,* Descartes conceives of a mathematical physics as the science which is closest to the identity of being and certitude which he seeks in first philosophy. And this suggests to Descartes that it is precisely the certitudes of mathematics which survive both his doubt of the veracity of his senses and his doubt of his capacity to distinguish whether he is now dreaming or awake. Whether he is "awake" or "asleep" and dreaming, "when two and three are joined they form five, and the square can never have more than four sides." Two and three *not* equaling five and a square *not* having four sides are impossible even to imagine or to dream as existing.[8]

This leads Descartes to propose the third principle which founds his former opinions and which he now subjects to doubt, namely, the veracity of God. He has long had "fastened in" his mind, he tells us, the "old opinion" that God is an all-powerful Creator. But how does he know that God has not made it to be that there really are no simple extended things and yet, nevertheless, he has the impressions of all these things and they seem to him to exist exactly as he now sees them? How does he know that he is not deceived (fallar) whenever he adds two and three or counts the sides of a square? Perhaps it could be argued that God could simply not will (noluit) that he should be so deceived, since God is said to be supremely good. But if it is contrary to God's goodness to have created Descartes in such a way that he is always deceived, then it would also seem to be foreign to God's goodness to permit him to be sometimes deceived. The existence of God, in other words, far from being a principle of certainty, turns out to be an occasion for doubting that anything is certain, even the truths of mathematics

---

\* See p. 13 above.

themselves.* And so Descartes must admit that there is nothing in those things which he previously thought to be true which does not "permit of doubt," and this not because of any lack of consideration or "shallowness" on his part but because of "valid and meditated" reasons. The conclusion is that in the future if he wishes to find what is certain, he must withhold (cohibendam) his assent from these doubtful matters no less than from what is manifestly false. It would seem that the foundations of all his former claims to knowledge (and, therefore, all the claims themselves) are doubtful.

Yet, his former claims to knowledge, being "commonly held" and longstanding, tend to revert (recurrunt) to his mind. His long usage of and familiarity with them give them the right to occupy his mind, making them "easy to believe," even against his will. These former claims very nearly make themselves "masters" of his belief. Belief itself, it would seem, is readily subject to mastery by something that is not as such rational, namely, the mere perdurance of traditionally held but readily doubted opinions. Belief itself has no credentials which can lead to—or enable it to seek—understanding. The only credentials it could have would be those given it by reason—a reason which is completely *other* than it. Descartes will never extricate himself from the habit of assenting to and confiding in the three principles which ground his former opinions as long as he views them as what they really are, namely, in some way doubtful but nevertheless "highly probable," so that there is much more reason to "believe" than to "deny" them. In the face of the very

---

\* This might lead certain people, Descartes says, to deny the existence of a God so powerful rather than believe that all other things are uncertain. Even were Descartes not to oppose them, and even were he to grant this hypothesis of an all-powerful God (who permits him to be deceived entirely) to be fictitious, nevertheless, since to err and be mistaken is a kind of imperfection, to whatever degree these people consider the author of their being to be "fate" or "chance," in that degree it will be more probable that they are so imperfect that they are always deceived. Whether, then, the author of his being is all-powerful, i.e., God, or is not all-powerful, i.e., something less than God, Descartes can have no response by which he could exclude the possibility of his always being deceived—a possibility which follows from either alternative. The veracity of a divine creator is as much subject to doubt as the veracity of a less-than-divine creative agency.

credibility of his former opinions, Descartes must assume a contrary stance (contrarium versa), namely, "freely" permit himself to be deceived and for a certain time contrive (fingam) all his beliefs to be "false and imaginary," until something like an equality (velut aequatis) obtains between his former prejudices and his new "prejudice" that he is entirely deceived.

Only in this way shall his judgment not be "turned away" by habit or tradition (consuetudo) from the "right perception of things," from the little traveled and straight path (droit chemin) leading to the knowledge of the truth. He can assure himself that there is neither "danger" nor error in assuming this stance, nor is he able to overindulge in his mistrust (diffidentiae) of his former opinions, since what he is doing is only done within the domain of first philosophy and is not a matter of things which are to be acted upon (rebus agendis) but only of things which are to be known (cognoscendis). Even though reason can show his former beliefs to be more worthy of belief than they are of disbelief, this reason must focus on the slightest occasions for doubting these beliefs and treat these occasions *as if* they had the same "weight" as falsity itself.[9] Belief itself can no more constitute a *terminus a quo* in first philosophy than can falsehood. If belief is to have *any* place in first philosophy, it would seem to be either a belief that has been arrived at by understanding in some way or a belief that has ceased to be a belief because it is now *fully* understood to the extent that it is demonstrated as certain.

Descartes must, therefore, fabricate a world—in a sense, "create" a world in the first of six days of meditation—in which he could be totally deceived. He must "suppose" not the supremely good God (optimum Deum) of Anselm's first philosophy but some malign spirit[*]—not the fount of truth (fontem veritatis) of Anselm's first philosophy, but a being at once "supremely powerful" and deceitful (callidum) who has employed all his "assiduity" in order to deceive Descartes. What he must suppose, it would seem, is the very incarnation of evil (the very initiator of the fall of man, the devil) in pos-

---

[*] genium aliquem malignum

session of the power of God: God-as-if-devil *or* devil-as-if-God—a God, it would seem, in power but not in truth and goodness, a God who could do anything, a God who could, therefore, deceive. And so, Descartes must suppose that all the furniture of the world is nothing but an elaborate game, a mockery dreamed up (ludificationes somniorum) by a seemingly all-powerful* deceiver by which he "insidiously" catches man's credulity. Descartes must remain inflexibly "fixed" on this hypothesis in this meditation, even to the point, if need be, of realizing that if no truth is to be known by his methodic doubt carried to this extreme, great care will at least have been taken in *not* assenting to anything false by virtue of the mind's having prepared itself so well against this deceiver. Such an undertaking (institutum) is, of course, laborious, and, as Descartes tells us, a certain slothfulness leads him back to his ordinary and accustomed life (consuetudinem vitae). Like a captive who in sleep enjoys an "imaginary liberty," when he begins to suspect that he is asleep, fears to be awakened (timet excitari) and conspires with his "agreeable illusions," Descartes also insensibly sinks back (sponte relabor) into his old opinions, and he dreads "being awakened" from this sleep, because he fears that the laborious wakefulness (laboriosa vigilia) that would follow the "quiet of this repose" would be spent not in some light but in the darkness (tenebras) of difficulties which he has previously discussed and from which he has not been extricated.[10]

Belief—to the extent that it has no credentials in and of itself which would enable it to seek understanding, to the extent that it is completely other than reason, and to the extent that it is readily subject to mastery by the sheer inertia of tradition which is not as such rational—is a kind of sleep illuminated by the tranquil repose of agreeable dreams to which Descartes is constantly summoned

---

   * Richard Kennington, however, argues that "whereas an omnipotent being, in virtue of his power alone, could suspend the law of non-contradiction, only an omnipotent being who is evil would do so. Hence, as regards the context of Cartesian doubt, God may be replaced, as a *ratio dubitandi*, by a genius who is evil but not by one who is [really] omnipotent. Otherwise, the further course of Cartesian doubt as a reasoning inquiry would be impossible."

and from which he fears to be awakened since, by comparison, the laborious wakefulness of methodic doubt would be a darkness. In sum, the calling back (revocari) of belief into doubt turns out to be what Anselm called an awakening. But for Descartes this "excitatio"* is not for the sake of contemplating God, not for the sake of belief's seeking its understanding, but for the sake of traveling a straight and little traveled path—one unmediated by belief—leading to the knowledge of a truth that would require that he *first* be more concerned with *not* assenting to anything false, rather than with assenting to the truth itself. The very straightness of the path to truth consists not in a dialectic of belief and reason, which attempts to prove what was doubted,° but in the withholding of assent to what is doubtful. The path to truth is through a wakefulness that is unilluminated—through the night of doubt. And if there is to be any illumination, it cannot come from any other source than the doubter himself. It would seem, then, that the identity of intelligibility and existence (i.e., of certitude and being), which Descartes seeks in first philosophy, is an indubitable existence which is more truly his than the ordinary life which he leads within the context of what nature makes accessible to him—that is, within the context of the world.

### iii. The Being Beyond Doubt

Descartes begins his second day of meditation on first philosophy by picturing himself as having suddenly "slipped down" into a deep whirlpool (profundum gurgitem) of doubt where he is able neither to fasten his feet on the bottom nor to rise to the surface (enatare ad summum). Nonetheless, he must continue to treat every belief which admits of the least doubt as if it were entirely false, until he has found "something certain" or until he has come to know for certain that "nothing is certain." In order to move the entire earth from its place, Archimedes asked nothing more than a

---

\* See pp. 104, 57 above.
° See p. 88 above.

"firm and immovable point," and in the same way, Descartes says, he shall "be able to hope" for much if he can discover at least one thing which is certain (certum) and unshaken (inconcussum). He must suppose, therefore, that everything which he sees is false. He must believe that nothing of what his "mendacious memory" represents at any time existed. In sum, he must entertain the possibility that nothing will be true unless this one thing, viz., that there is nothing certain.

But, in doing this, does he know that there is nothing "different" from all these things which he has doubted—no thing that in the slightest degree is unable to be an occasion for doubting? Is there not some God or something else, by whatever name it is spoken, which gives him these thoughts? But why should he think this to be true, for perhaps he himself is able to be the author of these thoughts? At least, therefore, is he himself not something (aliquid)? Yet, he has now denied that he has any senses or body. But is he himself so "bound" to the body and the senses that without them he is not able to exist (esse non possim)? If he was persuaded that there was nothing which exists in the world, was he not also persuaded that he himself does not exist? Certainly this does not follow, for if he persuaded himself of something or even if he only thought of something, then certainly he himself existed. Even if there is some deceiver, "supremely powerful," who employs his assiduity in order always to deceive him, then by no means is it doubtful that he exists, if he is so deceived.* If this deceiver tricks Descartes as much as he is able, he nonetheless cannot bring it about that Descartes is "nothing" as long as Descartes "thinks" that he is something. Having thought sufficiently on all these things, Descartes must finally maintain that this proposition (hoc pronuntiatum)—*I am, I exist*°—is necessarily true as often as he "mentions" it or conceives it mentally (mente concipitur).[11]

It cannot, consequently, be true that nothing is true except that nothing is certain since it cannot be certain that nothing is certain.

---

   * etiam sum, si me fallit

   ° Ego sum, ego existo

## The Cartesian Refounding of First Philosophy 113

At least one certainty is built into the very structure of negativity, of doubt, as a method for thinking. Doubt is able to withhold assent from the existence of things in the world and (it would seem) from the very existence of God, but it cannot withhold assent from the existence of the doubter. This "I" who doubts—even were it persuaded that nothing exists in the world (not even minds)—would nevertheless be persuaded of something, i.e., that it thinks of itself as something. Not even a seemingly all-powerful deceiver could bring it to pass that this "I" is nothing so long as the "I" thinks of itself as something. One thing at least is certain and unshaken, in the sense that it cannot be asserted as false, namely, that whether or not there is anything in the world, the "I" cannot doubt that it is, that it exists.

But this "I" does not yet sufficiently understand what kind of thing it is, and so it must beware lest perhaps it imprudently take up some other thing in place of itself and in this way "err" in that very knowledge which it affirms to be most certain and evident. Descartes must thus meditate on what he "once believed" himself to be before he arrived at this certitude which excludes all doubts, and he must "withdraw" anything that is able in the slightest degree "to be weakened," so that what will remain will be only what is certain and unshaken.

Formerly he thought himself to be a man, but shall he say that a man is an "animal rationale"? Certainly not, he answers, for were he so to reply he would have to inquire what an animal is and what it is to be rational, and from a single question he "would fall" into many more difficult questions. Rather, he must consider the thoughts which arose "spontaneously and naturally" whenever he considered what he was. Formerly, he thought he had a distinct knowledge of his nature as all of that able to be "bounded" by a "certain figure." But now that he supposes a most powerful and malicious deceiver bent upon deceiving him, he can no longer affirm that he possesses the least of all those things which pertain to "corporeal nature." He finds here that it is thought and this alone which is unable to be separated from him.* It is certain that "ego sum," that "ego existo," but for how long? For as long, doubtlessly, as this *ego* thinks, for it might perhaps happen that if all thought were to cease this *ego* would entirely cease to exist (esse desinerem). Descartes now admits nothing except what is necessarily true, and so he concludes that he is only a thinking thing (res cogitans), i.e., a "mens," or "animus," or "intellectus," or "ratio"—the significance of these terms being formerly unknown to him. But he is a "true thing" and truly existing (vere existens).[12]

From this Descartes knows that nothing of those things which he is able to comprehend by the "imagination" pertains to the "notion" he has of himself, and thus that the mind ought to be most diligently called away (avocandam) from the mode of comprehension peculiar to the imagination in order that it most distinctly perceive its own nature. What cannot be "separated" from this nature is his thinking (mea cogitatione) which is itself a *particular thing*, an "aliquid," for which it is as true as it is certain that it exists and that it would exist even if he were always sleeping (dormirais toujours) and always deceived. It is his "cogitatione" which is the particular thing that makes him what he is, viz., a "res cogitans," and his doubting, understanding, imagining, and feeling are attributes which could not exist apart from this "res cogitans." The problem, however, is that his attempt to understand the nature of this "res cogitans" is hampered by the tendency of his mind (mens mea) to "rejoice" in its "wandering" and not yet to suffer itself "to be constrained within the limits of truth." The best course, then, would be to give the mind the "loosest" rein, so that afterwards, when it is opportune to pull it back (reductis), it may suffer itself to be "more easily ruled." This might best be done by considering something which is "commonly thought" to be most distinctly comprehended of all things, namely, the bodies which we touch and see, not, however, bodies "in general"—since general perceptions are more confused than particular ones—but some one body "in particular."

---

\* cogitatio . . . haec sola a me divelli nequit

Descartes thus proposes that we consider this piece of wax (hanc ceram), fresh from the hive, in which all the things held to be requisite for our knowing a body most distinctly are met with. When brought close to the fire, its taste, color, smell, figure, and magnitude change. No one denies, however, that this is the "same" wax, and yet what is comprehended distinctly in this thing cannot be anything which can be "touched by the senses," for now, although the wax remains, all these sensible things about it are changed. What remains is a certain extended thing which is flexible and changeable; and this extended thing does not consist in anything that can be imagined, for it can be imagined only as undergoing innumerable changes. But if neither the senses nor the "imaginandi facultate" comprehend what this wax really is, then this particular piece of wax cannot be perceived "unless by the mind"—and as to wax in general, this conclusion is even clearer. To perceive this wax as the same wax—as the same wax that he sees, touches, and imagines—Descartes' "perceptio" can neither be vision, touch, nor imagination but only an act by which the mind looks into itself (mentis inspectio) which may be as imperfect and confused as it formerly was or clear and distinct as it now is.[13] What Descartes has done is to appropriate the very act by which thinking looks into itself—the "cogitantis inspectio" of Anselm's first philosophy*—(which Descartes now calls "mentis inspectio") as the very principle for the sensible perception of sensible things.

But, given the way we speak, we say that we see (videre) the same wax and not that we judge (judicare) that it is the same; and from the way we speak we are inclined to conclude that we know the wax by means of a vision of the eyes (visione oculi) and not solely by "mentis inspectione."° From this we can see that a good

---

\* See pp. xvi, 42, 48, 53, 54, 91, 94 above.

° Thus, when we look from a window, we say that we "see" men passing by, and we are inclined to conclude that we see them by a vision of the eye. But what we really see from the window are hats and coats that might just as well have been covering automata but which we judge to be men. As it is with this, so also is it with the wax: by the "faculty of judgment" alone (which is in "mente

deal of the feebleness of the mind and its proneness to fall insensibly into errors is due to the fact that words themselves (verbis ipsis) "impede" the mind which is very nearly deceived by the usage of language itself. When we attempt to think beyond and beneath this usage of language, and when we attempt to distinguish the wax from its "external forms," we see that we could not perceive it as it "really" is without a "humana mente," and it is this mind itself which is "me myself"—"me ipso."

This self, which seems to perceive this wax so distinctly, actually knows itself not only more truly and more certainly but also more distinctly and evidently, for if this self judges that the wax exists from having seen it, it certainly is more evident that this self, this "me ipsum," also exists from the fact that it sees the wax.* In this way, Descartes can say that he has insensibly or spontaneously "reverted" to the point he wished to make. Since bodies are not properly perceived by the senses or by the faculty of the imagination but are "perceived" by the understanding alone, "solo intellectu," and since they are not perceived because they are touched or seen, but only because they are understood, it must be concluded that there is nothing which is easier or more evident to be able to perceive than the mind—"mea mente."[14]

Descartes has thus attempted in this meditation to establish the principle that when he sees (or, what is the same thing, when he thinks he sees), it cannot be the case that he himself who thinks is not something. The impossibility of his own non-existence seems to have been given the role of the impossibility of the non-existence of God in Anselm's first philosophy. For Anselm, in thinking that than which nothing greater can be conceived, something is

---

mea") that is comprehended which is falsely thought to be "seen" with the eyes.

* Although it may be that what is seen is not truly wax, it cannot be intelligible that when this self sees or "thinks" it sees—and these two are no longer to be distinguished—that it itself is not something (aliquid). What can be said of the wax can be applied to all things posited as external to the self (extra me posita), for all the reasons which are able to help in the perception of the wax (or any other body whatsoever) actually prove better (melius probent) the nature of the mind—of "mentis meae."

being thought which exists in the understanding but which could *not only* exist in the understanding—something, in fact, which would exist even if it didn't exist in the human understanding. But for Descartes it is not a matter of his thought's affirming the existence of something that would be *there* without his thought. Rather, it is a matter of his thought's affirming the existence of itself as a really existing thing. For Descartes, in the negativity of doubting (which seems to take the place of the negativity of the denial of lived faith as the starting point of Anselm's reflection on first philosophy), the self thinks the existence of something which is inseparable from its thinking, something which could not exist were the self unable to think. This something—what Descartes calls "res" and (in keeping with Anselm's terminology) "aliquid"—is the very particular thing which his thinking is. Descartes has not simply affirmed his own existence—for that in itself would be no decisive event in the history of first philosophy—but he has established his existence as the particular something (the "aliquid," the "res") which thinks his existence.* And this particular something, this "ego cogitans," would presumably exist (from what has been said thus far) even if there were nothing else for it to think, nothing from which it could distinguish itself—even if there were, so to speak, no wax ("sine cera")°[15] or any other body.

### iv. Addressing the Self Alone

Having given his mind free rein to consider what is involved in the perception of objects other than itself, and having seen that this perception is nothing more than the act by which the mind looks into itself, Descartes can now in the third meditation pull the mind back to itself. He shall now call off (avocabo) all his senses and efface (delebo) from his thought all images of corporeal

---

* Descartes here both presupposes and goes beyond Anselm's assertion that the human mind's thinking is the very image of its own existence. See p. 37 above.

° "Cera," interestingly enough, may have been derived from "cerno" which means "to sift" or "to separate."

things—or at least consider these images "empty and false." Addressing himself alone and looking into the interior of himself,* he shall attempt to "restore" little by little what is more known and familiar to himself. As a thinking thing or "res cogitans," he realizes that the things which he senses or imagines could perhaps be "nothing" apart from him and in themselves, but he is nonetheless certain that these modes of thinking (cogitandi modos) which he calls "sensation" and "imagination"—only insofar as they are modes of *thinking*—exist *in him*. Very circumspectly and diligently he must now see if there are other things about himself which he has not yet looked backed upon (respexi), in the confidence that what he can perceive as exceedingly "clear and distinct" is entirely true. This confidence, in fact, is a "general rule" that he has discovered in concluding to the necessity of his own existence as a thinking thing.

In examining the contents of his mind, Descartes notices the "preconceived" opinion which he has of God as the highest power. As often as this opinion occurs to him, he is unable not to acknowledge that God could easily will to cause him to err even in regard to those things which he thinks he has seen (intueri) as most evident with the mind's eye (mentis oculis).° Granted, even if there is a deceiver-God, the self-certainty of Descartes' own existence would still obtain. Unless the possibility of a deceiver-God is eliminated, however, there is nothing other than his own existence which Descartes would be able to know with certainty. Admittedly, the occasion for entertaining this possibility arises only in first philosophy and in a *refounded* first philosophy at that, since for Aristo-

---

  * meque solum alloquendo . . . penitus inspiciendo meipsum. Cf. Anselm's "alloquium," p. 56 above.

  ° Cf. pp. 24, 77, 78 above. Since there is no occasion for "reckoning" that there is "some deceiver-God," and since Descartes does not yet even sufficiently know whether there *is* some God, the reason for doubting which depends on this opinion is "exceedingly tenuous" and might even be said to be "metaphysical." Nonetheless, if he is to remove altogether any possible occasion that might occur in this regard, he ought to examine whether there is a God (an sit Deus), and if there is, whether God can be a deceiver. As long as he is ignorant of this, he would not be able to be certain distinctly of any other contents of his mind.

tle deception makes no sense when predicated of the pregiven unity of the prime unmoved mover, of thought thinking itself.[16]

Descartes, then, must examine the question of the existence of God in his refounding of first philosophy, even though that philosophy is not theology. This would seem to entail that the question of the existence of God is not as such the question of being *qua* being in Descartes' first philosophy but is in function of the certainty and nature of Descartes' own existence as "res cogitans." Thus, the question of God's existence must be examined without interrupting the order of meditations which Descartes has proposed for himself—an order in which he passes by degrees from those notions which he discovers to be first in his mind to those notions that he is able to discover afterwards. He must then methodically "divide" his thoughts into certain kinds. The most generic kinds which he proposes are those ideas which the term "idea" (ideae nomen) alone properly fits and those ideas which are something else besides ideas since they have other "forms" attached to them.

The *first* kind, pure ideas, are representations, somewhat like images of things, but which can be considered only in themselves and not as referring to anything "other" than themselves. To the extent that these ideas exist only as certain modes of his thinking, they are scarcely able to afford any "matter for erring"; they are not able to be "properly false." The *second* kind, impure ideas, as for example, to will, to fear, to affirm, to deny, always add something "more" to the idea itself by which is comprehended the likeness of the thing (rei similitudinem). This second kind of idea is capable of being false to the extent that something other than an idea as a pure representative reality is involved. Of this kind, some are called "volitions," others "affections," and still others "judgments." When the sub-kind is volition or affection, the falsity is not as such in the will or affections themselves, for even when "bad things" or things that never were (nusquam sunt) are desired or willed, it is no less true that there is an "I" who desires them. Because of this, the principal location of falsity is to be found in judgments wherein the

"I" or self judges that the ideas which are in itself are similar or conformable to those things which are outside itself.

The first kind of idea, namely, idea properly so called, has three sub-kinds: "innate" which are neither made by nor come from outside the self; "adventitious" which are not made by (but seem to come from outside) the self; and "factitious" which do not come from outside (but seem to be made by) the self. In all three, however, that by which the self understands a thing, a truth, or a thought is had by it from no other source than its own nature (mea natura). In regard to adventitious ideas, then, Descartes must inquire what is the cause which moves him to esteem them similar to external objects.*[17] The cause which he finds here is not a certain judgment, "certo judicio," but only some "blind" impulse which pre-

---

\* In the first place, it seems that he is taught this by nature (doctus a natura), and in the second place he "experiences" within himself that these ideas do not depend on his will and, therefore, do not depend on himself. Whether he wills or not, he now feels heat from the fire, and so he can persuade himself that the idea of heat is produced in him by something different from himself (a me diversa), something that imprints its "likeness" upon him. But are these reasons sufficiently firm? To say that he is instructed of this by nature only means that there is a spontaneous "impulse" by which he believes in the connection between the idea and the external object, and not as such a certain natural light (lumine aliquo naturali) which shows it to be true to him, as when he was shown that his existence follows from the fact of his doubting (ex eo quod dubitam, sequatur me esse). He has, in fact, no other faculty which could teach him that what this light of nature shows him as true is not true; and "natural inclinations," he has observed, frequently lead him as much to things "worse" as to things "good," so that he can see no reason to have "faith" in these natural inclinations in regard to distinguishing the true from the false. Nor does he find the argument convincing that adventitious ideas must *in fact* proceed from objects outside him since they do not depend on his will, for perhaps there is in him some faculty able to effect these ideas which is not yet sufficiently known by him. It would seem, after all, that in sleep these adventitious ideas can be formed in him without the aid of "external things." But even if these ideas did, in fact, issue from things different from himself, it would not as such follow that these ideas ought to be similar to these things. To illustrate this, Descartes proposes the idea of the sun which is derived from the senses (where the sun appears extremely small); this idea, when compared to the idea of the sun proposed by astronomy (where the sun is presented as greater than the earth), is seen to be more greatly dissimilar to the sun itself.

viously led him to believe that things existed different from himself and impressed upon him (through the organs of his senses) their "images." Yet, there is another way to inquire if, among the things of which he has ideas, there are some which exist outside him (extra me).

If he considers only the first kind of idea, namely, the idea as only a "particular mode" of thinking, he would not be able to recognize any difference or inequality, for all ideas would appear to proceed from him in the same way. But if he considers the second kind of idea, namely, the idea as representing something in "one thing" and something else in "another thing," it becomes clear that these ideas differ greatly among themselves. Included in this second kind of idea are those ideas that would present substances, and these ideas would be greater (majus) than the rest and would contain in themselves more "objective reality." They would participate by representation in a higher degree of being or perfection than those ideas that only represent modes or accidents. And among these ideas which present substances, the idea of God as something supreme (summum aliquem), eternal, infinite, immutable, all-knowing, all-powerful, and Creator of all things which are other than himself would assuredly have in itself more objective reality than those ideas through which "finite substances" are presented.*[18]

---

\* In regard to Descartes' use of the term "objective reality of an idea," it should be noted that by "idea," he understands a "form of each of our thoughts"—a "thought" being anything that exists in us in such a way that we are "immediately conscious" of it. Objective reality means the entity or the being of the thing (l'être de la chose) inasmuch as this entity is *in* the idea. If, then, it is manifest by the "light of nature" that there must be at least as much existence in the efficient cause as in the effect of this cause, then it follows that what is more perfect, i.e., what contains "more reality" in itself, cannot proceed from what is less perfect, and this would apply to ideas considered only in terms of their objective reality. Hence the idea of heat or of a stone is not able to exist in the self unless it is displayed (profita) in that self by some cause in which there is at least as much reality as can be *conceived* to be in heat or stone. This cause is no less real for not pouring out (transfundat) any of its actual or formal reality into the idea.

The nature of an idea is to be a work (un ouvrage) of the mind (l'esprit) which requires no other "formal reality" than that which it borrows (mutuatur) from the thinking of the self of which it is a mode. However, although one idea is able to be born of another idea, this cannot be an "infinite progression." If among the ideas had by the self, which are like images or pictures (tableaux), one is found whose reality does not exist in the self formally or "eminently," and consequently the self is not able to be its cause, it would follow necessarily that it is not only the self which exists, but some other thing (aliam rem) exists which is the cause of this idea. Were no such idea to be found in the self, no argument could be had for the existence of anything different from the self.

The ideas which display (exhibent) other men or animals or even angels might easily have been formed of the ideas which the self has of itself, even if there were (apart from these ideas) no men, animals, or angels in the world. And even when it comes to the clear and distinct ideas of "corporeal objects," such as substance, duration, and number, these "could have been borrowed" from the idea of the self (mei ipsius). Only the idea of God is an "aliquid" which would not be able to "proceed" from the self, since the name of God (Dei nomine) denotes an infinite and independent substance, "supremely intelligent" and "powerful," by which the self (ego ipse) and "everything else," if anything else exists, have been created.

Although the idea of substance is in the self from the very fact that this self is a substance, there would be no idea of an infinite substance, "substantiae infinitae," in a finite self unless this idea had proceeded from some substance which is "really" infinite. The self does, in fact, "perceive the infinite" through a true idea and not only through the "negation of the finite." This is because the self understands more reality to exist in infinite than in finite substance; and so the perception of the infinite is in some way in the self "prior" to that of the finite. There is a sense in which the notion of God is prior to that of the self. For by what reason would this self understand that it doubts and desires, i.e., that something is lacking in it and that it does not exist as entirely perfect, unless it had within itself the idea of an entity more perfect—by comparison with which it would recognize the defects of its own nature? It is, consequently, the idea of God that is not able to exist from nothing (a nihilo), that cannot be "materially false" but can only be most greatly (maxime) clear and distinct, and that contains more objective reality than any other idea. No other idea can be found to be "more true" in itself or less suspect of error and falsity. Although, perhaps, it is able to be represented in thought (fingi potest) that such a being does not exist, it is not able to be conceived that the idea of this being displays *nothing* real[*] to the self. Whatever is perceived clearly and distinctly and conveys (importat) some perfection is totally contained in this idea of God.[19]

Could it be, however, that Descartes is something more than he understands himself to be, and that all these perfections which he "assigns" to God are in some way "potentially" in himself, even if they do not yet put themselves forth (exerant) or are not "reduced to act"? He has already had the experience of his own thought (cognitionem meam) increasing little by little, and he sees nothing which would prevent it from increasing more and more unto infinity (augeatur in infinitum). Yet, when he reflects on the matter, he realizes that his knowledge could never be "actually infinite," since it could never reach a point where it would not be capable of still greater increase, a point, that is, where (as in God) absolutely nothing is potential, where nothing can be added to his perfection. In this way, the fact that the certainty of his own thought increases by degrees (gradatim augeri) turns out to be a most certain argument for Descartes' imperfection. It is only, then, when the keen vision of his mind (mentis aciem) is "blinded" that he does not easily recollect (recordor) why the idea of a being more perfect than himself necessarily proceeds from an entity which is really more perfect. Descartes must, consequently, inquire whether he himself who has this idea would be able to exist (esse possem) at all if no such entity existed.

---

[*] Cf. pp. 69, 48-49, 27 above.

He knows for certain that no thing more perfect or even as perfect as God is able to be thought (cogitari) or formed mentally (fingi). Were Descartes the source of his own being, he should neither doubt nor desire, nor should anything be lacking (deesset) to him, for he would have given himself (mihi dedissem) every perfection of which he had some idea in himself and thus "would be God." But as it is, Descartes experiences nothing to exist by which he could effect that he who now is shall *continue to be* in the future. Since the "light of nature" makes manifest that the distinction between creation and conservation in being is only a "distinction of reason," he can know very evidently that he "depends" on some entity (aliquo ente) different from himself.*20

It must be concluded, then, that from the fact alone that Descartes exists and that he has the idea of a most perfect being (entis perfectissimi) or of God, it is most evidently demonstrated that God *also* exists (etiam existere). Since this idea of God is not drawn (hausi) from the senses, is never presented "unexpectedly" as is the case with ideas of sensible things, and is also not "effected" by the self, it must be innate in the self in the same way as the idea of that self is innate in the self.

It is not to be wondered at that God, in creating the self, imparted (indidisse) this idea to it like the mark of an artificer printed on his work.° Nor is the mark necessarily something different from "the work itself." If God has created the self, it is "exceedingly believable" that in some way he has made it in his own image and likeness and that the self perceives this similitude in which the idea

---

* To say that he is simply produced by his parents or by some other cause less perfect than God is to forget that there must be at least as much existence in the cause as in the effect. Therefore, since he is a "res cogitans" having the idea of God within him, his cause must likewise be a thinking thing having all the perfections which he assigns to God. Likewise, to say that many "partial causes" may have "concurred" in effecting his self—so that from one was taken one of the perfections which he assigns to God and from another a second of the perfections which he assigns to God—is to forget that the unity, or simplicity, or the inseparability of all things which are in God is one of the principal perfections which is understood to exist in God.

° nota artificis operi suo impressa. See pp. 101-102 above.

of God is contained by the same faculty by which it perceives itself (ego ipse). When Descartes turns "the keen vision of his mind" into himself, he understands that he exists as an imperfect thing, an "incomplete thing" dependent on another, as something which indefinitely aspires (indefinite aspirantem) to become greater and better. At the same time, Descartes understands that what he depends on has infinitely in itself—not indefinitely and only potentially—that to which Descartes aspires, and thus that it is God (Deum esse).

The entire "force of the argument" used here to prove the existence of God consists in the impossibility (non posse) that the self exists in such a way, having as it does the idea of God in it, unless God also (etiam) truly exists. This God has in himself all those perfections which the self does not comprehend, but which in some way the self is able to come in contact with by thinking (attingere cogitatione). From this it is sufficiently manifest that God is not able to be a deceiver, since it is revealed by the "light of nature" that all fraud and deception depend on some defect, and God is palpably subject to no defects. At this point, Descartes concludes, it would be well to linger for a little while in the contemplation of this God (Dei contemplatione), for just as we believe by faith (fide credimus) that the highest happiness of that "other life" consists only in the contemplation of the divine majesty, so also we experience that a similar "meditation," although incomparably less perfect, permits us to have the greatest delight (voluptatem) that we are capable of in "this life."[21]

Having claimed in the second meditation that his perception of anything other than himself *is* the very act by which his mind looks into itself, Descartes in the third meditation addresses himself alone. Grounded though it is in Anselm's "cogitantis inspectio," the Cartesian "mentis inspectio" never makes Anselm's move from solitary meditation to dialogue in first philosophy. Far from being raised, consequently, in function of what truly ought to be believed, the question of the existence of God is raised by Descartes in function of the question of his being deceived about everything *except* his own existence.

Descartes does ask whether he himself would exist at all if God does not exist, but his answer is indirect: to the extent that he doubts and that he cannot guarantee his own existence in the future, his existence would have to be caused by God. He never says that he himself would not necessarily exist if he could not doubt (i.e., would not need to doubt) or if he could guarantee his own existence in the future. What he does say is that it is from the fact alone that he himself exists that God is demonstrated to exist. He only knows God to exist to the extent that he infers God to be a creator, an artificer, whose mark is imprinted on his own *ego*. He only knows God to exist by the same faculty by which he first knows his own *ego* to exist necessarily. Admittedly, his own existence, insofar as it is marked by entertaining the idea of God, would be impossible if God does not really exist as his creator. But he never explicitly says that he would not exist at all (or even not necessarily exist) if he did not have the idea of God. Instead, what he does say is that his notion of God, even though it is not discovered first, is prior to his notion of his own existence in the sense that his perception of an aspiration to the infinite within himself is prior to (or conditional for) the perception of himself as a *finite ego*.

The idea of God would seem to have priority, then, in the sense that it would not be able to proceed merely from the finite *ego* itself. This is what enables Descartes to say that—like his capacity to think the necessity of his own existence—this idea of God is innate. But, given his insistence that the nature of an idea as such—an idea in its purity, an idea *qua* idea—is to be a work of the mind of the finite *ego* which requires no other formal reality than that which it borrows from the thinking of that mind, it would seem that the idea of God as an infinite substance is *not quite* innate (namely, as an idea *qua* idea) but is rather innate as an idea which has something added on to it—presumably a volition, a will-to-the-infinite.

It is this idea of God (which is not purely an idea)—the idea of an infinite substance which the finite *ego* aspires to be or wills to be—which Descartes needs if he is to know anything other than himself. The thinking of this idea entails the thinking of the actual existence of God on the part of the finite *ego*. But the actual existence of God in and of itself, it would seem, is required by Cartesian first philosophy only indirectly. For Descartes to show that he cannot be deceived about everything other than his own existence, he must show that God cannot be understood to be a deceiver. And to show that God cannot be understood to be a deceiver, he must show that if the idea of God is thought, God cannot be conceived not to exist actually. What counts, then, in Descartes' refounding of first philosophy is not precisely what counts in Anselm's transformation of Aristotle's founding of first philosophy, namely, that God actually exists in the sense that he would exist even if nothing else existed. What counts in Cartesian first philosophy is that the finite *ego* thinks God as actually existing, thinks God as what this *ego* would be if it could attain that to which it aspires, namely, the infinite. That to which it aspires must actually exist if the finite *ego* is to be capable of aspiring to it. But if the existence of the finite *ego* were not *first* found to be necessary, there would be no way of discovering the priority of the existence of that to which it aspires. Something like what stands behind Anselm's single and self-sufficing argument for God's existence in his dialogue in first philosophy emerges in the third of Descartes' solitary meditations on first philosophy, namely, the *desire* to be, *to exist in the existence of the infinite*. But this desire *to be in* (the rectitude of) God now becomes the desire *to be* (or to have the absolute self-certainty of) God, for Descartes. God is what the self would be if it did not *merely think* the idea of God, if it transcended the possibility of doubting, if it could guarantee its own existence in the future.

What the self merely *would* be if it had the power to do these things must *actually* exist if the self is to account for the fact that it doubts and that it cannot guarantee its own existence in the future—that it *merely thinks* the idea of God. Descartes, it would seem, can only claim in his third meditation that the necessity of his own existence, discovered in the second meditation, is the image or mark of an infinite artificer to the extent that this artificer is discovered to be the infinite image of the necessity of Descartes' own existence. True to his announcement, he has addressed himself alone in the third meditation on his refounding of first philosophy—a first philosophy that is not to be identified with theology (as it was in Aristotle's founding of first philosophy or Anselm's transformation of this founding) but with the theoretical foundations for the physical sciences.

### v. The Supra-Substantial Human Subject

In the beginning of his fourth meditation, Descartes remarks that when he attends to the fact that he could not doubt unless he were an incomplete and dependent thing, the idea, so very clear and distinct, of an independent and complete being, that is, God, "occurs" to him. From the fact alone that such an idea is in him—or that he who possesses this idea exists—he manifestly concludes that God *also* exists and that his own existence at every single moment so entirely depends on God that nothing could be known more evidently and certainly by the "human mode of thinking." It now seems that he has some path (aliquam viam) which will lead from the contemplation of the true God—in whom are "hidden" all the treasures of the sciences and wisdom, "omnes thesauri scientiarum & sapientiae"—to the knowledge of other things in the world.

This is possible because as long as he thinks only of God and turns himself (converto) entirely toward him, he seizes upon no cause of error or falsity, whereas, afterwards, when having "reverted" to himself, he experiences himself to be subject to innumerable errors. Upon investigating this, he finds that not only does he have a real and positive idea of God as a being of "supreme perfection," but he also has a certain negative idea of that which is supremely removed (summe abest) from every perfection, that is, an idea of "nothingness." In this sense, he discovers himself to be a mean between God and nothingness[*]—his existence constituted as in between the highest being (summum ens) and nonbeing (non ens).

Insofar as he is created by this highest being, there is assuredly nothing through which he can be deceived or "led into error." But

---

[*] medium quid inter Deus & nihil

insofar as in some way he participates in nothingness or in nonbeing—i.e., insofar as he himself is not the supreme being and thus finds himself exposed to an "infinity of shortcomings"—it should not be marveled at that he is deceived. Descartes can now understand that error as such does not exist as something real (quid reale) which depends on God but can only exist by way of "being a defect." There is, then, no faculty which has been assigned by God to the self for the purpose of erring; rather, erring depends on the fact that the faculty for judging truth which the self has from God is not infinite in the self. Error—far from being a "pura negatio" or a simple deficiency or shortcoming of some perfection which, in point of fact, is not owed to the self—is a "privation" of, or being-without (carentia), some acquired knowledge (cognitionis) which in some way ought to exist (esse deberet) in the self. It would not seem possible that God bestowed on the self some faculty which is not perfect "in its kind." For if it is the case that the more skilled the artisan is, the more perfect is the work "intended" by him, what could have been made by the supreme framer (conditore) of all things that is not finished or complete in all its members? Certainly, God could have created the self in such a way that it would never err, and certainly God always wills what is best. Is Descartes, then, to conclude that it is better for the self to be able to be deceived than not to be able?[22]

But one should not be astonished, Descartes remarks, at not understanding the reasons why God does what he does, and this would not be a reason for doubting his existence. There are, after all, innumerable things which God is able to do, the causes of which man is ignorant; and it would be "rashness" on man's part to think it possible to investigate the purposes of God. This itself would suffice to esteem the kinds of causes that are called "final" to have no use in regard to the "things of Physics." But in inquiring whether the works of God (opera Dei) are perfect, one should not consider some one creature "separately," for the same thing, that might seem to be exceedingly imperfect if it is by itself, might be found to be most perfect when considered as part of the order (rationem) in the world. Although Descartes only knows with certainty, so far, that he exists and God exists, he is not able, given the boundless power of God, to deny that God may have made many other things (or at least is able to make them) in such a way that Descartes himself might have a part in the order of things in the world.

It would seem, then, that the best way that Descartes can account for his errors is to appeal to a "simultaneous concurrence" of two causes, namely, the faculty of recognizing what is already known (facultate cognoscendi), i.e., the understanding (ab intellectu), and the "faculty of choice or free will," i.e., the will (a voluntate) as such. By the understanding alone, the self neither makes certain of nor denies anything but only perceives the ideas with which it can form a judgment. It cannot, then, be properly said that any error is in the understanding. Even if, perhaps, there are innumerable things which exist of which there are no ideas in the self, it cannot be said that the self is "deprived of them" as something which is owed to the nature of its understanding, since there is no reason able to prove that God should have given the self a greater faculty of recognizing "what is already known." However "skillful an artificer" God is understood to be, he need not place in each particular thing (in singulis) all the perfections which he is able to place in some of his works.

But it cannot be said of the will or liberty of choice that the self has not received it from God as sufficiently "large and perfect," since the will is experienced as "circumscribed by no limits." Of all the perfections that are in the self there is none so perfect or so great that it could be understood to be more perfect or greater than the will. At the same time that the faculty of understanding is found to be very small (perexiguam) and exceedingly limited in the self, the idea is formed of another faculty "much greater" than the understanding and "even infinite." From the very fact that the idea of this faculty can be formed, it must follow that this faculty pertains to the very "nature of God." It is will alone or liberty of choice which is experienced as so great in the self that no greater idea can be apprehended.* Thus it is by reason of its will that the self can principally understand that it carries the image and likeness of God. In God the will is comparatively greater than it is in the self by virtue of the "knowledge and power" which, when conjoined to it in God, render it "more solid and efficacious" than it is in the self, and also by virtue of its object in God, viz., that it extends itself to so many things. Nevertheless, the will does not "seem greater" in God than in the self when it is considered "formally and precisely in itself." When so considered, apart from knowledge and power, the faculty of will consists only in this: to do or not to do, to affirm or to deny, to follow through or to avoid. In order to affirm or to deny, to follow through or to avoid those things placed before (proponitur) the understanding, the will performs in such a way that the self feels itself determined by no "external force."[23]

But if the will as such is so large and perfect in its own kind and is had from God, it can no more be the cause of errors than the understanding which is also had from God and by which whatever is understood is understood rightly (recto intelligo). Error, then, can only arise from the fact that the self does not "restrain" the will—which is "wider" than the understanding—within the same limits as the understanding but, rather, extends it to those things which are not understood, so that the will (being indifferent) is easily turned away (deflectit) from the true and the good, and in this way the self is "deceived" and transgresses (pecco). Were it to abstain from passing judgment on anything that it did not perceive with sufficient clarity and distinctness, the self would act rightly (recte agere) and would not be deceived, since, by the light of nature, it is clear that the "perception of the understanding" ought always to precede the "determination of the will." It is when the free will is not "used rightly" that there occurs the privation which constitutes the "formam erroris." This privation is in the operation itself of the will, insofar as it proceeds from the self (a me procedit),

---

\* ut nullius majoris ideam apprehendam

but not in the faculty of the will received from God (a Deo accepi) and dependent on him.\*

When Descartes considers himself alone, as if he were alone in the world, he infers that he would be much more perfect than he now is if God had created him so that he never made a mistake.° Yet he cannot deny that in some way the number of things considered as a whole\*\* might be more perfect if some of its parts were not immune from error, while others are so immune, than if all of its parts were simply the same. Whether he considers his self as a part of or apart from this whole, Descartes experiences a "weakness" in this self, namely, that he is "not always able to cleave to or to be fastened onto one and the same thought." Yet he is able by attentive and frequently "repeated meditation" to effect this on occasion. To the extent that he is willing and able to make no judgment except upon matters clearly and distinctly displayed by the understanding, Descartes can thus restrain his will within the

---

\* In recognizing the infinity of this faculty and the way its operation (as proceeding from the self) can be misused, Descartes realizes that he has no cause for "lamenting" that God did not give him a greater power of understanding (vim intelligendi) or a natural light greater than what he gave. On the contrary, Descartes has every reason to "give thanks" to God who owes him not the slightest thing but has "bestowed so much" on him. The privation in the operation of the will, which is alone the formal reason of falsity and faults, does not need any concurrence from God, since it is not a thing (res) and is not related to God as to a cause. The privation in the operation of the will is given its signification, then, only in the negative mode (tantummodo negatio). It is no imperfection in God to have given the self the liberty to assent or not to assent to things which he has not placed as clear and distinct perceptions in the human understanding. Rather, it is an imperfection in the human self not to use this liberty well and "to pass judgment" on those things which it does not rightly understand.

° God could have made the self, had he so willed, so that it never erred and yet remained free and possessed of a finite acquired knowledge (cognitionis finitae), namely, by either giving to human understanding a clear and distinct perception of everything about which it should ever have to deliberate, or by impressing so firmly on human memory, so that it would never be able "to forget" it, the resolve never to pass judgment on anything without clearly and distinctly understanding it.

\*\* in tota rerum universitate. Cf. p. 27 above.

limits of his judgment; and to this extent he simply is not able to be deceived, and he acquires a "kind of habit" of "never erring."

What makes the general rule of clarity and distinctness of perception the very criterion for acquiring such a habit is the fact that every clear and distinct perception is indubitably "something" and, as such, is not able to exist "from nothingness" but necessarily has "God as its author," a God who, in being "summe perfectum," would be incompatible with deception. In learning what he must beware of in order "never to be deceived," Descartes has also simultaneously learned what is to be done "to arrive at the truth," for he shall arrive at this goal if only he sufficiently attends to all those things which he perfectly understands and if he sunders apart (secernam) from these things what remains as apprehended more confusedly and obscurely.[24]

When Descartes in the third meditation raised the question of the existence of God in function of the question of his being deceived about everything *except* his own existence, he found that the idea of God in him is a representation of what he would be if he did not *merely* think the idea of God. The idea of God is the representation of the necessity of the finite self's existence as if it were infinite—a representation, i.e., which is more than an idea but has attached to it Descartes' own aspiration to be infinite, to be God. Having shown that this representation could not have proceeded only from himself, i.e., having shown the actual existence of what is represented here (God), Descartes now claims in the fourth meditation to have discovered a straight path from the existence of this God to the knowledge of other things besides God and himself, that is, a path to the *existence* of what is addressed by the modern physical sciences.

Descartes can now account for the error which he finds in himself by virtue of his being a mean between the actual existence of that which is represented by the idea of himself as infinite (a positive idea, the idea of God) and a negative idea of absolute nonbeing or nothingness. To the extent that he meditates on the representation of himself as if he were infinite, he is not subject to error; to the extent that he does not meditate upon this idea of God, he participates in the negative idea of nothingness and thus is subject to error. Error, consequently, is not something real but consists in the self's being deprived of God's having created it in such a way that it does not have the capacity for error. The idea of God as the representation of the necessity of the self's existence as if it were infinite is, in fact, the framing of an idea than which no greater idea can be thought, namely, the idea of the will, that is, the idea of the self's acting in such a way that it feels determined by no force external to itself. This idea of liberty of choice is the principal reason why Descartes understands himself to bear the image or mark of God as his creator. This idea, therefore, is the principal reason why he understands God to be a representation of the necessity of his own existence as if it were infinite: considered by itself, apart from power and knowledge, the will is not something greater in God than it is in himself. It is the human self, then, by virtue of its will, which is presented as the supra-substantial subject—that "essentia" which is "extra omnem substantiam."\*

Error as a privation, consequently, arises in the operation of the will as it proceeds from the self (and not in terms of its being given as a faculty to that self *by* God)—i.e., the will does not keep within the same limits as the self's understanding but extends to things not understood, so that the determinations of the will precede the clear and distinct perceptions of the understanding. What constitutes the infirmity, the finitude, of Descartes' own necessary existence is that he lacks the knowledge and the *power* to be God, the power to be *always* fixed upon one idea—while possessing the *will* to be God. Although he can never be God and, thus, can never know God's purposes in creating—and, thus, in turn, can never know why God did not create him without the capacity to err—Descartes claims to have clarified a method which, if it were perfectly practiced, would permit him to acquire a habit of never erring, namely, the method of making no judgments except upon matters first clearly and distinctly perceived. These matters could not have come from the

---

\* Cf. pp. 48, 33 above.

nothingness that is the source of the form of error; these matters, therefore, must have God as their author. In claiming to have learned how not to be deceived, how not to assent to anything false, Descartes claims to have learned what to do to arrive at the truth of the treasures of the physical sciences hidden in God as the author of clear and distinct perception. It would seem that the contemplation of God enjoined upon us at the end of the third meditation turns out, at the end of the fourth meditation, to be an admonition for us to uncover these treasures within the chamber of the supra-substantial Cartesian self.

### vi. Truth as Certitude

Throughout his prior meditations, Descartes has been confident that whatever he has perceived clearly and distinctly is entirely true, and this confidence has, in fact, served as a general rule. This confidence must now be rationally grounded. Certainty must now be *shown* to be the essence of truth.

Descartes remarks at the beginning of his fifth meditation that his previous meditation has disclosed to him innumerable ideas of things which, even if they exist nowhere outside the self, are nevertheless not able to be said to be nothing and which, although they are thought at will (ad arbitrium), are not feigned but have "true and immutable natures." Thus, for example, when a triangle is imagined, even though, perhaps, no such figure exists outside thought in the world, there is nonetheless in this figure a certain determinate nature or essence or form which is immutable and eternal and which has not been effected by the self (and, therefore, does not depend on its mind).

No less than any such figure or number, Descartes finds the idea in his mind of a supremely perfect Being, and he understands that actual and eternal existence belongs to its nature no less clearly and distinctly than he knows that what he can demonstrate of some figure or number also belongs to the nature of figure or number.

The idea of God here is presented not as a "preconceived" opinion*
but as among the immutable and eternal ideas of mathematics.

    The existence of God, then, ought to have at least the *degree of certitude*° which hitherto was found in the truths of mathematics that pertain only to numbers and figures. Having become accustomed in all other things to distinguish between "existentiam" and "essentiam," Descartes might be able to persuade himself that the existence of God is also able to be separated (sejungi posse) from God's essence (and, thus, that God is able to be thought of as nonexistent). But when he attends more diligently to this matter, it is clear that no more than he can separate from the essence of a triangle the fact that the magnitude of its three angles equals two right angles, or from the idea of a mountain the idea of a valley, can the existence of God be separated (separari) from the essence of God. Thus, it is not more repugnant to think God, i.e., a "summe perfectum" who "lacks existence," or who lacks some perfection, than it is to think of a mountain which lacks a valley.[25]

    Of course, from the mere fact that anyone thinks a mountain with a valley, it does not follow that there is such a mountain in the world, for human thought, i.e., "cogitatio mea," "imposes" no necessity on things, as when a winged horse is imagined, although no horse with wings actually exists. From this it might be inferred that existence is able to be "attributed" to God, although no God actually exists. But we must remember that from the very fact that the self is "not able to think of God unless as existing," it follows that "existence is inseparable from God" and that he really exists. It is not thought or "mea cogitatio" which effects this, but it is the necessity in the "thing itself," i.e., in the existence of God, which determines the self in thinking this. Although the self is free to imagine a horse with or without wings, it is not free to think (cogitare) God without existence, that is, a supremely perfect Be-

---

  \* See p. 118 above.

  ° The role played in Anselm by the "graduum distinctio" of existence and goodness (see pp. 26, 36, 68, 88 above) is now played in Descartes by the "certitudinis gradu" (see p. 123 above).

ing without a supreme perfection. Although it is not necessary that the thought of God ever be inscribed (incidam) on anything, much as it is not necessary that a circle ever be inscribed on anything—that is, not necessary that the self should ever have the idea of God—nonetheless whenever the self wills to think (libet cogitare) of a being that is first and supreme and draws this idea forth from the treasure chamber (thesauro)* of its mind, it is necessary that there be attributed to this idea all perfections. When the mind is "directed" to the realization that existence is a perfection, it can be rightly concluded that this first and highest being exists.

This idea of God—an idea alongside other ideas—cannot be something "fictitious" depending on thought but must be the image of a true and immutable nature, as is the case with the ideas of mathematics. Descartes knows this to be the case because he is not able to find out by thinking (excogitari) any other thing to whose essence existence "belongs" except "God alone," and because he is not able to understand two or more gods in this way. Given the conclusion that it is one God who so exists, he must exist "before" from eternity and in the "future" for eternity and possess qualities which the human mind is not able to diminish or change.

Could there be anything, then, more uncovered (apertius) than that the "summum ens" or God exists as that alone to whose essence existence belongs? Only the fact that human thought is "covered over by prejudices" and "besieged" by images of sensible things prevents it from recognizing God first or more easily than anything else among those things which are perceived clearly and distinctly and which alone persuade completely. Although so attentive a consideration on Descartes' part had to be made, he finds that he is not only equally certain of God's existence as he is of all else that seems most certain, but that the certainty of the rest of these things depends upon the certainty of God's existence than which he can know nothing more perfectly. Although it is the case

---

\* The metaphor here is Augustinian. See Bk. X, ch. viii of the *Confessions* where Augustine refers to the treasures of innumerable images (thesauri innumerabilium imaginum) hoarded in his memory.

that as soon as he perceives something exceedingly clear and distinct, he is "not able not to believe it to be true," it is also the case that he is not able to have his mind always fixed (semper defigere) on this same thing so as to be able to perceive it clearly. In this way, other reasons might be able to be offered to him which would easily cast aside his original opinion and, instead of leaving him with true and certain science, would leave him only "vague and changeable opinions"—were he ignorant of God. It is only after having perceived that God truly exists, and having understood at the same time that all other things are dependent on God and that God is not a deceiver, that Descartes can collect together all those things (collegi illa omnia) which he perceives clearly and distinctly as being necessarily *true*.

In this way, the certainty *and* truth of all the sciences are seen to depend upon the knowledge acquired of the "one true God," in the sense that Descartes, before he came to know God, was able to know nothing perfectly of any "other thing." But now he can know innumerable things, not only of God himself and other matters of the understanding, but of "corporeal nature" insofar as it is the object of "pure mathematics," that is, insofar as it is the object of the demonstrations of geometricians who do not consider the point of the existence of this object in nature.[26]

Descartes' seeming equation of his admonition to contemplate God (at the end of the third meditation) with his admonition to uncover the treasures of science hidden in God (in the fourth meditation) is now seen (in the fifth meditation) to be a contemplation which uncovers the contents of the treasure chamber of his own mind. The treasures of the physical sciences hidden in God find their chamber in his own mind and are thus shown to be no longer hidden. The most decisive content to be uncovered from this chamber is the idea of God, since this is the only one of the true and immutable natures locked inside this chamber that will enable him metaphysically to secure the existence of corporeal nature for the physical sciences.

Like the true and immutable natures of mathematics which cannot be fictitious, even though they may not exist outside the treasure chamber of his mind, the idea of God presents itself in this chamber in such a way that the existence of this God can no more be separated from the thinking of his essence than the equality of the three angles of a triangle with two right angles can be separated from the thinking of the essence of a triangle. But it is the necessity of God's existing outside the chamber of his mind which determines him to think God's existence as inseparable from God's essence, and which prevents him from being free to think God *without* existence in the way that he is free to think a horse *with* wings. Existence in God is a perfection that God could not be thought to be without; and God could not be thought to be without this perfection only if God actually exists. But just as the true and immutable natures of mathematics must be thought in one way once they are thought, but need not be thought at all, so also God must be thought as existent, once he is thought, but he need not be thought at all. Once the thought of God is willed, i.e., once man wills his aspiration to the infinite, the thought can only be willed as referring to one, and only one, God, a particular something (like the "aliquid" of Anselm's first philosophy), possessed of qualities that the will of man cannot alter—a particular but infinite "res" whose existence belongs to its essence, whose entire essence it is to exist.

This particular but infinite something whose entire essence it is to exist, that is uncovered from the treasure chamber of Descartes' mind, would be seen to be that which is most evident, most uncovered, that which would be recognized *first*, were it not for the fact that Descartes, like the rest of men, has (or, rather, *had*) a mind covered over by prejudices and besieged by images of sensible things. The necessity of God's existence, in other words, rather than the necessity of his own existence, would be first recognized by Descartes *were* Descartes, in fact, what his will aspires to be, namely, God. As matters stand, Descartes has first discovered his thought to be inseparable from his existence. But his will has not been discovered to be inseparable from (his) existence to the extent that it can participate in nothingness. Existence is inseparable from his thinking but separable from his will. Were his will incapable of participating in nothingness, and were he incapable of doubt in the past and capable of assuring his existence in the future, his entire essence would be inseparable from his existence.

Since this is not the case, it is only after the *recognition* of the absolute inseparability of essence and existence in God—and God alone, whose past and future are an eternal now—that all certitudes can be collected together and perceived as necessarily true—that certitude itself can be identified as the essence of truth. The very truth of the certainty and the very certainty of the truth of all the physical sciences depend on this recognition. But the value of this recognition lies precisely in its grounding (in first philosophy) of the possibility of the existence of corporeal things for the mathematical method at the heart of the physical sciences—a method which is not as such concerned with the physical existence of the things it thinks. The metaphysical foundation of physical science requires not only (mathematical) certainty but a certainty that constitutes the essence of the truth (of the physical world). Descartes' treatment of the existence of God in his non-theological first philosophy turns out to be the instrument for establishing certainty as the essence of truth—as the essence of representation by the self of what is other than the self. Without the idea of God, Descartes has the certainty of his own existence but no truth. With the idea of God as an absolute identity of essence and existence, this certainty becomes the essence of truth. The essence of truth shifts from the Anselmian rectitude of the Divine Will to the Cartesian certitude aspired to by the human will.

### vii. First Philosophy as the Foundation of Physical Science

There remains, in Descartes' sixth meditation, the task of examining whether material things exist. Descartes at least knows that they are "able to exist" insofar as they are the object of pure mathematics. Since the faculty of imagination is a certain application of

## The Cartesian Refounding of First Philosophy 141

the faculty of knowledge to the body which is inwardly present (intime praesens) to it, it seems to follow that material things exist. In imagination there is a peculiar exertion of the soul (animi contentione) which is not to be found in the understanding, as, for example, when a triangle is imagined, it is not only understood to be a figure compassed by three lines but at the same time the three lines are attended to (intueor) as present by a keen vision of the mind (acie mentis).* This "vim imaginandi," insofar as it differs from the "power of understanding," is not required for the essence of the self or "mentis meae," for were the power of imagining absent, the self would remain no less the same than it is now. From this it seems to follow that the power of imagining depends on some "other thing" different from the self.

Descartes could easily understand, consequently, that if some body exists to which his mind is thus "conjoined" in such a way that his mind can look into (inspiciendum) this body whenever it "freely wills" to do so, it could be in this way that corporeal things can be imagined. On the one hand, imagination as a "mode of thinking" is such that the mind would "turn toward" the body and attend to something in the body conformable to an idea either understood by itself or perceived by the senses. On the other hand, pure understanding (pura intellectione) as a mode of thinking would differ from the imagination in that the mind, when it understands, turns in some way "to itself" and regards some one of the ideas which are in itself. Descartes could easily understand the imagination to differ from pure understanding in this way *if* the body exists. Since no other way occurs to him that is "equally fitting" for explaining the imagination, Descartes conjectures (conjicio) that the body exists, but only that it probably (probabiliter tantum) exists. He does not yet, however, see how from the distinct idea of corporeal nature, which he discovers (invenio) in his imagination, he can derive an argument which would "conclude necessarily" to the existence of some body.

---

\* Cf. pp. 125, 123, 56, 42 above.

He must, then, see if—from the ideas which he perceives by that mode of thinking which he calls "sensation"*—he can derive some certain argument for holding the existence of corporeal things. On the one hand, he knows that no other thing belongs to his nature or essence except that he is a thinking thing; and so he rightly concludes that he is a substance whose whole essence or nature is nothing but to think. He can have a clear and distinct idea of himself only insofar as he is a thinking and "non-extended" thing. On the other hand, Descartes has a distinct idea of body only insofar as it is an extended and "non-thinking" thing. He finds in himself faculties of imagining and sensing without which he is able clearly and distinctly to understand himself as a whole (totum me) but which themselves cannot exist without him (sine me), i.e., without an "intelligent substance" in which they abide. For in their "formal concept," they include understanding and so are distinguished from the self as the modes of a thing are distinguished from the thing.°27

---

\* At first, he says, he thought it was not without reason that he judged (arbitrabar) that this body, which by a certain special right he called his own, belonged to him more than any other body. But afterwards many "experiences" shook (labefactarunt) all of the faith which he had in the senses not only in regard to "external things" but also in regard to "internal things" as well, such as pain. Those who have had limbs amputated report that they have felt pain in the limb which had been removed, and this led him to the conclusion that he could not be clearly certain that it was a particular member that pained him even though he felt pain in that member. But now, after he has begun to recognize himself and the "author" of his "origin" better, although he would still think it to be "rash" to allow admittance to all the things which he seems to hold by the senses, he realizes that not all of these things should necessarily be "called back into doubt."

° Descartes also finds other faculties, such as that of changing position and assuming various shapes, which are also not able to be understood (and, therefore, are not able to exist) apart from some substance in which they abide. These faculties, if they exist, ought to inhere in some extended or "corporeal substance" and not in an intelligent substance. There is a sense, then, in which the body is more than a bringing together of accidents (see p. 101 above) and can be said to be a substance. But what is certain is that the self—that by which Descartes is what he is (par laquelle je suis ce que je suis)—is entirely and truly distinct from his body and is able to be or to exist without the body.

Descartes would have "no use" for these "passive" faculties for sensing or "receiving" and becoming acquainted with the ideas of sensible things, unless there also existed a certain "active" faculty for effecting or producing these ideas either in himself or in something else. Given the fact that this active faculty clearly presupposes no understanding, and that these ideas are produced without his cooperation and frequently even when he does not summon them, it follows that this active faculty is not able to exist in the self inasmuch as this self is a thing which thinks. This active faculty must exist, then, in some substance different from the self in which all the reality which is objectively in the ideas produced by this faculty ought to be formally or eminently found. This substance, which is different from the self, is either a corporeal nature or else it is God or some creature "more noble than the body" in which is contained eminently—that is, in a sufficiently great way so as to be able to make up for the defect (défaut) in their excellence—all the reality contained objectively in the ideas produced by this active faculty.

But since God has been discovered not to be a deceiver, it follows that he does not immediately by himself send these ideas into the self (mihi immittere) and does not mediately—through some creature in which their reality is only contained objectively but not formally or eminently—send these ideas into the self. Since God has given the self a "great propensity" for believing these ideas to be conveyed by corporeal things, Descartes cannot see by what reason God would be able to be understood not to be a deceiver, if these ideas were conveyed by something other than corporeal things. Thus, it can be concluded that corporeal things exist (existunt), though all of them, perhaps, are not such as to exist entirely as they are comprehended by the senses, since their comprehension by the senses in many cases is exceedingly obscure and confused. What must be conceded, at least, is that whatever is understood clearly and distinctly in them, that is, whatever in them is comprehended as the object of pure mathematics, is really *in them*.

If this is so, there must be something of truth in all those things which Descartes is taught "by nature," whether nature is considered "generaliter"—that is, either God himself or else "the coordination of created things instituted by God," namely, the order and the arrangement (la disposition) which God has established in created things—or whether nature is considered "in particulari"—that is, Descartes' nature (naturam meam) as the combination of all those things which have been assigned (tributa) him by God. When Descartes considers nature in particular, there is nothing that it more expressly or sensibly teaches him than that he has a body which is badly affected when he feels pain, which is in need of food or drink when hunger or thirst is suffered, and that what ought not to be doubted, henceforth, is that there is something of truth in these things. This entails, furthermore, that Descartes is not only in (adesse) his body as a pilot is *in* his ship, but that he is "most closely" conjoined with it, as if he were intermingled (quasi permixtum) with it. The self thus seems to compose with "its" body something like a whole. All these sensations of hunger, thirst, and pain are nothing other than certain confused modes of thinking,[*] as if they arose (exorti) from the union and admixture of the mind with the body. When Descartes considers nature in particular, it teaches him "to flee from" those things which bring in the feeling of pain and "to follow" those which bring in the "feeling of pleasure." It does not, however, teach him, beyond this, that he should draw a conclusion from these sense perceptions about anything outside himself, unless the examination of the understanding comes before what is concluded about these perceptions. For it is the mind alone, and not the composite of mind and body, which is able to know the truth of these things. In fact, the reason why men are accustomed "to subvert" the order of nature, the "ordinem naturae," is that they use these sensible perceptions—which were properly given by nature only for signifying to the mind which things are suitable or unsuitable for the composite—as if they were "certain rules" for immediately distinguishing the essence of bodies placed outside the self.[28]

---

[*] confusi quidam cogitandi modi

## The Cartesian Refounding of First Philosophy 145

There is, then, a great difference that exists between the body, which by its nature is always divisible, and the mind which is completely indivisible. The mind, or the self (meipsum) insofar as this self is only a thinking thing, is understood to be entirely "one and whole" with no parts being able to be distinguished. What we call the faculties of willing, sensing, and understanding are not able to be said to be parts of the mind, since it is "one and the same" mind which wills, senses, and understands. But in the case of corporeal or extended things, Descartes is not able to think of one which is unable to be divided by his thought into parts and which he does not understand to be divisible. This suffices to show that "the mind is entirely different from the body." Experience itself, then, would "testify" that there is nothing put into all of our sensations by nature which can be ascertained not to confirm the "power and goodness" of God. But it is also clear that, notwithstanding the boundless goodness of God, the "nature" of man (naturam hominis) as a composite of mind and body is unable not to be "sometimes" deceived.*

But knowing now that all his senses more frequently indicate truth rather than falsehood in regard to those things which are "suitable" for the body, and being able by memory to connect the present with what preceded it, and by understanding to look into all the causes of his errors, Descartes ought no longer fear that false things are displayed by his senses. He must now drive out

---

* Descartes, in fact, singles out "internal sensations" as matters in which he sometimes detects errors in what is displayed to him by nature when it is considered in particular. These errors seem to indicate that he is directly deceived by his own nature (directement trompé par ma nature) here. It is not a rare occurrence for men to err even in those things to which they are urged on by nature, as in the case of the sick who are afterwards harmed by the very food or drink which they desire. To say that they are in error because their nature is corrupted does not remove the difficulty here, for a sick man is truly no less the "creature of God" than is the healthy man. Therefore, it seems no less inconsistent for the sick man to have a deceptive nature (fallacem naturam) from God than for the healthy man. The only conclusion to be drawn, then, is that the "goodness of God" does not "hinder" nature, when it is considered in particular, from being "deceptive."

(explodendae) the doubts of the preceding days as exaggerated (hyperbolicae) and "worthy of laughter."*29

It is, then, as a composite being—a being which happens to have a body in addition to the self or mind which constitutes his essence—that man is subject to error in regard to his sense perceptions. But these perceptions cannot be entirely in error. Because the necessity of "acting on things"—a necessity not, as such, examined in Cartesian first philosophy—frequently obliges men to decide and does not always afford them the leisure to examine things so accurately, human life in particular things is "fated" to be frequently subject to errors. In the end, the weakness (infirmitas) and feebleness (la faiblesse) of human "nature"—i.e., the composite of mind and body—must be acknowledged.[30]

With this acknowledgment of the errors of human life, Descartes draws to a close his refounding of first philosophy. But this acknowledgment does not pertain to the self, the subject, the *ego* that Descartes has discovered or (more precisely) invented. For this *ego* is a "res cogitans" whose essence would be absolutely inseparable from its existence were it not an aspiration or will to an infinity which it cannot become—were it not an orientation into the negativity of nothingness as well as into the positive actuality of infinity. Among the modes of thinking peculiar to this self in its conjunction with a body are the faculties of imagination and sensation; but these modes are not required for the existence of this self and, consequently, require a substance other than the self to which they can refer. In examining imagination, Descartes finds that it proceeds from his will, his aspiration to infinity, but that it seems to turn to something (other than his self) which should, in all likelihood, be

---

* Particularly the one concerning his distinguishing sleep from wakefulness, for he can now find a very great difference between the two. Dreams can never be "conjoined" with each other or with all the actions of life by the memory, as it does with things which occur in wakefulness. If, without any interruption, Descartes can connect his perceptions of things, when he distinctly knows "where" and "when" they appeared to him, with the entire course of the rest of his life, then he can be certain that these perceptions occur in wakefulness and not in sleep. Since God is not a deceiver, it follows that Descartes cannot be entirely deceived in such things.

*there*—namely, bodily entity. In examining sensation, Descartes finds an active faculty for producing the ideas of these sensations—a faculty not dependent on his will and, therefore, requiring something other than his self. This other substance cannot be God or some non-bodily creature, since Descartes has a propensity to believe that this active faculty is a bodily substance. And since God has been discovered to exist and, therefore, not to be a deceiver, this God would not so radically deceive Descartes in giving him this propensity.

Bodily substances must, therefore, exist, probably not exactly in the way they are comprehended by sensations, but at least in the way they are comprehended by pure mathematics. The physical sciences are thus metaphysically guaranteed an object which really exists for their mathematical method. The treasures of the physical sciences are thus unlocked and made unhidden by virtue of the idea of God locked in the chamber of the *ego* or human subject. The idea of God is the idea of what that human subject would be were it not merely an aspiration to the infinite but, rather, the full positive actuality of the infinite. First philosophy, refounded as the ground of physics, as the handmaiden of physical science, and no longer as theology, is this very unlocking of the treasures of the modern physical sciences.

But if bodily substance exists, it follows that the *ego*, the self, as the will to be the infinity it cannot be in the full actuality and positivity of this infinity, is fittingly conjoined to bodily substance so as to form a composite whole, a body-soul *system*. For the Greeks σύστημα meant a composite whole, a whole that is put together; and for Descartes the body-soul system is what has been put together by the Creator-God. It is this body-soul system which constitutes nature when considered in its particularity (i.e., the combination of all things assigned to the self by God). But "soul" here is not really soul in the ancient and medieval sense (viz., something that is a part of nature) but stands for the self, the *ego*, as a pure undivided essence—something particular, an "aliquid," that would exist without the nature assigned by God, inasmuch as the human aspiration or will to be infinite is a will to be beyond nature. This nature, this put-together whole assigned by God, deceives man in regard to both external and internal sensations; but it is now clear that it deceives him to a lesser degree than it doesn't deceive him. Since man's pure undivided essence, his self, which has an existence beyond this system of self-body, is not deceived in any way except when the will overextends the compass of the understanding, and since Descartes has discovered a method, essentially the mathematical method of the new science, for overcoming this overextension, it follows that this deceptive composite nature which man has received from God is not inconsistent with God's goodness. To this extent it can now be recognized that all of the doubts of the first meditation are hyperbolic.

Radical subjectivity is now clearly in view in first philosophy. The grammatical first person has been ontologically reified. It is only as a system of body and self, as a composite whole, as a being among the beings of nature, that I am subject to error and that *my* infirmity must be acknowledged. But this infirmity is not really "mine"—not really a part of my pure "partless" essence, of my *ego* which is not really a being among the beings of nature. Anselm's dialectic of God as a being among beings and a being beyond beings is the paradigm here. What is really *me*, for Descartes, is not, as such, something that belongs to nature; and because of this I am able, in the modern physical sciences, to be the master and possessor of nature,* the victor over the very sickness of the corporeal substance to which I am so intimately connected.

### viii. Descartes' Response to Criticism

Much as the criticism of Gaunilo was an occasion for Anselm to *deepen* reason's response to the impenetrability of the suprasubstantial, more-than-natural, essence of the divine subject, so also the criticism of his contemporaries was an occasion for Descartes to *clarify* the supra-substantial human subject. The more-than-nat-

---

\* See Part VI of Descartes' *Discourse on Method*.

ural essence of this human subject or *ego* is clarified by Descartes in his "Replies to Objections Urged Against 'The Meditations'."

The existence of his own self (moi-même), Descartes tells his critics, does not depend on any "series" of causes and can be used "to support" his proof of the existence of God. But he has not asked for the cause of his own being insofar as he is composed of body and soul but precisely insofar as he is a thing which thinks. Yet, he has not only asked what is the cause of his own being as a thinking thing but also insofar as there is in him, *among* his other thoughts, the idea of a supremely perfect being. It is on this idea alone that the whole force of his demonstration of God's existence depends. In the case of the idea of God, we clearly and distinctly conceive that "to exist" belongs to his true and immutable nature. As the being who preserves himself in existence, as the cause of himself (soi-même), God is such that it is impossible that he not be always existent. God cannot be comprehended (compris) or "grasped" in his entirety, but he can be understood (entendu), or clearly and distinctly apprehended, as that which is the infinite *qua* infinite.

This demonstration, however, requiring as it does the necessity of the existence of the thinker having the idea of God, presupposes something more fundamental than demonstration, namely, a simple act by which the mind looks into itself* and recognizes itself, without a syllogism, as a thing (une chose) that is known through itself (de soi). "I think, therefore I am or I exist" is not demonstratively or syllogistically deduced because it does not explicitly include the premise "everything that thinks is or exists." But the individual who never moves on from this intuition to that demonstration, the man who does not recognize a God, the atheist, can never be certain that he is not being deceived in the things that seem to be "most evident" to him.[31]

The idea of God is, however, an idea among other ideas that can be held by the *ego* or human subject, and there is nothing that this subject thinks of which it cannot be asked "What is the cause of its

---

\* une simple inspection de l'esprit. See p. 115 above.

existence?" In the case of the idea of God, however, it is discovered that it is the very boundlessness of his nature that is the cause or the reason why he needs "no cause in order to exist." Existence is contained in the idea or concept of each thing because we are not able to conceive of anything except "under the form of something which exists." But it is only possible or contingent existence which is contained in our concept of a limited thing, whereas perfect and necessary being is included in the concept we have of a supremely perfect being.

Anything, then, that we attribute to God is not able to come from "objects external" to our selves, for there is in God nothing of the same kind as in external things, that is to say, in corporeal things. But this idea of God is developed into ideas of God's attributes. Anyone who conceives something perceives that he does so, and by extending this infinitely (étendant à l'infini) he forms the idea of "the divine understanding," and so also with the other attributes of God. Such "unlimited power" is contained in this idea of God, in fact, that we conceive that it would be repugnant, if God truly exists, for anything else to exist unless it were created by God.[32]

The power in this idea of God can only be thought by an entity or subject whose very essence is to think, a subject for whom to be united to a human body is no part of its essence.* The fact that there is a "close conjunction" between soul and body is not denied

---

* This subject whose essence it is to think does not need any object other than itself to exercise its proper activity. And there is no activity of which this subject can be wholly certain, in the sense of metaphysical certitude, except thinking (la pensée). Hence, from any other activity (such as, e.g., walking) that this subject can think that it performs, it can very well infer the existence of its essence as the mind which so thinks this activity, but it cannot infer the existence of the body which performs this activity (i.e., walks). Thus, for Descartes to find that he is "a substance which thinks," or for him to form a clear and distinct concept of this substance in which is contained none of those attributes which belong to corporeal substance, is quite sufficient to convince him that he is (insofar as he knows himself) *nothing but* a thing which thinks. The composite of soul and body, in other words, is not what he really is, i.e., is not the subject that he has "discovered" himself to be, but is only what he formerly thought himself to be.

by Descartes, for this is what we all "experience." But what is denied by him is that there is no "real distinction" between the one and the other and that together they constitute his essence, i.e., the subject which he really is.³³

This means that the term "soul" has ceased to function in Descartes' thought as signifying in any way the principle by which the body is animated. Descartes rejects the notion of the soul as a form for a natural body, i.e., the actuality of that body, as proposed by Aristotle.* As Descartes sees it, the principle by which the body is "nourished" is to be entirely distinguished from the principle by means of which it "thinks." To use the term "soul" to signify both principles is "equivocal"; it can only be legitimately used to signify the primary activity or "formal principle" of man, i.e., the principle by which man thinks. Precisely to avoid equivocation, Descartes, whenever possible, uses the term "mind" (nom d'espirit) rather than the term "soul" (nom d'âme). It would seem that much as the term "soul" is inappropriate for designating a principle in the God of which Descartes speaks, i.e., the Christian God, it has become expendable for designating the primary principle in the human subject—given the fact that this subject is in a fundamental fashion defined in terms of its aspiration to be what it cannot be, namely, God. The sense in which God is the supra-substantial subject in Anselm has become, in Descartes, the sense in which man is the supra-substantial subject. Unlike the human mind or "mens humana" of Anselm which has no concept of nothingness *in* its reflexive understanding, the human subject of Descartes has a certain "negative idea"—an idea of nothingness°—to the extent that this subject "participates" in nonbeing (non-être) by not being the Supreme Being that it strives to be. Although there is nothing which this subject "wills" which it does not "conceive" in some fashion, what it understands (entendre) and what it wills are not equal, for it wills things of which it knows (connaître) very little.³⁴

---

\* See Aristotle, *De Anima*, Bk. II, 412a, 20-22.

° l'idée que nous avons du néant

It is, in fact, in relation to this subject that it would be impossible for God to be a "deceiver," since the form or essence of deception is nonbeing, toward which the Supreme Being cannot ever be "turned"; this is the very "basis and foundation of the Christian religion" upon which all the certainty of its faith—"la certitude de sa foi"—depends. What deception there is, then, of the human subject appertains to the will's overextending the understanding and, therefore, proceeds from this subject and not from God. And when the bodily nature deceives us, it is not the subject as such which is being deceived but the composite system of self and body, so that the deception which the will of God, as "supreme legislator," permits here does not touch the pure essence of the human subject. This subject even has within its power the overcoming of this deceptive nature through its conquest of that nature, made possible by physical sciences, the foundations of which have been provided by a first philosophy whose refounder has renounced the "profession of the study of theology." If the God examined in the first philosophy which Descartes has refounded is still very much the God of Christian faith, it is nonetheless the case that this faith is no more the object of that first philosophy than that first philosophy is a theology.*35

In his "Conversation with Burman," Descartes attempts to clarify further the status of the supra-substantial human subject at the center of his refounding of first philosophy. In this conversation he reiterates that the *ego* or supra-substantial human subject is

---

\* Much as there is no necessitation for the human subject to think the idea of God, but when this subject does entertain this idea, God cannot be thought as nonexistent or as a deceiver in relation to this subject, so also there is no necessitation for this subject to think God's justice in conceiving of God's boundlessness (l'immensité). But when these two attributes are presented to his mind, Descartes is not able to believe that "God could be boundless without being just." Likewise, it is possible to conceive clearly of the existence of God without any knowledge of the persons of the Trinity, but to think these persons is not to think a "distinction réelle" in essence, no matter what can be said by reason of their relations. Neither God's mercy (in relation to his justice) nor the real distinction of relations within the Trinity can be *explicit* contents of a non-theological first philosophy.

## The Cartesian Refounding of First Philosophy    153

"composed partly of nothingness and partly of being" and so is partly "inclined" toward nothingness and toward being, whereas God (since he is "l'être suprême et pur") is not able to be partly inclined toward nothingness. The human subject or *ego* can never be without thought, even for a moment, much as the body cannot be without extension. The necessity of the existence of this subject is precisely what is first affirmed in its having any thought. Descartes can thus say that "explicitly" we are able to be acquainted with our own imperfection before we are acquainted with the perfection of God, since we are able to direct our attention to ourselves before we direct it to God. Thus we conclude to our own finitude before we conclude to God's infinity.

But since the absolute inseparability of essence and existence is what is afterwards affirmed in the human subject's having the idea of God, Descartes can say that "implicitly" the knowledge of God and of his perfections must always precede the knowledge of ourselves and of our imperfections. This is because the infinite perfection of God is prior (antérieure) to our imperfection, for our imperfection is a "defect and negation" of the perfection of God, and every defect (as does every negation) presupposes the thing of which it is a defect and negation.* Because, in metaphysics, nothingness is comprehended in terms of the comprehension of being, it is the existence which is represented by the idea of God that is preconditional for the human subject's discovery of its own finitude in first philosophy. This discovery is precisely a realization that this subject, unlike God, does not have an understanding of everything in a single act (acte unique)—"unu intuitu" as Anselm called it.°

If this subject had given itself its own nature and that which it is, it would also have given itself all the perfections of God—in keeping with its "indefinite" conception of these perfections.** But

---

\* See pp. 122-123 above.

° See pp. 77, 79 above.

\*\* For example, this subject would have given itself greater knowledge than it now possesses, and when it had that, still greater knowledge; indefinites multiplied in this way become "infinite" or, rather, *the* infinite. Having increased

since this subject knows by experience that it is not able to do this and that it cannot, in fact, increase its knowledge to infinity as it "would will," it also knows that it does not derive its existence from itself.

God, then, is not the cause of the finite subject in the sense in which a builder is the cause of a house, namely, merely applying "active forces" to "passive things," but is the "cause totale," the cause of being itself (l'être lui-même), that is, the cause which brings something into being from nothingness. In this way, the finite subject must be "like" its total cause and must represent the image of that cause. So much, in fact, is the finite subject like its total cause that it is capable of forming the idea of a pure spirit that is less than God, namely, an angel, from the idea of its own self or mind, so that there is nothing it can think of in an angel that it is not able also to take note of in itself.

Nonetheless, for this finite subject to want "to take flight" into the purposes of God in creating is "rash," since these purposes—at least insofar as one considers them as a philosopher and *not* in terms of divine "revelation"—are "hidden" from this subject. It was, in Descartes' view, Aristotle's "greatest flaw" to have argued always "from purposes" in nature. First philosophy is thus entirely ignorant of God's purposes, but anything that the finite subject can conceive as "an absolutely perfect perfection" is, by this very fact, something that, in the perspective of first philosophy, must belong to the nature of God.

The will is precisely such a perfection, for against the objection that the will (vouloir) is imperfect in the finite subject because it wills "sometimes" and not at other times, Descartes replies that this only proves that there is an "inconstancy" in the operation of the human will and not that there is a "defect" in this will itself—an inconstancy that has its source in not "judging well" which, in turn, has its source in the ignorance of the understanding (l'entendement). Since the finite subject cannot conceive of anything

---

its knowledge to infinity, this subject would also have "increased" its other attributes and, thus, "would become God."

## The Cartesian Refounding of First Philosophy 155

which can overtake it in terms of "the liberty of the will," it must have a "perfect and absolute will," and the will must be "above" the understanding and more "like unto God" than the understanding.[36]

If the will in itself is as perfect in the finite subject as it is in God (and it is precisely this perfection which leads this subject to attribute willing to God), the difference between this finite subject and God lies in understanding and power, not in the will. Given God's power and knowledge, his will is the cause not only of actual and future things but of "possible things and simple natures," so that nothing can be imagined that does not depend on God's will. When God's will is thus shown to be necessarily good (and, thus, God is shown to be unable to be a deceiver), the idea of this will grounds the existence of corporeal things for mathematical physics which—unlike pure mathematics that considers its object as possible, i.e., as something not actually existing in space but only capable of doing so—must consider its object as actually and specifically existing.

God, then, is not to be identified merely with the soul in its perfection or with Aristotle's νοῦς, for the term "God" signifies some particular thing (quelque chose), a singular being (un être unique), who includes in himself "absolutely every perfection," whereas the term "soul" does not signify absolutely every perfection. Lacking the power, knowledge, and goodness of God, the will-to-be-infinite in the finite *ego* cannot be the subject of absolutely all perfections. But were this subject to be without imagination as one of the modes of its thinking—and certainly imagination is not necessary for the existence of this subject—it would be the same as the angels who never imagine* and not a subject which relies on the body as a "machine" that functions as a "universal instrument." But as things stand, the hidden purposes of the will of God have determined the more-than-natural subject or *ego*, characterized as it is by a will-to-

---

* "Rational cognition," Jacques Maritain remarked, "is for Descartes a sort of *natural revelation*, and . . . our ideas, like the infused species of the angel, have their immediate pattern in God, not in objects." What Maritain calls "Descartes' angelism" is "the deepest spiritual and metaphysical *intention* of his thought." Cf. pp. 154, 122 above.

the-infinite, to exercise this will in conjunction with the imagination and the body-machine: the more-than-natural being of the finite subject lives out its existence in the order of nature. And so it suffices for the philosopher to consider man inasmuch as he is free in "the natural order." It is necessary for the Cartesian philosopher to write his philosophy in such a way that it is capable of being received everywhere, even among non-Christians.

But such a philosopher has for his purpose reflection on the finite subject as really distinct from the body and reflection on the existence of God *in order to* provide metaphysical foundations for the physical sciences. Thus, Descartes can admonish his critics not to be "weighed down" by his meditations or by "metaphysical things," for it suffices to have grasped the import of his first philosophy *one* time and in a "general manner," and "to recall" its conclusion—otherwise the mind will be too much turned away from physical and sensible things and will become unsuited for considering these things. It is precisely the physical sciences which are "the most suitable occupation for men," since in them men would abundantly find things "useful" for the life which they live out in the natural world. Descartes' intention, in other words, in dealing with "metaphysical things" in these meditations on first philosophy, is to establish the certitude of these things so that others would not have "to try their skill at this enterprise" or "torment their minds for a long time" in meditating on these matters.[37]

First philosophy can no longer argue from purposes in nature precisely because God's purposes in creating are hidden. But these purposes have determined the more-than-natural *ego* to live out its existence in the natural order. Unlike God, who has an understanding of everything in a single act, this *ego* cannot accomplish what it wills, namely, to increase its knowledge to infinity and thus be the total cause of itself, the cause which brings something into being out of nothingness. Precisely insofar as it is not the God it wills to be, the *ego* is not pure being but participates in nonbeing—is part nothingness. The will to be infinite, however, is an absolute perfection, something than which nothing greater can be conceived and, thus, something which is, in and by itself, as perfect as it is in God.* The liberty of the will of the *ego*, the liberty proper to the human mind, is in no way inferior to the liberty of God's will, and because of this the necessity of the existence of this *ego* is always what is first affirmed in its having any thought. Because this *ego* is explicitly prior to anything else, the simple act by which it looks into itself and recognizes itself as a thing that is known through itself is more fundamental than (and presupposed by) any demonstration—even the demonstration of God's existence. But since the pure being of God is what permits this *ego* to be a participation in nothingness, i.e., since this *ego* in its finitude is a negation of the perfection of God, it is the idea of God which implicitly precedes the *ego's* idea of its own finitude.

The power contained in this idea of God is so unlimited that the idea could only be possessed by a subject who does not need an object other than itself in order to think—by a subject who is really defined as what traditional theology would call an angel, by a subject whose existence does not depend on the body-machine it has been assigned (by God's hidden purposes) to use as a universal instrument. Such a subject has the power to gain mastery and possession of this and all the other instruments of corporeal nature by means of the physical sciences which really constitute the most suitable occupation for this subject—consigned as this *ego* is by God to live out its existence in the natural order. In the end, then, first philosophy does not have as its purpose the turning of this subject away from physical or sensible things but has as its purpose the turning of this *ego* to the tasks of physics—modern mathematical physics. The point of Descartes' refounding of first philosophy—the counterpoint to the Aristotelian founding—is that all who follow him will never again have need to engage in first philosophy.

### ix. Descartes and Anselm

The fact that Descartes first wrote the *Meditations* in Latin and the very nature of his dedication of this work indicate that he is ad-

---

* See pp. 130-131, 134, 154-155 above.

dressing "the heirs and guardians of the philosophical tradition," most particularly the tradition which began with Aristotle's founding of first philosophy. Descartes' use of the language of this tradition, especially the term "substance," tends to distort and hide the radical import of his notion of "res cogitans," as well as to hide what is really his assault on the Aristotelian founding.[38]

Speaking of his *Meditations* as containing the foundations of his physics, Descartes reveals his hope that his readers "insensibly accustom" themselves to his principles and recognize the truth of these principles before finding out that they "destroy" those of Aristotle.[39] The attack on the Aristotelian founding, the veritable refounding of first philosophy, consists in the assertion that *my* thinking is the principle of first philosophy, that reason itself is the *ego cogitans*, that *I* am the only thing that cannot be an object, that my *particular* reason displays to itself a limit to omnipotence and, therefore, a limit to deception.

What is at issue here is both the logical and ontological necessity of the self-assertion of reason, that is, an unshakable and absolute will which underlies the particularity of my reason and enables me to realize that I cannot doubt that existence is inseparable from my thinking (in the way I can doubt that it is inseparable from extended things). The gap between thought and reality experienced in doubt is not possible in the thinking of my own existence where the very being of what is thought is guaranteed by the thinking of it: doubt pertains to things which exist apart from me, but certainty pertains to me and my doubt. The very thinking of (or attempt to doubt) my existence makes this existence immediately present to my thinking as an *ego* that cannot be imagined but must be willed-as-known, must be asserted in its particularity. This ontologization of the self in its particularity as the principle of first philosophy is not, however, a negation of sense perception but the raising of this perception to the status of a mode of *thinking* of objects, a mode which is not inconsistent with the self-sufficiency of the *ego* (its capacity to think itself independently of the world) and the sovereignty of the *ego* (its projecting the necessary connection be-

## The Cartesian Refounding of First Philosophy 159

tween its own thought and its own existence as the paradigm for clear and distinct perception of the world of objects).[40]

Nonetheless, the Cartesian refounding of first philosophy, in proclaiming this ontologization of the self, does stand in some fundamental fashion within the tradition of Anselm's transformation of first philosophy and Augustine's emphasis upon a return or "reditus" of the self into itself.[41] Descartes' repeated allusions to the "natural light,"* implying as they do an emancipation of reason from the authority of faith, presuppose a kind of revelation internal to the *ego*, a kind of "natural revelation," of something previously revealed externally to the believer; and in this sense, "emancipated" reason is still informed by its prior guidance by faith. Granted, the modern physical sciences, for which Descartes attempts to provide metaphysical foundations, could not begin until the ancient (and particularly Aristotelian) presuppositions about nature were displaced; but this displacement became possible only when the Christian notion of God—as an object for systematic study and not simply for unanalyzed belief—had displaced the ancient or pagan notion of divinity.[42]

This primary displacement of the pagan notion of divinity finds one of its most powerful expressions in Anselm's transformation of the Aristotelian founding of first philosophy. Descartes himself was not beyond writing, "Je verrai saint Anselme à la première occasion."[43] Yet Descartes' attempt to show that God exists by a superabundance of being, by a coincidence of essence and existence by which he can be said to "deserve" to exist, presupposes something of what Anselm argues about the infinite freedom and uncircumscribed goodness and generosity of God.[44] This is the case even though the idea of God for Descartes is a positive one and not the negative idea to be found in Anselm's Ontological Argument.

Although faith is no longer an object for reason as it was in Anselm's first philosophy, the natural light or "lumen naturale" of reason in Descartes' first philosophy is informed by faith and imi-

---

* See pp. 102, 120, 121, 125, 131, xvii-xviii above.

tates the subjective certainty of faith which Anselm called "fidei certitudinem" and perceived as issuing from God. The Cartesian "lumen naturale" presents itself as what Heidegger will call a certainty which man himself has brought about (erwirkte) for himself. The Cartesian advancement of a "self-confidence" effected by man himself—far from originating in "an insurrection against the teaching of faith"—is the philosophical sequel to the highest truth's having the character of the "certainty of salvation." In this way, the domain of Christian faith remains authoritative not only for modern culture—which attempts to organize and care for what is actual—but for "the laying out of the actual in its very actuality" in modern metaphysics. Modern culture is Christian even when it ceases to believe.[45]

Heidegger sees in Descartes' *Meditations* a decided beginning of the metaphysics which supports modernity to the extent that this work first asserts that the essence of the actuality of what is actual lies in the permanence and unchangingness of what is represented in the "certain representation"—a permanence which is to be distinguished from Aristotle's notion of the permanence of what is realized in the individual thing in nature. This absolute and unshakable foundation* is a substructure (Unterbau) which is no longer suspended in reference to something else but, rather, "reposes in itself." It requires the existence of a subject or "subiectum" which is present beforehand in and for all representation, i.e., all "re-presentation." This subject is the "representer" itself, the "ego cogitans" or "res cogitans," whose existence is sufficient for the essence of truth in the sense of certainty.

The question of being *qua* being is precisely what is addressed in the *Meditations*. But since this work is only the beginning of the metaphysics of modernity, the subjectivity which it presents is at the same time spoken of as a "substantia finita," a "substantia creata," which is, in fact, the language of Anselm. It still remains for the subsequent metaphysics of modernity to remove entirely the language of substance and designate by the name "subject" what

---

\* fundamentum absolutum et inconcussum.

Anselm had first called the "mens humana" or "mens mea." Nonetheless, the supra-substantiality of the human subject is invented by Descartes even if this subject still expresses itself in the language of substance. Subjectivity is already in view in Descartes to the extent that he proposes the "transformation of actuality to the self-certainty" of the *ego cogitans*—a transformation that has Christian conditions.[46]

Heidegger's conclusion that Christian categories are preconditional for the Cartesian invention of subjectivity presupposes that no foundation for this subjectivity can be found in ancient philosophical thought. Erich Frank makes this presupposition explicit when he says that "the *ego* as a philosophical concept was unknown to classical Greek philosophers," for they "did not emphasize at all the notion of a self to which the outside world was in opposition," but instead "grasped the essence of the soul in the objective forms of this world alone."[47] Edmund Husserl, too, remarks that the Cartesian philosophical act, which seeks its ultimate foundations in the subjective, has no precedent in ancient philosophy. What Descartes, utilizing medieval philosophical resources, invented—and did not simply "discover" by himself—was the being or "Sein" of the pure *ego* which is prior to the natural being of the world. As meditator, Descartes attends only to his self—the pure *ego* of his "cogitationes"—whose existence is "absolutely indubitable" and cannot be done away with. The existence of this self is what would obtain even if this world did not exist.* It is to this *ego* that the words of Anselm are now seen to apply: in no way would it be less even if everything else returned to nothingness.° Carrying out a solipsistic philosophical act, Descartes seeks apodictically certain ways by which an "objective outwardness" can be made accessible to his pure inwardness.[48]

Here lies the center of the Cartesian refounding of first philosophy: the *ego*, the subject, is something that would exist even if the natural world did not exist. The human subject is something onto-

---

\* auch wenn diese Welt nicht wäre

° See pp. 80, 72, 49-50 above.

logically prior to the being of nature. In this is to be found the Cartesian transmutation of Anselm's transformation of the founding of first philosophy. What, for Anselm, was that Being which would exist even if there were nothing other than it, namely, God, is transmuted by Descartes into the *ego*, the human subject, which is finite but characterized by an aspiration to the infinite, a will-to-be-infinite. The human *ego*, as the will to be the full actuality of the infinite, is something particular and unique which is more-than-natural. And so, the human *ego*, as that which would exist were there no natural world, entails the existence of that which it wills to be, viz., God.

God is implicitly necessary to secure the finitude of this *ego*: without the existence of God this *ego* would *in fact* exist without a world in which to exist. That than which nothing greater can be conceived is the liberty of the will which, for Descartes, is no greater in God than it is in the finite *ego* or human subject. But in God this will has only being, pure being, as its object, while in the human subject it has both being *and* nonbeing as its object. In Cartesian meditation, the thinker attempts to hold thinking still, to liberate the inner essence of thought, and to think it the way God thinks this essence. Yet, incapable of being God (who thinks in such a way that finite reality is created out of nothing), the thinker must suffer what the Christian God could never suffer, viz., the alienation of thought from the essence of natural things. Cartesian first philosophy thus reports human thought meditating on itself—not unlike the thinking of the Aristotelian *God* which is a thinking of thinking. But, unlike the Aristotelian *philosopher*, the Cartesian philosopher does not bespeak a thought which has the essence of the things of nature made manifest to it.

The "mens humana," then, which in Anselm was a mean between what is completely beyond nature and the being of nature, is now, in Descartes, a mean between a more-than-natural pure being (God) and absolute nothingness. If in Anselm the Ontological Argument is about God but is also shown to be about man, then Descartes' transmutation of this argument requires that it be about man's essence as a more-than-natural subjectivity but *also* that it be

## The Cartesian Refounding of First Philosophy 163

shown to be about God.* But if it is only *also* shown to be about God, then the new beginning for first philosophy is the beginning of something which is not, as such, theology.

Should Descartes' proposal that first philosophy serve as a foundation for mathematical physics prove to be undesirable or unnecessary, the only alternative, it would seem, would be a reduction of first philosophy to anthropology. This would mean that the *also* or "etiam" of the Cartesian refounding of first philosophy would be held to be *only* the image or projection of human subjectivity. This, in fact, is the point made by Feuerbach who argues that the term "God" entails no ontological claim but only an anthropological claim.

---

\* See pp. 93, 96, 125, 128 above.

# V

# Feuerbach's Reduction of First Philosophy to Anthropology

In the Cartesian refounding of first philosophy, the *ego*, the "res cogitans," is known to be necessarily existent without any explicit appeal to the existence of God. But God is implicitly necessary in order to secure metaphysically the finitude of this *ego*, for were it not for the existence of God, this "res cogitans," in fact, would exist without a world in which to exist and would thus be unbounded. Although the refounding of first philosophy requires that such a philosophy cannot be theology, it is nonetheless the case that the infinite aspiration of the will of the Cartesian *ego*—that will which is at the center of subjectivity—has its very condition in Christianity. It is no less the case that this *ego*'s infinite will and that Christian condition are both presupposed by late modernity's attack on Christianity.

Ever since the beginning of the metaphysics of modern times, Heidegger remarks, being is will, that is, the thrusting-forth of essence ("exigentia essentiae"), and this means the beginning of a general "humanization" of being. As the metaphysics of modern times—and thus metaphysics in general—approaches its completion, anthropomorphism is required and taken over as the truth. As metaphysics approaches this completion, being is seen to be entirely a "selfhood," a self-willing (Sich-Wollen), a coming-toward-itself ("Auf-sich-zu"), the "will to will," the proper actuality which determines beforehand all that is actual. Basing itself on the will as manifesting itself in truth-as-certainty (Wahrheit als Gewissheit), a notion implied in the Cartesian refounding of first philosophy, the metaphysics of late modernity makes subjectivity into a system—a "systematic essence."[1]

It is in Feuerbach that the Cartesian manifestation of the will as certainty is brought to a conclusion, namely, in the reduction of first philosophy to anthropology. As Feuerbach saw it, the paradox of modern culture was the underlying *identity* of belief and unbelief, theism and atheism, theology and philosophy, Christianity and paganism. And so the contradiction endemic to modern philosophy is that it is a negation of theology which is itself based upon theology. The only way to resolve this paradox and to overcome this contradiction is to show that this contradictory modern philosophical "theology" is really reducible to anthropology. Anthropology, as a "devout atheism," ought to be exalted to the status of theology.[2]

To do this, Feuerbach must substitute for the Cartesian "cogito ergo sum"—with its seeming break from sense perception and its seemingly timeless will, both of which are impossibilities—a new "sentio ergo sum" which, against all previous first philosophy, entails that only existence in space and time is existence as such. All prior conceptions of the divine and the real must be shown to be "embalmed abstractions" of human qualities; only the human is real since only the human can be reasonable. Man must be proclaimed as the measure of intelligibility in order to bring modernity to its consummation, to bring it to the fulfillment of its hidden task, viz., the humanization of God, the final dissolution of theology into anthropology. It is this dissolution which alone can overcome the contradiction of modern philosophy.[3]

Christianity first related man to the world, Feuerbach argues, in terms of this world's being-for-him rather than in terms of its being-for-and-in-itself. In proposing the Incarnation, Christianity was but thinly disguising the admission that God is man, that Christ is a personification of human subjectivity, and that Christian religion is at bottom the religion of subjectivity. In claiming to deal with the supernatural, Christian theology, by proposing a God who is both infinite and particular, was unable to give the supernatural anything but a natural content. This theology was absorbed by modern philosophy's invention of the human subject. Feuerbach will claim to bring that philosophy to its consummation by showing this subject in its passivity to be the body against which the will, at the center of this subject, strives. Thought will be shown to be a function of the body, for whatever becomes actual becomes so only as a particular bodily thing. This will mean saving subjectivity from the theology that made it possible by showing that man as the ultimate subject, as *ego agens*, has the will at the center of his being forever tied to time and space.

Even the lowest senses in man, smell and taste, raise themselves to the level of cognitive acts, acts which always have as their fruition sensuous remedies which alone augment the freedom of the subject's will from evil. By elevating the bodily and the sensible in their *human* character, Feuerbach claims to bring the Cartesian invention of subjectivity into its truly systematic essence, an essence which will negate first philosophy's prior negation of the body and thus locate true philosophy in the very negation of what philosophy has previously been.[4]

### i. Religion and the Logic of Subjectivity

In his *Lectures on the Essence of Religion*, Feuerbach—having noted that Descartes-the-philosopher and Descartes-the-believer were two different individuals in conflict—proposes the elimination of this conflict in the two parts of these lectures. The first part shows how the essence of pre-Christian religions, which differentiated God from man, was nothing else than the essence of nature. The second part shows how the essence of Christian religion, which differentiated God from nature, is nothing else than the essence of man. God, initially an independent being, becomes an attribute of man; and this shows that God and (the human desire for) immortality are really one. The one and universal God of Christianity is a personified generic concept of the human race—of the human *species*, which is the only real immortality.

Protestant Christianity (with its antithesis of faith and reason—faith grounded in the particular and reason in the universal) no longer concerns itself (as did Catholic Christianity) with what God is in himself but only with what God is for man. In doing this, Protestantism transforms theology into christology, i.e., into religious anthropology. In the process, the Christian religion is brought to a recognition of its essence and thus to a recognition of the essence of religion as such, namely, its being an affirmation of human sensuousness in its very negation of sensuousness. The whole point of Feuerbach's exposing this essence is to enable man, who was always unconsciously governed by his own essence, consciously to take this essence as the measure of his ethical and political life in the modern world.[5]

At the beginning of religion is not merely fear but that of which fear is an expression, namely, dependency; and dependency requires not the organs of criticism and skepticism but the ear as the very "womb" of the gods. Even Christianity, with its emphasis on the Word of God, bases itself on the sense of hearing. The joy and love that fear gives way to are equally feelings of dependency in religion which always requires a god who can curse and bless, terrify and provide joy. But religion begins with man's dependence on nature, with his realization that the length of his life does not depend on his own will alone. In this way it is equally true that man's tomb is the very "womb" of the gods. Yet, if dependence on nature is the beginning of religion, the goal of religion is freedom from dependence: its *terminus a quo* is the divinity of nature, and its *terminus ad quem* is the divinity of man. But if the divinity of man (by virtue of Christianity's belief in a God above nature) measures the divinity of nature, then it can be said that the criterion which forms gods, from start to finish, is man's egoism. Both gods and God are created in terms of usefulness for man.

Only, then, a being beneficial and useful to man is conceded to be divine; and so the feeling of dependence with which religion begins is only a negative or inverted feeling of egoism. Not even in Christianity can this egoism be avoided, for even here "God" is not really a proper name but a generic name, since the Bible itself refers to the devil as the "God" of this world and the belly as the "God" of some men. Granted, in polytheism, "god" is a mere collective noun, but the same necessity which impels man to substitute number for quantities that he intuits, and eventually to substitute letters for numbers, also impels him to substitute, for the many causes constituting the genesis and preservation of the world, one cause and one name in Hebraic and Christian religion. The Christian God cannot be good if there is nothing else for him to be good to, nor can he be infinite if there is not something else which is finite: even this God throws us back on the world. God's goodness here, as much as Jupiter's goodness for the Romans,* is merely the utility of nature for man but ennobled by man's imagination and personified into an active cause.[6]

But if both the Judaeo-Christian God and the pagan gods throw man back on the world, they do so through a concept of divinity which is more or less universal, a concept from which the images of sensible things are more or less extrapolated—less in the case of the pagan gods, more in the case of the Judaic God, and still more in the case of the Christian God. If all sensuous imagery is extrapolated from the concept of God's essence by Christian theology, and if, as Descartes argued, God's essence is inseparable from his existence, then the existence attributed to God is the generic concept of existence abstracted from all particular properties. And since this pure universal (like all universals) can exist only in the mind of man, it follows that God is not thought and willed because he exists but he is said to exist because he is thought and willed. In this way, for first philosophy, insofar as it is theology, to examine the question of God's existence is to examine the question of whether the universal has an existence of its own.

To answer "yes" to this question is to treat the universal of man's own creation as a particular beyond the influence of his will, to

---

* Cicero remarked that Jupiter was known as *optimus* and *maximus* to the Romans: his benefits were the best and the highest. Always god is what feeds man, and Feuerbach can say, punning on the German words for "is" and "eats," that "Man is what he eats" (Der Mensch *ist* was er *isst*). No less is this true of the history of first philosophy. For what is substance but sustenance (Nahrung)? Or what is the beginning of existence except nourishment (Ernahrung)?

turn the subjective into the objective—to be misled by the very nature of human language, given the inability of that language to express the particular, and given the latent universality of its every word. But if the existence of God, in theology, is merely the concept of existence, merely the hypostatized essence of the human imagination in its unrestrictedness—so that God can be conceived as himself a miracle who creates the world out of nothingness—then theological explanations explain nothing. First philosophy, insofar as it is theology, explains nothing in asking the meaningless question, "Why is there anything at all?" If there is such a God, as has been claimed by *all* prior first philosophy, namely, a perfect being who is not man, then the existence of all other beings—the existence of the imperfect—cannot be accounted for. Why should there then be imperfection? For all else but God is superfluous, and nothing can follow from God. The only recourse, given the existence of the world, is to conclude that God is man's dream, a being existing only in the human imagination.[7] This is why, after Descartes-the-philosopher had discovered the human subject to be that which would exist if there were no world, Descartes-the-believer had to continue to doubt the world's existence in order to "demonstrate" the existence of God.

The logic of modern subjectivity begun by Descartes, then, has not yet drawn out the conclusion implicit in its premises, namely, that a God who can only help man through the advances man himself has effected—through doctors and medicine, for example—is an uttterly superfluous God who gives nothing that man's control of nature cannot give. If any attempt to make God and world coexist leads to contradiction, then the will at the center of the modern subject must find its context only in space and time. The will of the self is unable to be dissociated from the time in which that self lives; that self has become what it is in the context of this people, this place, this century. This is the only rational meaning of Descartes' claim that the finitude of the *ego* is contingent on the existence of God. The *ego* is particular and unique, and particularity is the only thing that can be understood in terms of itself; for whatever makes this thing a "this" is something that cannot be philosophically or theologically deduced from anything else, even though this thing requires a space-time context that is other than itself. Although Christianity has asserted autonomous human activity—in contrast to the religious teaching of the Orient—its assimilation by modern thought has led to an unpalatable mixture of theism and atheism, since the essence of the Christian God is precisely the essence of the word, of language itself, with its orientation into the universal. And since the universal can be found only in the mind of man, this God is simply man's striving for happiness fulfilled in his own imagination. Faith or belief is nothing but the activity of this imagination; and the power to provide consolation is the sole criterion for the truth and falsity of this belief.

The very omnipotence of this God is the all-powerfulness of man's prayer and desire turned into an objective being—an hypostasization of the essence common to all words. But this individual, personal being that Christianity represents as God, insofar as it is spoken of by theology as the Word of God, is nothing other than the concept of the word itself. In being a reification of the essence of human language, God is seen to be first by Christian theology only insofar as he is the instrument for human immortality, a hypostasization of the human future, of the future of the race, represented as a present being. It is precisely the identity of divinity and immortality—and thus the identity of God and man—that is the solution to the riddle of religion, especially Christian religion: in being the essence of the human imagination, God is the essence of the human heart. This, in fact, is what enabled Anselm to attempt to understand God by the dictates of his heart—"cor meum."[*]

But the point of this immortality, which the human heart yearns for in religion, is not a future life in which the evil of this life is done away with. Man, fundamentally, does not want to exceed his species; and this suggests that his yearning for immortality is an idealization of the continuance of his species. In its denial that this idealization exists as a divine person, atheism is not really negative. It is theism which is implicitly negative since if, as it asserts, God

---

[*] See pp. 79, 93 above.

existed before the world and man existed, then God can exist without them. God is really the nothingness of the world and of man. The essence of Christianity, insofar as it is the consummation of all religion, is the essence of religion itself. This essence proves to be the nothingness of the world and of man treated as if it were something, that is, the Cartesian subject freed by its own will from the limits imposed upon it by nature.[8] The point, in the final analysis, is not really God *and* subjectivity, but the point is that God is subjectivity—God is reducible to human subjectivity.

### ii. Negativity: Theology as Anthropomorphic

It is in *The Essence of Christianity* that Feuerbach claims to have arrived at a "resolution" of the "enigma" of the Christian religion—a resolution which amounts to a reduction of first philosophy, in its long history as theology, to anthropology. In this resolution, the thing (Gegenstand) is not derived from the thought (Gedanken), but the notion of Christianity is derived from the thing which Christianity really is. By saying what Christianity really is, Feuerbach really intends his reduction of first philosophy to anthropology as a resolution, i.e., a dissolution, of speculation itself. Feuerbach's first philosophy *qua* anthropology, consequently, lets the Christian essence of religion speak for itself, and Feuerbach is only its "hearer" and "interpreter" and in no way its "prompter."

It is the thing itself, Christianity itself, that worships man as the true *ens realissimum*, although theology (as the mere idea of Christianity) denies this. Feuerbach can only claim to have set forth the secret (das Geheimnis) of the Christian religion, to have extricated it from the net of contradictions constructed by theology. Atheism, in fact, is this "Geheimnis" not on the surface but in the ground of Christianity, not in its own opinion and imagination, but in its heart (Herzen), in its true essence (wahren Wesen); for this essence is at bottom nothing but a belief in the truth and "divinity" of man's essence.

Feuerbach divides his considerations of the essence of Christianity into two parts: the first sets forth the resolution of Christianity as the essence of religion in terms of its truth; the second sets forth this resolution in terms of Christianity's contradictions. The first part shows that the true meaning of theology is anthropology, that there is no difference between the predicates of the divine and the human essence and, therefore, no difference between the divine and human subject. The second part shows that the distinction which is made by Christian theology between the theological and anthropological predicates is really "nonsense." The first is thus the direct and the second is the indirect proof that theology is anthropology.

Taken together, both parts demonstrate that Christianity, as the essence of religion, is "the dream" of the human mind. But even in his dreams man finds himself not in nothingness or in heaven but on the earth, in the realm of actuality. Taken together, both parts show that the faith of the modern world is only an apparent faith (scheinbarer Glaube), one that does not really believe what it imagines that it believes, a faith that is really an undecided and feeble-minded "unbelief."[9]

In beginning his first part, his "direct proof" that first philosophy can only be anthropology, Feuerbach remarks that religion is based on the essential difference between man and the non-human animal. It is only man who can make his own "genus" an "object" and thus can live a double life (zweifaches Leben): an "inner life" in which he speaks with himself, by virtue of his genus' being an object for him, and an "outer life." It is only man who is at once "I" and "thou" to himself by virtue of his capacity to put himself in the place of what is other than himself. In this sense, religion is identical with the essence of man, with man's self-assertiveness (Selbstbewusstsein).* No other animals have religion.

---

\* This self-assertiveness is consciousness in the strict and proper sense; and since a consciousness of the limited is no consciousness in this strict and proper sense, this self-assertiveness is a consciousness of the infinite which is nothing else than the consciousness of the "infinity of consciousness." In religion the infinity of man's essence, the infinity of his self-assertiveness, is made an object. But this object is nothing "singular," nothing distinct from the being of man's self-assertiveness as an object to itself—a being which is satiated (gesättigten) by itself. What religion makes into an object, then, is nothing

In sensuous perception, i.e., the outer life of man, the object is "distinguishable" from man's self-assertiveness. In religion, i.e., the inner life of man, however, the object is in "immediate conjunction" with this self-assertiveness, so that the object here is nothing else than the essence of the subject itself treated objectively (gegenständliche). Consciousness of God is, therefore, the self-assertiveness, the self-willing of man; and the knowledge of God is the self-knowledge (Selbsterkenntnis) of man. But far from being directly conscious of this identity, religion requires for its "specific difference" a "privation" of this direct consciousness. In religion man sees his essence as outside of himself (ausser sich), as the essence of another object, so that the essence of religion is itself "hidden" from the religious man and can only be uncovered by "the thinker" who can see that the opposition (der Gegensatz) of the divine and the human is altogether illusory. The object and content of the Christian religion are "altogether human."

Incapable of recognizing that the divine essence is really the human essence set free from the limits of the individual man and "made objective," religious consciousness would "destroy its peace" were it to distinguish between what God is in his own being and what he is for man, for this consciousness requires a God without reservation, God himself, God in person. To the extent, then, that the idea that the religious predicates are only anthropomorphisms has entered religious consciousness, to that extent has "unbelief taken hold of faith," as it has in the modern world and its philosophy.

If, as modern man believes, love is a divine attribute precisely because he himself loves, and God is wise and good because he himself can find nothing better than goodness and understanding, then it follows that God exists, that God is a subject for these attributes, precisely because man himself exists and is himself a subject for these attributes. Given the Cartesian identification of essence and existence in God, and given that subject and predicate

---

but the rapture of feeling blessed in itself. God is pure, unlimited "free feeling."

are distinguished only as existence and essence, it follows that the negation of the predicate is also the negation of the subject.[10]

Since the reality of the predicate is the only "guarantee" of existence, it follows that God could be an existing and real essence only on the same ground that he could be this particular, specified (dieses bestimmte) essence. But the very particularity of such an essence would be undercut by the kind of predicates attributed to God. Whatever attribute is predicated of God, it is not thereby divine because God has it. God can only be said to have it because it is in itself divine, because without it God would be a "defective" essence. But where can these predicates be found except in the objects of the world, for religion has no unique contents (aparten Inhalt).

If, furthermore, each new man is a new predicate, a new aptitude of mankind, then the secret of the inexhaustible fullness of the divine predicates is precisely the secret or "Geheimnis" of the human essence as an infinitely "dissimilar," infinitely "determinable" but, for that very reason, "sensuous" essence. To the extent that the divine subject (göttliche Subjekt) is human in essence, to that extent the greater would be the seeming difference between God and man, for what man takes away from himself and dispenses with in himself, he only enjoys in an incomparably higher and richer measure in God. But if man only "negates" of himself what he "puts into" God—and because of this negation perceives so great a difference between himself and God, since he beholds his own essence as external to himself and as the good itself—it follows that God is the very subjectivity of man separated from man's essence.

In the contraction of the heart of religion (religiösen Systole), man thrusts his own essence from himself; he disowns and repudiates it as his own. In the dilation of the heart of religion (religiösen Diastole), however, man receives the "rejected" essence back into his heart. As religion comes closer to its true essence in Christianity, however, the contraction reaches a point where there is no more to be removed from man's essence. With the modern assimilation of this true essence, the dilation becomes preponderant, so that now man begins to take more away from God and awards more to himself.

If religion is the tearing asunder (Entzweiung) of man from himself in which he places God before himself as the "opposite" of his essence, then religion can be said to be the "unconscious self-assertiveness" of man. God *qua* God, that is, the object of theology which is not finite, not human, not materially specified, is only an object of thinking—only, through the "via negationis," the objective essence of intellectual power (Denkkraft), only reason in its highest essence made objective to itself. For the imagination of the religious man, reason is a "revelation of God." But for the reason of the theologian, God is the revelation of reason (Vernunft), the highest degree of intellectual power, the "quo nihil majus cogitari potest" of St. Anselm, the "realized, filled up, exhausted intellectual power." Only that which is itself nothing deduced, nothing derived, can construe everything other than itself as derived; and this means that the understanding (Verstand) is the original, primitive essence which posits itself as the first causal, preworldly essence (vorweltliche Wesen). As can be seen from Descartes' assimilation of theology, not even omnipotence can do what is against reason; and so the conclusion must be that over the very power of omnipotence stands the "higher power" of reason as the criterion of what can be affirmed and negated of God.

The fact, then, that God is what the understanding thinks as "the highest" in the old ontotheology proves that the understanding is itself the "ens realissimum," the "self-enjoying, self-sufficing, absolute subject" which cannot be an object for other beings. The ontotheological predicates are predicates of human understanding.[11]

The significance of the ontotheological (and especially Cartesian) identity of essence and existence in God is that God is the infinite being which does not stand as an individual under a genus but is an "Individuum" indistinguishable from a "genus." But the sense in which predicates and subject are identical in this infinite being is only drawn from the notion (Begriff) of the essence of the understanding. However, this God *qua* God of ontotheology has no more significance for religion than a general principle has for a special science. It is not, then, in the God-as-God of the understanding that we most clearly perceive the essence of religion which Christianity makes manifest but, rather, in the Incarnation, for here it becomes clear what theology will not admit, namely, that God is entirely a human essence (menschlichen Wesen). God *qua* God is the aggregate of all human perfections, but Christ is the aggregate of all human miseries, pure suffering, "passio pura," and not pure act, "actus purus"—the highest metaphysical thought, the "être suprême" of the heart.

What is made manifest through the human heart, freed from the contradiction of the theological element, is the better part, the "pars melior," of Christianity. And here it can be said that the Christian religion is so little a "suprahuman" one, that it even sanctions human weakness. The secret of the "suffering God" is the secret of human "sensation," the "self-admission of human sensibility," which reveals that God is the book which brings together (das Kollektaneenbuch) the highest thoughts and sensations of men, the family album (das Stammbuch) of mankind in which are entered the names which are most cherished and held most sacred by the human race. Only an essence that carries in itself the undivided man can satisfy the undivided man. In this way, man's consciousness of himself in his totality, which is projected upon Christ, is projected upon that which Christ projects upon, namely, the self-consciousness of the Trinity. The first thing met with in the Trinity is precisely "the objectivization of self-assertiveness"; and here being itself is seen to be one with self-assertiveness.[12]

What is decisive in the Trinity is the self-distinguishing (Selbstunterscheidung) of God from himself. It is this which enables God to be the ground of that which is distinguished from him. It is, in other words, the self-assertiveness conveyed by the Trinity which is seen to be the origin or "Ursprung" of the world. The world as that which is distinguished from God could not have come "immediately" from God but only from a "distinguishing of God in God." The Second Person of the Trinity is precisely God as an object to himself, and this is spoken of as the Word of God.

What the Trinity ultimately shows, then, is that God, as an objectivization of the essence of man's "waking dreams," is precisely an objectivization of the essence of man's speech, his words, for the word itself is only the essence of the power of the imagination (Einbildungskraft). This can be seen in the "narcotic effects" of words by which man is held captive under the mastery of the dreams of his waking life. What the Trinity ultimately discloses, then, is that God is the self-esteem (Selbstgefühl) of man freed from all repulsive elements, i.e., the subjectivity of man honoring itself,[*] enjoying only itself, retaining only itself in its innermost being. As that beyond which man can abstract no more, as the "id quo nihil majus cogitari potest" of St. Anselm, God begins where nature ceases, i.e., as the absolute essence of "Personlichkeit" in abstraction from nature. For in the personality of the Trinitarian God, man only honors the "supranaturalness," the immortality, the independence, and the "unrestrictedness" of his own peculiar personality.

But if the human subjectivity which constitutes the true meaning of the Trinity is what enables God to be conceived as creating the world, then the highest pinnacle of the "principle of subjectivity" is Creation out of nothing, wherein the "power of the will" to will that the world should exist overcomes the possible will (mögliche Wille) that it should not exist. But this highest expression of omnipotence, this subjectivity releasing itself from all objective determinations and honoring this release as the highest power and essentiality (Wesenheit), is nothing else than the power of the arbitrary will (der Willkur), the power *of* "the power of the imagination" as identical with the will. In this way, the whole point of "creatio ex nihilo" is not the truth and reality of nature or the world but the truth and reality of subjectivity distinguished from the world, that is, the truth and reality of the personality of man freed from the determination and limitation of nature. The entire meaning of the distinguishing of God from nature is the distinguishing of man from nature: God

---

[*] sich selbst feiernde Subjektivitat des Menschen

is the self-affirmation (Selbstbewährung) of man's "subjective essence" outside the world.

It is thus Descartes' own personality that constitutes the essence in relation to the existence of the God that he purports to demonstrate. An atheism hidden even from himself characterizes the refounding of first philosophy accomplished by Descartes, for he cannot derive God from his selfhood unless God himself is the idea of his own subjective essence. But even more fundamental here than Descartes, in Feuerbach's perspective, is the very revelation of God which can be nothing other than the revelation, the self-unfolding (Selbstentfaltung) of the human essence. In this lies the truth—the only truth—of Christianity as the developed essence of religion.[13]

### iii. The Being Beyond God

If the revelation of God is only the self-unfolding of the human essence, and if God himself is only the "omnipotence of human feeling" without regard to anything else, then it follows that both God himself and the revelation of God find their essence in man's prayer (Gebet) "echoing itself"—the mind audible to itself, the echo of man's "cry of anguish." God is the unpronounceable sigh (unaussprechlichen Seufzen) in the human heart which reveals that the deepest essence of religion is found in the simplest act of religion, namely, prayer. But prayer is nothing more than the "absolute conduct" of the human heart toward itself; and because of this, prayer is both essentially and outwardly a speaking in which man makes his heart objective and his feelings omnipotent, by treating them as the "omnipotence of goodness" that breaks through all the limits of the understanding and "soars beyond" all the boundaries of nature.

Prayer, of course, presupposes faith wherein the principle of doubt itself is vanquished and the subjective becomes for itself the objective and the absolute. The essence of faith is, then, precisely the absolute reality of subjectivity, the infinite self-certainty of man, freed of doubt, that his subjective essence is the objective essence, the "essence of essence," the essence of God. In bringing this essence into focus, Christianity closes off man's capacity to think of himself as in the universe or as a part of nature. In place of this capacity, Christianity offers man the Resurrection of Christ as the realized wish of man for immediate certainty of his personal continuance after death—personal immortality as a sensible, indubitable matter of fact.

As the doctrine that grounds—the "Grunddogmen" of— Christianity, the Resurrection is thus the "realized wish of the human heart," a "dream with the eyes open," a "dream of waking consciousness," presented as the immediate unity of will and fact, of wish and actuality. To *see* God is the highest wish and triumph of the human heart; and the resurrected Christ is this wish and triumph fulfilled, the blessed certainty (selige Gewissheit) that God exists and that he is what the human mind wills and needs him to be.[14]

As one particular personality*—and not the multiple personalities of the pagan gods—Christ is this bond of the "freedom" of man's waking dream and the "necessity" of his heart. As the particularity which overcomes death, as the "omnipotence of subjectivity," as the human heart delivered from all the "cords and laws" of nature, and concentrated only in itself, Christ is the notion of the human genus (Gattungsbegriff), the "essence of this genus," in the immediacy of existence and individuality. And this alone is what it means to say that essence and existence are identical in God. Whereas pagan thought made the understanding into a universal essence, Christianity individualized this understanding. But in doing so, it made difference of sex into an "external adjunct" of individuality. It made the individual into a "sexless," absolute essence complete in itself.

---

* The deathless personality of Christ presupposes something like Leibniz's principle of distinction, namely, that no existent thing is perfectly like another. Thus the deathless personality of Christ fulfills man's longing for one particular personality, a longing that can only be satisfied in the particularity of the "blood of Christ." This is a God who "experiences" and is himself "the identity of the human heart and its waking dreams."

But if the resurrected Christ presents individuality itself as beyond the distinction of sex, then it really "abolishes" the distinction between soul and person, between genus and individual, so that what belongs only to the totality of the genus is now placed immediately in the individual self. What is had in the God of Christianity is the immediate unity of the genus and individuality: the individual now has in him the significance (Bedeutung) of absolute essence; and the immanent sequel of this is personal immortality. This means that God is the self's sheltered, certain existence, the very "subjectivity of subjects" and "personality of persons." And the only interest which the human self has in knowing that God exists is the interest he has in knowing that he himself is "eternal." If the self will not always be, then God is not God. If there is no immortality, there is no God.

But given the this-worldly particularity of Christ, the life to come (Jenseits) is nothing other than this present life* (Diesseits) liberated from what appears in it as a barrier and an evil. What the deathless individuality conveyed by the particularity of Christ entails is that man "separates himself" from his self, negates himself (negiert sich) and this present life, but only to posit this life and self again in a future life. The more "suprahuman" God appears at the "start" of this process, the more human he is at its "end." So also, the more supranatural the heavenly life appears at the beginning of this process, the more clearly does it show its identity with the natural life (naturlichen Leben) at the end—an identity which encompases the flesh and the body.[15]

To say, then, that God is pure, absolute subjectivity with all "natural limits" transcended is to say that God is only what human individuals ought to be, what they will come to be. Faith in God, consequently, is the faith of man in the infinity of his own essence, in his own absolute freedom and limitlessness. Man is the "beginning," the "midpoint," and the completion (das Ende) of religion. This is the outcome of first philosophy, the truth of Christianity, conveyed by the first part of Feuerbach's treatment of the

---

\* Cf. pp. 125, 81 above.

essence of Christianity. What now remains is to elucidate his indirect approach to that essence—what he proposes as the contradictions in Christianity.

These contradictions fundamentally flow from the fact that God as a proper name or "nomen proprium" is only an object of religion (not of philosophy), of practical experience and the necessity of feeling (not of reason or the theoretical mode), and of the practical standpoint (not of the theoretical standpoint of the freedom of thought). When taken over into the sphere of the theoretical, most especially into the sphere of first philosophy, and made to serve as the "explanation" of the inexplicable (Unerklärichen), this "nomen proprium" explains nothing, since in itself it is the "night of the theoretical"—that night which is the "mother of religions." The only truth of the essence of religion, then, lies in its practical application to man's nature as a moral healing power (sittliche Heilkraft). Anything else—any ontological claim that religion pretends to convey about the nature of a reality other than man—is the source of its un-truth, its "Unwahrheit."

Of all these pretended ontological claims, the one that Feuerbach finds most interesting is the one that makes the claim itself the proof of God's existence, by proceeding from within the claim itself, i.e., the so-called Ontological Argument of Anselm. As Feuerbach sees it, the premise of this argument—namely, that the most perfect essence is that essence "above which no higher is able to be thought," that God is the "highest" that man thinks or can think—bespeaks the "innermost" and most secret (geheimste) essence of religion. That which is the highest for man is that from which he can make no further abstraction, the positive limit of his reason and sentiments—"id quo nihil majus cogitari potest." Where this proof succumbs to un-truth, however, is in what it claims to follow from this premise, namely, that this highest essence would not be highest if it did not exist apart from man. This proof fails when it attempts to make what is internal external (Innere zu veräussern)—when it attempts to separate what is internal to man from man himself. This "proof" raises us to the realization that the thought, "There *is* a God," is "inspiring." What it fails to recognize, however, is that the "is" here signifies inner reality alone—an existence which is a movement of inspiration (Begeisterung), an act of aspiration (Erhebung).[16]

Yet, behind the Ontological Argument—at the center of Anselm's first philosophy—is the hidden presupposition that God does not exist for man, if man does not exist for God, that there is no God for man if man believes in no God. Behind Anselm's argument, in Feuerbach's view, is the ungrasped insight that "the self-attestation of existence," God's revelation of his own existence, is the only true proof (wahre-Beweis) that God really exists or *is* really *there* (Dasein). The certainty of existence for man reposes in the certainty of revelation. But this means that man himself is the ground for the determination of God (Bestimmungsgrund Gottes), i.e., that revelation is only the "self-determination" of man in which he interposes between himself as "determined" and himself as "determining" an object, as if this object were another essence. But this object, this other essence, this God, is nothing but the substantial bond, the "vinculum substantiale," between man's essence or genus and his existence as an individual. The contents of divine revelation are thus of purely human origin, for they have originated not from God-as-God but from God as determined by human reason and needs. Revelation is merely the process by which man goes out of himself in order to return to himself (zurückzukommen) by a "circuitous route."

But if religion and divine revelation are simply the light of the mind, the "Licht des Geistes," whose rays are "broken apart" by the medium of man's waking dreams, so as to make the same essence illustrative of a "duplicate," it follows that man ought to cease to distinguish between psychology or anthropology *and* philosophy of religion or theology. Only when man "recognizes anthropology itself as theology," as the only true theology, the only permissible first philosophy, will he attain a true and satisfactory identity of the divine and human essence—the identity of the human essence with itself.

To fail to give anthropology the status traditionally accorded to theology, i.e., to fail to reduce first philosophy to pure anthropology, is to fail to carry through to its proper conclusion the logic of the Cartesian refounding of first philosophy. Failure here means failure to see that what theology has traditionally spoken of as the "grace of God" is really the "self-grace" of man, the "objectivization" of man's "free will." Not to complete the Cartesian logic is to leave the being of religion and the very being of man in modern times hopelessly alienated from themselves. Not to complete this logic means to continue to look at the essence of religion as the identity of the divine and human essence while, at the same time, envisaging the form of religion as the distinction between the divine and human essence. To fail to reduce first philosophy to anthropology, then, means to fail at liberating the power of love—which Christianity unleashes—from the contamination of the faith which Christianity proposes, for it is love which identifies man with God and God with man and thus identifies man with man, while faith separates God from man and thus separates man from man.[17]

Whereas, Feuerbach says, faith isolates God and makes him a particular, an *other* being, "love universalizes" and makes God a common essence, the love of whom is one with the love of man. Love practically denies the existence of a particular God to be contrasted with man, for love has God in itself. But faith has God outside of itself, so that it alienates (entfremdet) God from man and makes God an "external object." Whereas faith holds itself to the self-subsistence (Selbstandigkeit) of God, love cancels this self-subsistence, proposing the genus, mankind itself, as that than which "nothing higher can be loved." Where, in fact, there springs up the consciousness of the human genus as a genus, Christ "vanishes"—not, however, his true essence, for he was the representative of the consciousness of the genus, the image of humanity under which this humanity became the new law of "ordinary life." Thus it is that what is first for religion is in truth second, and that which for religion is second, namely, the essence of man, must "come to be pronounced" first. "Homo homini deus est": Man is God for men.

This is the practical principle which is the true "turning-point of world history."*18

Love, consequently, is not holy through being a predicate of God but, on the contrary, is only a predicate of God because it is "through and for itself divine." It is precisely eating and drinking themselves which are the mystery, "die Mysterien," of the Lord's Supper. The point, for Feuerbach, is no longer to pursue the transcendent otherness proposed by theology but, rather, by means of a reduction of first philosophy to its properly anthropological essence, to render to the common an uncommon significance—"dem Gemeinen ungemeine Bedeutung," to render to such a life as this, in its totality, a "religious significance." The yearning of man for what is "above and outside himself" is the yearning to be free from the limits and defects of his individuality.

If reason is man in his "universal" essence, the heart is man in his "specificity" as a personal being, so that reason relates to the "thing," whereas the heart relates to the "person." Thus the yearning after God, the yearning of man to be free from the limits and defects of his individuality, is a yearning for a perfect and unlimited individuality, a yearning for "unlimited, unbroken, and unalloyed feeling." The alienation of Descartes-the-believer from Descartes-the-philosopher is thus due to the fact that, having banished theology from first philosophy, he did not make first philosophy into anthropology but, instead, insisted on treating God as an object and not as the subject in its unlimited yearning, its infinite will. The Cartesian "I think" or "cogito" is a thing of the "head," but the Cartesian "I am" or "sum" is a thing of the "heart." The conclusion that Descartes drew, "cogito ergo sum," reflects the split between the believer and the philosopher. Had the believer been the same as the philosopher—and the philosopher been a true philosopher, i.e., an anthropologist—the conclusion would have been "sentio ergo sum."

---

* Feuerbach plays here on Hegel's notion of the axis on which the history of the world turns. But for Hegel this axis is the silent mystery of the *triune* God, the comprehension of which is the work of philosophy.

Descartes' hesitancy—his reluctance, perhaps his inability—to draw the proper conclusion must now be overcome by and in Feuerbach. Christianity made man an "otherworldly" and "supranatural" essence. But in Catholicism, humanity is the attribute (Eigenschaft), the predicate of Godhood, of Christ—the God who is man, the God who is God first and man second. Only in Protestantism is Godhood the attribute and predicate of humanity, that is, of Christ—the man who is God, the man who is man first and God in function of his being man. In the Catholic consciousness, man exists for God; but in the Protestant consciousness, God exists for man. It is thus that the entire history of Christianity has for its task the "unveiling of this secret"—the actualization and recognition of theology as anthropology, an actualization and recognition which Feuerbach merely permits to happen in first philosophy as anthropology, in first philosophy's addressing being *qua* being as purely human.[19] It is first philosophy, having now proclaimed its anthropological essence, which discloses that there is a being "beyond" God, a purely human being, the being of human desire itself, of human love itself. And it is this being "beyond" God which lies behind subjectivity and to which subjectivity must now be led.

### iv. From Subjectivity to Intersubjectivity

Given the importance of Protestantism for the recognition of theology as anthropology, it was fitting that Feuerbach should address Martin Luther's notion of faith in another work which he entitled *The Essence of Faith in Luther's Sense* and which he intended as a supplement to *The Essence of Christianity*. Luther's notion of faith, Feuerbach points out, is anything but humanistic in its presuppositions. One must either have faith in God and doubt man or one must have faith in man and doubt God. But its consequences are decidedly humanistic. Taken in and by himself, man can do nothing; but through faith in God, man can do everything, since this faith is a virtual power over God. The object of faith is not outside but is within the believer whose will God accomplishes.

The mysteries of faith are locked inside the believer, and it is *for* the believer that God is what he is—Christ for us. God can only be said to be omnipotent in the sense that he is omnipotently good, for a diabolical being might also be omnipotent in the sense that he is omnipotently omniscient, but only God can be omnipotently good to man. It is in man, therefore, that we find the meaning of God's goodness: man can be said to be the highest good of man. The truth, consequently, of the goodness of God is the humanness of God-in-Christ who is the "sensual essence" of God. Even the pagan divinities testify that God cannot be reached through intellectual investigation. But what for the pagan is only an imagined divinity is for the Christian a sensual and therefore certain divinity. This means that for Luther, as Feuerbach sees it, "God" is already a word which has man as its sole meaning.[20]

Although God-in-Christ once was an object of the senses to man, and although he will be so again, he is not presently such an object; his being is not now before our eyes, although his Word has entered our ears—those ears that are the womb of the gods. This must mean that faith does not attach itself to what is present: for faith the most distant thing is near and the closest thing is most distant. Faith "sees" in the dark where nothing is to be seen, and it has to do with future, not present or past, things. In this sense, faith is a subjective certainty[*] that the good shall not be subjected to the evil but, rather, the evil *will be* subjected to the good. Without Christ, however, God would be a God of terror and fear and, to that extent, an evil being, for an evil being can put himself in the garment of majesty and seeming omnipotence but can never take upon himself the Cross.

Luther's God, so Feuerbach infers, thus has his basis outside himself: he is necessary not in or to himself but for those who think him necessary. Without man there would be no God, or rather there would be only a God-in-himself, a metaphysical being, a being of thought. The true God is essentially Lord, but there is no lord without a servant. The essence of God, consequently, is to

---

[*] See pp. 42, 97-98, 152, 159-160 above.

be nothing in himself, and this essence is actual in Christ. This means that the essence of faith lies in the indubitable proposition that God's essence is love for man, that love for man is the supreme being. The whole point of conceding everything to God in faith is precisely to concede everything to man in life. Faith is its own object, which means that the essence of its object is itself; but it is the "I" of the believer who is the essence of faith itself. God is thus given as a "tabula rasa" on which is to be written only what this "I" writes.[21]

But if in faith God is "you" to the "I", this "you" calls out to man what man himself is: the essence of the human heart as the most actual of beings, the blessedness of the "I" related only to itself. This deified *ego*, this blessedness of self-love, is at the heart of Luther's notion of faith which is to be distinguished from life and, therefore, from the love of others in life—a love where the "you" of others is the God of the "I". But although faith is to be clearly distinguished from life, the whole point of conceding everything to God—and, therefore, to the self—in faith is to concede everything to the love of man, of humanity, in life. In examining Luther's notion of faith, consequently, Feuerbach claims to see in it a confirmation of his own premise that the world, if it is the creation of God, is superfluous, a mere luxury, for God would be able to do by himself, without the world, what he does with the world. This must mean that if this life and this world are to be considered more than superfluous, more than a mere luxury, God must be considered to be nothing in and of himself. To the extent that faith is distinguished from this life and this world, it has for its object something that is nothing in itself (God), which means that it has as its object nothing but the *ego* of the believer, i.e., the undyingness of the self of the believer. It is not, then, *for* life that one needs the God of faith but *against* death.* In this way, the Resurrection of Christ is, for Luther, the chief article of faith, the "Grunddogmen" of Chris-

---

* In this regard, Feuerbach quotes from Luther's letters: "[There is] far more fear of death than under popery, when men lived in a secure ignorance concerning the significance of death and the wrath of God."

tianity, and to deny the future life of the particular human self is to remove God entirely.[22] As Feuerbach sees it, if faith is superfluous for this life, its whole point, in being ego-love, is to make room for the love of the other in this life, for the love of humanity.

The antithesis of faith and reason examined by Feuerbach in his treatment of Luther's notion of faith comes up for examination in some of his other writings. Faith, Feuerbach indicates, as conceived by Protestantism and thus by the modern world, has become the object of faith. The original object of faith, namely, God, affirmed only under the determination of particularity, raises the particular and the "something" to the status of the absolute. This itself already entails a vision of the object of faith in terms of the particularity and determinateness of the *ego*. But the deathlessness of this *ego* cannot be maintained by the modern transformation of faith except over against reason—a reason which celebrates in the last moans of dying individuals the victory march of the species over the remains of the single phenomenon. For reason, the *ego* at its end, as at its beginning, exists only in the consciousness of others.[23]

The notion of rationality as presented by modern philosophy, according to Feuerbach, begins with the premise of the antithesis of faith and reason. In its attempt to begin first philosophy anew by removing all presuppositions, modern philosophy attempts to abstract from everything which it is possible to abstract from without ceasing to think at all. This means that philosophy must set itself over against faith which is itself the act of presupposition. But in presenting itself as an abstraction from all objectivity, as that which is without presupposition, modern philosophy is really arrogating to itself the presuppositionlessness and *aseity* of the God who is the object of faith. Implicitly, modern philosophy—in order to think itself as presupposing no external object—must think the object of faith as a being that does not presuppose any other being or object. The *ego* which pronounces that it exists simply because of its own thinking of its existence, the *ego* as pure self-assertiveness, self-willing without presupposition, is precisely the object of faith, the God of the old theology.

Paradoxically, to do for reason—as the antithesis of faith—what Luther did for faith—as the antithesis of reason—modern philosophy must proceed from a presupposition which is hidden to itself, namely, the identity of faith and reason. In other words, to particularize reason as self-willing *ego*—much as Luther particularized faith as self-willing *ego*—modern philosophy must presuppose an underlying identity of faith and reason. Although secretly presupposed by modern philosophical reason, this identity is no longer lived by faith in the modern world which has effectively destroyed the "organs" for apprehension of the supranatural. Reason in the modern world has essentially the presupposition of Christian faith, but its *telos* is anti-theological and, in the last analysis, anti-Christian. Much as the natural sciences turned from the examination of light, as such, back to the eye, philosophy turned from the objects of thinking to the "I" that thinks, holding that the reality of seeing is precisely (as Descartes would have it) the consciousness of seeing,* holding that all being is being-for-*ego*-consciousness, that being *qua* being is subjectivity as the horizon of the world. Descartes' definition of man as the particularity of ego-consciousness is modern philosophy's definition of itself. But what Descartes did was to transform Anselm's proposition—because God is thinkable he exists—into the proposition that I exist because I think. The inseparability of being and being-thought in God is now seen to be the inseparability of being and being-thought in *me*.[24]

In modern philosophy, then, thought has claimed for itself the particularity that is the essential form of sensation. This particularity, as the negation of generality, is now made a moment of thinking itself, i.e., the *ego* thinking itself. In this way, modern philosophy opposes itself to the first philosophy founded in antiquity which left something existing in the world apart from thought, a residue not absorbed by thought, an irrational substrate for reality, i.e., a matter against which reason finds its bound or limit. But, for modern thought, matter and particularity are inherently intelligible by virtue of that thought's presupposition of the theological

---

* See p. 115-116 above.

notion of the Christian God whose creation, being his direct product, can contain nothing irrational. It is, then, through Christian theology that modern philosophy postulates the antithesis of faith and reason, i.e., the antithesis of faith and modernity. And it is from Christian theology that the anti-theological consequences of modern thought flow.

But the time has now come, Feuerbach contends, to remove the paradox of an anti-theological "theology." The time has now come to admit that the very grandeur of theology in first philosophy is nothing but anthropology itself. Far from being a rejection of modern philosophy, this admission requires a completion of modern philosophy by removing the contradiction of belief and unbelief, by showing that the reason which this philosophy is talking about is really the will of man, and that the faith it presupposes (but puts to the side of itself) is really the will of man. The particularity which thought, in modern philosophy, claims for itself, Feuerbach says, belongs not to itself but to being; this particularity is something distinct from thought, added on to thought. The being of particularity always was and can only be material being, sensible being. But this sensible being, Feuerbach contends, can now be seen to be human or humanized. It is a sensible being which embodies the human will—the will which is really at the center of the Cartesian "res cogitans." What accounts for the isolation of this "res cogitans" is the *aseity* of the God it presupposes. But this God has now been shown, Feuerbach claims, to be nothing in himself—to be nothing but the infinite aspiration of the human will—and so the *aseity* of God has been removed and with it the isolation of the human *ego*. Cartesian subjectivity is now freed to be inter-subjectivity.

The only truth in Christianity, then, has been shown to be the infinite aspiration of the human will as the infinity of love. The only truth in the Ontological Argument of Anselm has been shown to be love as the only actuality that can establish an existence apart from the mind. But the love addressed here is a human love, and that means a materially embodied, a sensible, love. The *ego* of modern philosophy is now liberated to be the body in its totality.

My essence is now free for the first time to be *my* body. My will is now able to be an embodied will that *is* insofar as it is in relation to other embodied wills and that can love these others in their particularity and universality. Man is now able for the first time to be exclusively a lover of man. And modern philosophy's dissolution of theology into pure reason can now be completed by a dissolution of theology into the heart, into pure love.

The passion of man's love of God can now be released for the amelioration of the human condition, that is, the material, sensible being of man. The *eros* operative in first philosophy can now be liberated for the work of anthropology, the only pure and first philosophy, which has as its highest principle the "unity of man with man."[25] It is only first-philosophy-as-pure-anthropology which can be the systemization of modern subjectivity. And this systemization, this completion, of the logic of subjectivity is the notion of the *intersubjective* essence of man as the Being "beyond" the God of all prior first philosophy.

### v. The Inversion of Anselm

It is of the utmost significance, Ernst Bloch remarks, that Feuerbach considers the Christian "treasures" in the vault of the life-to-come (Jenseits-Tresor) to be superior to the less human treasures of pagan religion. No one has made a more resolute attempt than Feuerbach to "transfer" the Christian movement of human ideals into the life-to-come back to man himself. But Feuerbach could only do this because his method was obligated to the "radically human line" in Christianity.

The powerful solemnization of the subject (Subjekt-Feier) "held back" from the life-to-come, which we find in Feuerbach, does not quite have a common, "naturalistic, this-worldly" quality. It might almost be said that his genus-man or "Menschgenus" becomes—like the Christian "deus absconditus"—a "homo absconditus," a man who has not seen himself "face to face."[*] In this way, both Feuerbach's

---

\* Cf. pp. 44, 45, 48 above.

emphasis on subjectivity and his peculiar atheism would not have been possible without the Christianity which he subjected to anthropological criticism. In keeping with Christianity, Feuerbach presupposes that a reality of nothing-but-nature, "Nichts-als-Natur," is insufficient because man's own essence would have no actuality. Of course, Feuerbach wanted to make men "students of this life" rather than "candidates for the life-to-come," but it is precisely the Christian notion of the "kingdom of freedom" of the "children of God" which is the precondition for a "better this-life." Feuerbach's "decision" for this life could not have been effected with the astral myths of paganism but required the "Christian myth" with its "Son of Man."[26]

If, as Bloch suggests, Feuerbach's appropriation of the Christian 'myth' is preconditional for his emphasis on subjectivity and his peculiar atheism, it would be no surprise that his attempt to reduce first philosophy to anthropology is pre-conditioned by the appropriation of that 'myth' in Descartes' refounding of first philosophy and in Anselm's transformation of the Aristotelian founding of first philosophy.

It is quite clear, in the first place, that Feuerbach's reduction of first philosophy to anthropology—entailing as it does the notion of God as the objectification of human subjectivity—is faithful to the tradition of the Cartesian "cogito" in which the world is constituted as intelligible only through self-consciousness. Feuerbach, of course, elevates sensation as a Cartesian mode of thinking into the primacy of sense experience absolutely confined to spatio-temporal existence. But this elevation, which seems to go considerably beyond Cartesianism, presupposes a rejection of the traditional Christian theological assertion that the estrangement (i.e., sin) peculiar to man arises from a deflection of the human will from God to self. But this rejection is at least tacitly contained in the Cartesian attempt to ground first philosophy in the intuition of the *ego* as thought by itself. In this sense, Feuerbach's overhauling of Cartesian subjectivity, his elevation of materialism into a piety toward sensible experience which is rooted in intersubjectivity, might be construed as an attempt to make Cartesian first philosophy entirely consistent with itself—a systemization of subjectivity which overcomes the tension in Cartesian philosophy between the explicit primacy of the "cogito" and the implicit primacy of the "deus est."*[27]

The ambiguity, as Karl Löwith remarks, between the finite *ego*, as the "starting point" of the Cartesian refounding of first philosophy, and the proof of God's existence, as the "Endpunkt" of that refounding, resides in the fact that both starting and end-points appear to be simultaneously part of the instrumentation for the "mathematical reconstruction" of the physical world and the very ground of this reconstruction.[28] This reconstruction requires the inhibition of man's naive acceptance of a world that is pregiven, that is accessible in its truth to ordinary human sensible experience, and which is the context for self-consciousness.[29]

Yet the inhibition of sensory experience is itself absorbed by Descartes into the finite subject's thinking, and is so thoroughly absorbed that there is a kind of instantaneousness of thinking consciousness—a kind of immediate bridging of the gap between the intention thought and the embodiment of that intention. Although the *ego* as such is in no way embodied, its thoughts can be "embodied intentions" in space and time.[30] What Feuerbach seems to be attempting to resolve, then, is the Cartesian ambiguity of the explicit priority of the finite *ego* and the implicit priority of the demonstration of God's existence. Feuerbach attempts to resolve *both* the ambiguity of self and God as part of the instrumentation (and yet ground of the project) of mathematical physical science *and* the ambiguity of the inhibition of sensory experience and the elevation of that experience.

There is, however, yet another Cartesian ambiguity which is decisive for Feuerbach's reduction of first philosophy to anthropology. There can be no doubt that certainty is the most basic epistemological notion in Descartes' first philosophy. Descartes is more concerned with the distinction between what is certain and doubtful than he is with the distinction between what is true and false as

---

* See pp. 153, 157 above.

such; truth, in fact, comes to be defined in terms of certainty. Yet, unless God exists, it just might happen that what the *ego* perceives clearly and distinctly is false. The indubitability of the "cogito" and its reality as a finite *ego* cannot be coextensive unless the infinite toward which this *ego* aspires is established as existent. The mere fact that the *ego* cannot be doubted is not sufficient assurance of the truth of its finitude. In this way, the demonstration of God's existence establishes the truth of the "cogito" as a finite existence by eliminating every hypothesis (but especially the hypothesis of a malign deceiver) that might serve as a basis for mistrusting the reason of a finite but infinitely aspiring *ego*. Because of this, there is a sense in which certainty is seen, by Descartes, to be in function of truth.[31]

The residue, then, of the notion of God as "the truth of truth,"[*] the residue of Anselm's notion of truth as rectitude, is very much *there* in Descartes' first philosophy, even though that philosophy has ceased to be a theology. The Cartesian essence of truth is the certainty of the finite *ego*, and yet this *ego* must be in relation to the goodness of the divine will, the rectitude, the *truth* of that will. The finitude of the *ego*—i.e., the impossibility of its being either God or nothingness, or the necessity of its being a mean between God and nothingness—requires the existence of God. But this existence can be established in no other way than by demonstration from the "cogito" of this *ego*.

Feuerbach's attempt to overcome, to resolve, this Cartesian ambiguity amounts to an inversion of the Cartesian logic here. For Feuerbach, the infinity attributed to God requires the finitude of the *ego*, but the 'cogito' of this *ego* (what Feuerbach calls the "sentio" of this *ego*) requires the objectivization of itself, i.e., the projection of itself as God. Whereas Descartes argued that God is the ground of the finitude of human subjectivity, but God is only discovered through that subjectivity, Feuerbach argues that the finitude of human subjectivity is the ground of God (that God is nothing in himself), but that subjectivity is only discovered through

---

[*] See p. 39 above.

the human invention of God. By removing the residue of truth as the rectitude of the divine will, certainty as the essence of truth can now be located by Feuerbach entirely in the human will without relation to divine will. This is precisely because divine will, for him, is only a reification of man's aspiration to infinity or deathlessness. In effect, Feuerbach shifts the burden of illusoriness. The Cartesian illusory pregiven-world of sensible experience is replaced, in Feuerbach, by the illusory aseity of God. This enables the sensible world (as implicitly humanized) to become a certainty. Only in this way can the Cartesian ambiguity be overcome and the Cartesian refusal to identify first philosophy with theology be promoted to anthropology as the "first" philosophy.

By arguing that the very *fact* of human subjectivity is unleashed in the modern world by virtue of the *belief* in the personal God of Christianity, Feuerbach claims to have shown that the *belief* can never be related to a metaphysical statement about the world but only to an anthropological statement about human consciousness and sensibility. When made an object of reason, belief in this God can only result in self-contradictions. When conceded to be an object of feeling (the objectification, in fact, of feeling), belief in this God points to a certainty (i.e., a truth) in man, namely, his extension of self-love to the human race. But if the belief has only anthropological significance, and if the thrust of the method of modern mathematical physics is the de-mystification and de-anthropomorphization of the world, then what could be more obvious than that the "main source of the present-day conflicts between the spheres of religion and of science," as Albert Einstein once said, "lies in the concept of a personal God."[32] And yet, Feuerbach was philosophically astute in seeing that it was precisely the belief in the existence of a personal Creator-God that made the science, alluded to by Einstein, possible in the first place.

What Feuerbach will not or cannot recognize, however, is that the notion of the God of revelation—to whom the human subject ascribes existence—ultimately requires a modality which is not merely logical or phenomenological but metaphysical.[33] The requisite modality can only be anthropological for Feuerbach. But even in Descartes, the modality is still metaphysical: unless the world is entirely intelligible and, therefore, unless the existence of a personal Creator-God has metaphysical warrant, modern mathematical physics has no metaphysical foundation. Feuerbach, however, inverts the Cartesian logic and argues that unless the existence of a personal Creator-God has no metaphysical warrant, the sensible world, which man makes humanly controllable by modern mathematical physics, is superfluous. But this inversion is only possible by virtue of Feuerbach's reduction of all metaphysical claims to anthropological descriptions—by virtue of Feuerbach's attempt to show that the faith which Descartes brackets off from his first philosophy has nothing more than anthropological significance and thus would have to be disbelief in order to be consistent with Descartes' own logic. In this way, the inversion peculiar to Feuerbach's justification of anthropology as the "first" philosophy is not only an inversion of primary elements in the Cartesian refounding of first philosophy but is, even more fundamentally, an inversion of Anselm's first philosophy with its peculiar treatment of the relation between belief and unbelief. At bottom, Feuerbach proves to be Anselm "stood on his head."

Anselm's attempt in first philosophy to make the incomprehensibility of God comprehensible centers itself on a God who is at once "deus absconditus" and "deus revelatus"; and this hiddenness and unhiddenness of God finds its reflection in a kind of dialectic between unbelief and belief. Unbelief finds its embodiment in the "fool," but the fool himself has significance in terms of an unbelief that the believer himself must struggle against within himself.[34] In this dialectic, the lived atheism of the fool (the denial of his heart) can only be a kind of perverted imitation of the belief of the believer when that belief is lived (when the heart and the understanding are congruent). Throughout Feuerbach's anthropology, this Anselmian dialectic of *what is split* in the fool as an imitation of *what is united* in the believer reappears but precisely as inverted. It is now the unlived theism of the believer—the theological and, therefore, conceptual antithesis of man and God—which is a perverted imitation of the lived atheism of the believer himself—that is, the omnipotence of the human heart made into a "God" by the imagination. The primacy of belief over unbelief in Anselm has been transformed into the primacy of unbelief over belief in Feuerbach.

In the "Commendatio" (addressed to Pope Urban II) of his *Cur Deus Homo*, Anselm remarks that the understanding which we take hold of in this life stands in between faith and sight, and sight is that to which we all "aspire."[35] Again, in the first chapter of his *Epistola de Incarnatione Verbi*, Anselm says that whoever has not believed shall not understand—"qui non crediderit, non intelliget"—since in not believing, he has "not experienced," and in not experiencing, he has not known (non cognoscet).[36] Understanding, in other words, in this life is in between faith and sight, but faith, far from being in opposition to sensory experience, is seen to lead to (or to seek) a sensory experience which would enable it to be knowledge.

In Feuerbach, however, the relationships here are inverted. Faith is in opposition to reason and, therefore, cannot be made an object of reason—except to the extent that any illusion of the imagination can be made an object of rational investigation. Love, furthermore, is in opposition to faith—in contrast to Anselm's notion of "viva fides" as embodied in the "vitam delectionis"*—and, therefore, the sensible orientation of love cannot be said to characterize faith. There is, then, no sensible experience to which faith could possibly lead. The condition, the content, and the *terminus ad quem* of faith are all the same, namely, "sensory deprivation." Whereas, for Anselm, faith is one of the poles between which understanding in this life stands, faith, for Feuerbach, has *only* the status of an in-between. Faith stands in between human feeling (with its necessities) and human imagination (with its freedom). Faith, for Feuerbach, is what derives its "necessity" from the human heart and what derives its "freely willed" character from the imagination. Faith has no being of its own; it is a creature of the human heart and imagination.

---

* See pp. 62, 60, 46 above.

If for Anselm the reality of lived faith is made an object for first philosophy, and if for Descartes this reality is bracketed off from first philosophy (but nonetheless supplies contents to the reason or "light of nature" operative therein), then for Feuerbach faith is no longer something lived but has significance for first philosophy only as the illusion that must be overcome if that philosophy is to be pure anthropology. But this means that what is common to Descartes and Feuerbach is their rejection of lived faith as an object for reason in first philosophy. It is this rejection that enables them to agree that God is the infinity of subjectivity known only in subjectivity,[37] although they are diametrically opposed as to the conclusion to be drawn from that on which they agree. Both their agreement and disagreement here make sense only as a response to the conjunction of the inwardness of faith and reason proposed by Anselm.

The paradigm here, consequently, is the single and self-sufficing argument of Anselm's dialogue in first philosophy—an argument which claims that when we comprehend the signification of the name of God, we inevitably posit the existence of God, in such a way that the argument presents itself as an immediate reduction to absurdity of atheism.[38] This argument—which insists on the bond between God as the object of faith and faith as the object of reason in the innermost recesses of the human heart *and* understanding—is the paradigm for the invention of subjectivity in Descartes and the systemization of subjectivity in Feuerbach. To transpose the force of this argument from God as the object of faith to mankind as the object of man's feeling, Feuerbach must reject Anselm's presupposition that human words are derived ultimately from the Word of God—that this Word is that from which diverse human languages gain their meaningfulness. Feuerbach must also reject Anselm's contention that God is the very exception to the laws of space and time which enables these laws to be laws for everything else.*[39] But in rejecting these presuppositions, Feuerbach is really inverting them—arguing that "God" is merely the objectifi-

---

\* See pp. 80, 32 above.

cation of the very essence of language treated as if it were an individual existence, and arguing that time and space are the very exceptions to the laws of faith which prove that the object of this faith is only an objectification of the human subject.

Yet, Feuerbach's inversion here presupposes that the true, essential, or logical form of the sentences pronounced by faith must be contrasted with the apparent, merely grammatical, and sometimes false forms countenanced by ordinary usage. But this presupposition of a distinction between the inner word of thinking and the *usus loquendi*[40] is precisely the distinction proposed for first philosophy by Anselm and utilized by Descartes in his refounding of first philosophy.* Descartes attempts to call into doubt the linguistic vehicle for the ordinary, sense-perception-laden view of the world; he discovers that, in contrast to the names which are given things from the outside, "ego," when pronounced by thought, comes from within[41] and is the identity of namer and named, thinker and thing-thought. Whether, in sum, we are talking about the *ego cogitans* of Descartes' refounding or the *ego agens* of Feuerbach's reduction of first philosophy, we are talking about a subject over against an object.[42] Our very talking here presupposes an inner truth for words and an outer usage for words in their diversity which is displayed by diverse languages—a presupposition first made a working principle of first philosophy by Anselm.

It is, of course, Feuerbach's contention that the inner truth of the words which man speaks in (Christian) religion is precisely human feeling, and that the inner truth of the words man has spoken in (first) philosophy is precisely anthropology. The word "God" signifies the inner truth of the subjectivity of man honoring itself alone, the substantial bond between man's essence (his genus) and his (individual) existence, the immediacy of individual existence containing the human genus, the wish of man for immediate certainty of his personal continuance after death. The word "being" signifies the inner truth of the sensible embodiment of the human will, the *ego* freed from the *aseity* of God, so as to be the body in its

---

\* See pp. 115-116, 51-52, 40, 32, x above.

totality and intersubjective relations—man liberated to be exclusively a lover of man. The yearning after God bespoken in (Christian) religion has for its inner truth the yearning for an unlimited (infinite) individuality; and the being bespoken by (first) philosophy is a "sentio ergo sum," an "is" that signifies only the inner human reality of an existence which is an act of aspiration. The inner truth of (Christian) religious language is thus the rendering to the common things of this human life an uncommon significance; and the inner truth of the language of first philosophy is a veritable dissolution of speculation itself, an anthropology in the service of the practical or lived identification of man with man.

First philosophy, in effect, as Feuerbach sees it, has been an historical travail, a resistance against its own immanent and ultimate truth, namely, the truth that what is at once sensible and human is to be accorded the dignity, the devotion, the "uncommonness" of what has been thought (by speculation) to be more-than-human and more-than-sensible. The travail of first philosophy has been an historical movement from substance to subject which is centered in God *and* subjectivity, but its final realization lies in the superfluousness of the word "and"—in the reduction of God to human subjectivity.

And yet, to attain this realization, the word "God" was required; and the signification afforded this word by what, at this point in time, has become the "ordinary usage" of the Christian religion was necessary. Feuerbach's systemization of the logic of subjectivity presupposes this necessary signification and can do no more than turn it upside down. In the end, the "logic" of this systemization is that God must exist in the human understanding *alone* if, in fact, God is to be conceived as existing independently of the human understanding. This "logic" is nothing but an inversion of the primal logic of Anselm: God must exist independently of the human understanding if, in fact, God is to exist in the human understanding *at all*.

# VI

# The Historical Travail of First Philosophy

In founding first philosophy, Aristotle treats being *qua* being universally as an occurrence which is inherent in particular things and which has its *telos* in that which is separate from sensible things. *To be* means to be present as permanent, and although sensible things have this principle of permanence operative within them, they are not as such this occurrence that manifests itself in being*s* but is never hypostasized. The substantiality of substances is not a predicate but an immanent completion of nature for which all natural things strive. Thus, first philosophy is theology, the highest science, which deals with the most important (but in no way infinite) aspect of nature—a nature in which nothing can be higher than the form which is operative therein. Substance can be visible in particular sensible things only because, in its pure actuality, substance is the pure universality of thinking which thinks itself.

The representational thought of Christian belief, however, entails an hypostasized substantiality which is a primal subject of being completely other than this world. In transforming Aristotle's founding of first philosophy, Anselm makes the existence of particular things supremely problematic. The Aristotelian ἐνέργεια* operative in nature is transformed into the "actualitas" of a creative substance which transcends form as such. Being *qua* being is not the being-of-beings but a "creator spiritus" which, unlike the God of Aristotle, does not require the world in order to exist, since its

---

* See pp. 6, 10, 18, 19 above.

divinity does not require the non-divine alongside it. The human mind can rationally comprehend that this Supreme Spirit is incomprehensible, and the more eagerly this mind stretches forth to learn of itself, the more effectively is it raised to the conception of the creative essence of all things. The human mind is a mirror of itself in which it contemplates the image of what it is not able to see "face to face." The thinking of the divine subject of being is seen, in fact, to constitute the very being of the human mind in its singularity—"mens mea"—as this mind seeks to embody a lived faith in the life of love.

The desire for a perfection immanent in nature has thus been transformed by Anselm into a desire of "mens mea" for existence in a perfection which transcends nature. It is truth—as a rectitude of understanding and will—and the dialectic of the submergence and emergence of his own self that underlie Anselm's attempt to gain a finite comprehension of the infinity which constitutes the object of this desire. The very nature of the human mind is a striving to be *in* that existence that it ought to-be-in. This means that "that than which nothing greater can be thought" is, as such, something particular (an "aliquid") which is greater than what can be thought by the human mind. The human mind thinks the existence of what is beyond its capacity to think and, in its own negative way, comprehends the necessary existence of that more-than-natural (suprasubstantial) essence which is incomprehensible to it. God is wholly and always that which all contingent things desire if they are to be and to be *well*.

There is, however, a split in the being of fallen man. The fool or "insipiens" is the extreme instance of this split: what he says in his heart is at odds with what he thinks in his understanding. The self of the "insipiens" and of the philosophical investigator (the believer) is now seen to be matter for metaphysical speculation itself, since God can be investigated only insofar as the investigating-self attempts to speak to—to address—God. If God were able to be thought not to exist, he would exist in no way, not even in the understanding of the investigator and the "insipiens." In this way, the very denial of God's existence, as an act of the will and not a judgment of the understanding, presupposes the incomprehensible existence of that which faith seeks to understand. The impossibility of God's nonexistence and the incomprehensibility of his intelligibility are inseparable in the human mind, which cannot think beyond the impossibility of the nonexistence of God, but which can grasp the significance of its being grasped by an absolutely unique subject of being which it, itself, cannot grasp. Herein lies the ground for the act by which thinking looks into itself in man, i.e., the "cogitantis inspectio."

Modern philosophical subjectivity is only invented when the human mind attempts to do without Christian faith something which previously it would have had to renounce without this faith, viz., its release from the bondage to death imposed on it (as a particular thing) by nature. This Cartesian invention proceeds from the transformation of truth as rectitude (the certainty of truth in Anselm) into truth as representation (the truth of certainty). The liberty proper to the human mind in its particularity entails that the impossibility of the nonexistence of the human subject of being is what cannot be thought beyond. First philosophy can only begin by beginning anew *in me* and in a presuppositionless state, so that faith has no credentials which can enable it to seek understanding, and reason is entirely other than faith. First philosophy is now a search for an indubitable existence which is more truly *mine* than the ordinary life which I lead within the context of what nature makes accessible to me.

Whether or not there is anything in the world, I cannot doubt that I exist, and I would exist even if I were always sleeping and always deceived. What is unshakable and beyond doubt is the act by which my mind looks into itself, the "mentis inspectio," which is its own ground and is the very principle of the sensible perception of corporeal things. It is no longer a matter of my thought affirming the existence of an "aliquid" which would be there without my thought, but it is now a matter of my thinking the existence of something which is inseparable from my thinking, something which could not exist were I unable to think. My own existence is the *res* which thinks my existence: that by which I understand is had by me from no other source than my own particular thinking nature. This means that the question of the existence of God can only be raised in terms of the question of my being deceived about everything other than myself; the idea of an infinite substance is necessary (as that to which the *ego* aspires) if this *ego* is to know the corporeal things of nature. But the necessity of the existence of this *ego* in its finitude can, in fact, only be said to be the image or mark of God to the extent that God is discovered to be the infinite image of this *ego*'s existence.

Existence, which Descartes saw to be inseparable from the thinking of the *ego*, is now seen by him to be separable from the will of the *ego*. This will, although it seems to be the unlimited power contained in the idea of God, is capable of participation in nothingness. The idea of God can only be entertained as an object by a subject for whom to be united with a body is not part of its essence. Yet the more-than-natural (supra-substantial) being of this human subject lives out its existence in the order of corporeal nature. This means that first philosophy does not have as its purpose the turning of this subject away from or above sensible things to theology but, rather, the turning of this subject to the tasks of mathematical physics and the mastery of nature. The ontologization of the self, in its particularity, is a raising of sense perception to a mode of the thinking of objects. First philosophy is not theology but a metaphysical foundation for the mathematical reconstruction of the physical world. The human—not the divine—subject's lordship over nature is what is now at issue.

Yet, the anti-theological, Cartesian refounding of first philosophy presupposes a kind of revelation internal to the *ego* of something previously revealed externally to the Christian believer and made an object for theology. The purely human *ego*—which is ontologically prior to the natural being of the world, in Descartes' first philosophy, and which would exist even though this world did not exist—is modeled on the inseparability of the essence and existence of that which it wills to be, namely, God who, in Anselm's first philosophy, would exist if there were no world. The Cartesian "mentis inspectio" has its paradigm in the Anselmian "cogitantis inspectio" which, in turn, finds its ground in the human mind's being grasped by that which this mind cannot grasp. Without the existence of God, the Cartesian *ego* would be without a world in which to exist. But it is precisely the liberty of the will, that is no greater in God than in the human *ego*, which is that than which nothing greater can be conceived. First philosophy is now seen to take will—the thrusting forth of essence—as the intelligibility of being; and this begins a humanization of being *qua* being.

It is Feuerbach's aim to enable modern man to appropriate consciously this humanization—to take consciously, and no longer unconsciously, his own essence as the measure of his ethical and political life. The mystery, the secret, the "Geheimnis," of the representational thought of Christian belief is no longer the "impenetrabile secretum" of Anselm but is now uncovered[*] and shown to be atheism—the self-satiation of man's self-assertiveness, the essence of the human subject of being treated objectively, man's seeing his own essence as outside of himself, the hypostatization of the future of the human race represented as a present being in which the evil of this life is done away with. The distinguishing of God in God (the Trinity) is preconditional for the distinguishing of God from nature which, in turn, means only the distinguishing of man from nature. God is the self-affirmation of man's subjective essence imagined as beyond the world.

The Anselmian "nomen personae" of God is now seen by Feuerbach to be a "nomen proprium" devoid of any ontological claim. God means nothing in himself; the *ego* is the ground for the determination of God—a determination interposed between the human subject as determined and the human subject as determining. Substantiality is nothing but the cognitive bond between man's essence (his genus) and his existence as an individual. The only "truth" of the representational thought of Christianity is its liberation of the power of love which identifies man with God and thus identifies man with man. Feuerbach's aim is to free this power from the con-

---

[*] See pp. 186, 177, 175, 172, 38 above.

tamination of Christian faith which separates God from man and, thereby, separates man from man.

Feuerbach thus claims to have overcome the modern paradox of an anti-theological "theology." The Cartesian will is a sensibly embodied will, and with the final removal of the aseity of God there is removed the isolation of the Cartesian *ego*. Subjectivity can now be systematized as embodied intersubjectivity, and the passion in man's love of God can now be fully released for the melioration of the human *sensible* condition. The *eros* endemic to first philosophy can now be released for the work of anthropology. By removing the residue of the Anselmian notion of the rectitude of the divine will—which still remains in the Cartesian invention of subjectivity—Feuerbach can now claim to have systematized subjectivity and thus to have brought to a halt the travail of first philosophy in its journey from Aristotelian substantiality to modern subjectivity. From start to finish, first philosophy has been a protracted resistance against what alone can be its truth—anthropology possessed of the dignity of theology. The inner truth of the travail of first philosophy turns out to be the realization that what is at once sensible and human is to be accorded the "piety" that has been reserved by (prior) speculation for what is more-than-human or more-than-sensible or both.

### i. The Removal and Perdurance of Mystery

It is not accidental that Feuerbach's claim to have brought the travail of first philosophy—in its journey from substantiality to subjectivity—to a conclusion, to a close, is preconditioned by his claim to have removed the mystery, the "Geheimnis," the "impenetrabile secretum," of the meaning of Christianity. Mysteries, however, really remain mysteries, even when they are thought to be comprehended, precisely because they exceed the grasp of the human mind. Yet, it is with Descartes' notion of clear and distinct perception that the process of excluding mystery from first philosophy is begun, since the Cartesian notion implies that to understand a thing at all is to understand it fully.

The elimination of mystery which characterizes modern philosophy, as Michael B. Foster remarks, is in precise contrast to the revelation of mystery characteristic of Greek philosophy. The end or purpose of Aristotelian first philosophy, for example, was purely theoretical—a wondering contemplation of the divine in which mystery was not dispelled but more fully disclosed. This contemplation was a kind of union of the divine element in man with the divine nature of the world. Foster notes the contrast between the Platonic notion of science as "propaedeutic to contemplation" and the modern notion of science as "hostile to contemplation." But he also points out that the ancient conception of a divinity in man and nature was decisively different from Christian theology in which both nature and man are creatures and, therefore, *not* divine. The God of biblical revelation is hidden in contrast to the manifestation of the being-of-beings for ancient philosophy. Yet the biblical God makes himself manifest by an act of the will, so that it is seen, at the same time that he is made manifest, that it is not his nature to be unhidden. The word $\mu\nu\acute{\epsilon}\omega$ itself means to keep the mouth closed, and in the Greek mystery religions the initiate was not allowed to disclose to the uninitiated what he had heard. But in contrast to this is the Christian imperative to preach the gospel to all men, since to disclose or not to disclose is not the prerogative of man but only of God. The ancient philosophical confidence in the self-disclosure of the reality of nature to the contemplating mind of man is not the same as the biblical conception of God's holiness from which is derived his hiddenness.[1]

Paradoxically, the modern de-mystification of nature and man is rooted in the biblical conception of mystery, if only to the extent that the impoverished forms of mystery (the occult and the magical) are dispelled from nature, and the purposes of God (final causes) are held to be unknowable[*]—thus fitting the biblical sense that God has acted but that one cannot always specify exactly what God has done. Modern scientific reason involves, in Francis Bacon's terms, putting a question to nature, a method of commanding

---

[*] See pp. 100-101, 129, 154 above.

nature to answer man's questions, which, in turn, implies that nothing shall be admitted as evidence except what is accessible to the faculties common to all men. This means that modern science is applicable to all the things which are subject to man in his universal humanity. This is not inconsistent with "Thou hast put all things under his [man's] feet";* nor is it inconsistent with the biblical proclamation that "There is none holy like the Lord."° For this proclamation might be said to imply that if God alone is perfectly holy and mysterious, then there is no unfathomable mystery in the world, in nature.

If the modern de-mystification of nature is consonant with the biblical view of mystery, however, there is a certain biblical element which is noticeably absent from the modern worldview, viz., what Foster calls "something like a repentance in the sphere of the intellect," a repentance which is alien to the notion of the divinity of the understanding inherited from Greek philosophy, a repentance which is dependent on divine revelation and never supersedes that revelation. It is this repentance, interestingly enough, that we meet so forcibly in Anselm's first philosophy, which finds its final context in prayer where what is prayed for is the comprehension of the incomprehensible (being grasped by what one cannot grasp)—something that cannot be specified beforehand as to what it would be like to have it granted. Both repentance of the intellect and prayer are noticeably absent from both the Cartesian refounding of first philosophy and Feuerbach's reduction of that philosophy to anthropology. And yet, both Descartes and Feuerbach take their cue from Anselm who was working with the biblical notion of God as beyond nature and, therefore, with the assumption that there is no hierarchy of divine and non-divine elements either in human or non-human created nature. Anselm was no longer working with the Greek notion of the divine as dwelling within nature side by side with the non-divine. Descartes and, in turn, Feuerbach progressively extrude from man divine elements by replacing the

---

\* Psalm 8:6.

° 1 Samuel 2:2.

faculties of a soul which abides in nature with, respectively, the "ego cogitans" and the "ego agens."[2]

The travail of first philosophy, then, in its historical path from substantiality to subjectivity would seem to be a transformation of mystery which involves a progressive exclusion of mystery from man and nature and finally (with Feuerbach) from God himself. At the center of this travail, however, stands the "quiet eye" of the mystery of God made an object of reason in Anselm's first philosophy, especially in the single argument of Anselm's dialogue in first philosophy, where it is first shown on purely rational grounds that "that than which a greater cannot be conceived" really exists apart from conception, and where it is then shown that the *mystery* which is the object of faith, viz., the person of God, properly names what has been arrived at on purely rational grounds.[3] Always, the mystery of God (his complete otherness to the world and man) grounds the interweaving of God into the world and things. It is only the God who would exist if there were no world who, in Anselm's words, waited upon the response of the Virgin Mary in order to make himself from her and thus "remake all the things that he had made."[4] It is precisely the way Anselm holds the mystery of God in communion with reason—the balance he strikes between "aenigmata" and lucidity—which enables him to shift the burden of mystery away from the Aristotelian concern with the disclosure of the things of nature and into the presence of God to the intentional consciousness of man.

In Aristotelian first philosophy, the soul is not a "subject" but simply the first act of an organic entity; nor does "object" in this philosophy pertain to an intentional act of man, but it refers to an act operative in nature manifesting itself as efficient and final causality.[5] But the mystery of God's holiness in communion with reason, with "mens mea," in Anselm turns first philosophy toward human intentionality. It is this intentionality which eventually penetrates the extra-theological realms proposed by modern philosophy. It is this intentionality which enables Francis Bacon to exhort men to study nature with minds that are unpossessed and "washed clean from opinions" and which becomes the primary metaphysical principle in Descartes.[6] The fact that Anselm conceives of certainty entirely in terms of truth indicates that the divine mystery is still at the center of first philosophy. The fact that Descartes begins to consider truth in terms of certainty indicates that the divine mystery has retreated from the center of first philosophy. But the fact that Feuerbach dissolves the divine mystery into the attempt of the *ego agens* to will and gain freedom from nature and from the "fate" and risk implied by the classical irrational material substrate indicates that mystery has been banished from first philosophy.

Certainly this is no mere act of Feuerbach alone, for the nineteenth century itself makes visible the evolution of a modern social machinery which has been designed as a struggle against risk[7] and, to that extent, as a de-mystification of being. This breaking with tradition, decisively begun in Descartes, has now become part of our tradition (as Feuerbach tacitly confirms by treating Cartesian subjectivity as his "tradition"). But the break here is by no means as total as its proponents suggest. Anselm's fidelity to scriptural tradition is not inconsistent with his being as much a component of the tradition of rationality as Descartes. And in their own ways, Descartes and Feuerbach cannot escape both scriptural tradition and Anselm's assimilation of that tradition to the tradition of rationality. In the final analysis, what is owed by Feuerbach to Descartes is only equaled by the debt which Descartes bears to Anselm. In this way, the Augustinianism which Anselm transmutes into first philosophy resurfaces in the divine identity of knowing and willing which Descartes withholds from the finite *ego*. The idea which we have of God, Descartes says, instructs us that there is in him only a "single activity, wholly simple and wholly pure," and this is well put by the words of St. Augustine: "They [created things] are so because you [God] see them to be so,"[*] because in God *seeing* (videre) and *willing* (velle) are one and the same thing.[8]

What we find, then, in the historical travail of first philosophy from substance to subject, from the Aristotelian founding of first philosophy to the reduction of that philosophy to anthropology by

---

[*] *Confessions*, XIII, 38.

Feuerbach, is the progressive exclusion of mystery from nature, man, and finally God. But this exclusion is itself centered in a new sense of the mystery of the divine being and, therefore, in a new intelligibility for being itself. In Aristotle there is something of a conflict between the universal which is alone entirely true and the particular which, in its givenness, can be said to be alone entirely real. This conflict, by virtue of what Anselm takes to be the problematical character of existence, becomes a tension to be resolved by his harmonization of faith and reason. Of course, the shift is visible in broader terms than those proposed by Aristotle and Anselm. The classical or ancient statue, for example, represented man largely in terms of a function: man is essentially an idea, i.e., a form, a harmony of perfect proportions. But in the new art of the high Middle Ages the personality of the individual shines through the statue to be found on the porch of the cathedral.[9]

In a similar way the personality of the philosophical investigator and the personhood of God are given dialectical expression by Anselm—the former emerging and yet submerged before the attempt to see the latter. The soul-body distinction is now seen to be in function of the God-self distinction. The individuality of the soul—and not merely the classical particularity of the body—emerges in Anselm's first philosophy. But both soul and body are still very much a part of nature, even though nature is no longer the starting point of first philosophy. In Descartes' refounding of first philosophy, the soul-body distinction is dissolved into the dualism of mind and matter, and the God-self distinction is left, so to speak, to stand alone. Subjectivity is what replaces the soul, and it is not as such a part of nature, nor is it an object of theology but is, instead, offered as a purely "rational" metaphysical principle. Finally, in Feuerbach, the God-self distinction itself vanishes and we are left only with the intersubjective human self and its sensible embodiment.

Feuerbach's comprehensive expulsion of mystery from philosophy, if it cannot free itself entirely of reliance on the prior philosophical speculation which it hopes to strip away from first philosophy as a pure anthropology, also cannot free itself from internal inconsistencies. If, for example, God is the alienation of human excellences, it follows that human excellences are projected in terms of a human defect. We can readily understand the defect in man, but Feuerbach's analysis would seem to entail that the defect persists in the projection (namely, God). But he can never really make explicit why this defect is in what is supposedly (or held to be) a *perfect* being. Obviously, Feuerbach can have only one thing in mind, viz., the problem of evil, that is, the nothingness that seems to touch a created being which is (and must be) entirely rational if a Creator-God exists. But evil as a defect would seem to be bound up with the very nature of God for Feuerbach—a situation which is radically at odds with the claims of Christian religion. Feuerbach's reduction of first philosophy to anthropology, then, stands to be haunted by the specter of the problem of evil. One might even suggest, furthermore, that this "problem" is unresolved by his reduction—that this "problem" is the inexpungible residue of mystery lurking behind the attempt to extrude mystery completely from philosophy.

If the dialectical transformation of substantiality into subjectivity in the historical travail of first philosophy is a movement from God in his majesty (Anselmian "theology") to the commendation of the human self privately related to God (Cartesian "philosophy") to the self stretching-forth only to intersubjectivity (Feuerbachian "anthropology"), then the substrate of the entire historical development is nothing less than the impingement of the "problem" of evil on the dialectical transformation.* Anselm's realization that if God is possible then God is necessary becomes in Descartes the realization that if man thinks the necessity of God then man in his particularity is absolutely free and stands above nature as a "subject." Descartes' realization, in turn, becomes in Feuerbach the realization that if man is absolutely free, then God is nothing more than man-for-men. The upshot of all these realizations, however, would be the contradictoriness of God and evil. If God exists, there can be no evil. If evil exists, there can be no God. God, for

---

* See pp. 59-60, 69, 74-75, 109-110 above.

Feuerbach, would then have to be a something which is really nothing, and evil would have to be a nothing which is really something—in contradistinction to Anselm for whom evil is a "something" which is really nothing, and God is what appears to the fool to be nothing but really is the absolutely unique something.

The logic of Feuerbach, consequently, *should* leave us with the explicit realization of the reality of evil in the intersubjective human condition. But this is precisely what it fails to do. In this failure lies the most important internal inconsistency in the attempt to reduce first philosophy to pure anthropology. The success of the attempt, the success of the effort to vanquish the mystery or holiness of God, should leave the human condition in stark confrontation with evil. But the plain fact of the matter of Feuerbach's reduction is that it becomes clear that without God there is no evil but only the irrational substrate of nature—fate in one or another modern guise, most notably the failure of cells in a random sensible being. In point of fact, Feuerbach sets the intellectual tone for the contemporary world in his refusal to recognize either God or evil. But in recognizing neither, he has no metaphysical ground left for his "faith" in intersubjectivity, since anthropology as such can never yield a properly *meta-physical* ground if the human is tied only to space and time. Anthropology, in other words, cannot be an object to be investigated by anthropology. In order to have a truly metaphysical status, the notion of God as the alienation of human excellences would have to confront "faith" in human subjectivity with the stark "reality" of evil. This notion would have to lead to the questioning of subjectivity itself in the face of evil, and this Feuerbach never does.

Ironically, in being thrown back on the problem of evil as the problem which underlies the whole transformation from substance to subject, we are forced to question the outcome which Feuerbach proposes for this transformation. Evil, according to Anselm, is nothingness spoken and thought of as if it were something. This nothingness is powerlessness that is spoken and thought of as a power—the sin that is put to the side of Descartes' first philosophy, and entirely excluded from Feuerbach's anthropology, but which is the fundamental issue addressed in Anselm's inclusion of the "insipiens" in his first philosophy. The "problem," as it is called, lies in this: evil comes into the world through sin, and yet sin comes through evil—a nothingness from nothingness in a being brought out of nothingness, a being which is, throughout time, on the brink of falling back into the nothingness from which it was brought out. One man sins and suffers and another escapes the penalty of his misdeed. The just and the unjust suffer alike—like the elements of a dwelling that is to be demolished in order to be rebuilt. And like the elements of such a dwelling, the hairs of our heads are numbered by God;* and if the new and profound significance of particularity, of *every* singular existent thing, is now in view, so also is the demolition of the particular in clear view—as clearly as the death that has been vanquished by the Resurrection.[10]

Ultimately, in the face of the "problem" of evil, the late modern faith in a subjectivity without God, Feuerbach's love of a humanity without a divine ground, the utilitarian maximization of a happiness which is defined as satisfaction—all of these are disclosed to be the very "idealisms" which Feuerbach castigates, idealisms without ontological support. If, as is presupposed by Anselm's Ontological Argument, there is a personal desire for God, a desire which man does not simply have but which he *is*, then there is also a desire for nothingness. And modern subjectivity promoted into intersubjectivity—in terms of the nothingness of God—will have to be examined very closely so as to ascertain whether or not the attempt to promote human self-assertiveness without a confidence in God is precisely the desire-for or the will-to nothingness. In an age such as the one we today are living through—where the very debate between atheism and theism, generated by the nineteenth century and most especially by Feuerbach, seems no longer to be at issue[11]—the question, perhaps the only question left, might very well be the status of subjectivity in the face of evil. Why do we today persist in taking the human subject, at least our own individual self, with so much seriousness? Why do we dote upon our own individ-

---

* See Matthew 10:30, Luke 12:7.

uality in a statistical world—in what has been presented as a universe of evolutionary chance? The problem of evil may be the only remaining cord for the retrieval of philosophy's relation to mystery. If so, it would draw us to the center, the midpoint, of the history of first philosophy, the still Anselmian *vortex* of the travail of the concept of being.

Reflection on this vortex would have to involve two considerations. The first is the misinterpretation of the Ontological Argument by Descartes, Feuerbach, and most of modern thought—a misinterpretation which is not unrelated to the modern philosophical attempt to bracket off theology from philosophy. The second is the operative presence of this Ontological Argument as a kind of regulative notion for the development of modern philosophical subjectivity—a notion which operates, beneath the very bracketing-off of theology from philosophy, as a largely unverbalized dynamism both for the Cartesian invention of the radical human subject and for the Feuerbachian and contemporary attempts to sustain subjectivity without God. For the moment, we will turn to the first of these considerations: the modern misunderstanding of the single argument for God's existence which Anselm presented in his dialogue in first philosophy.

### ii. The Modern Misunderstanding of Anselm

The *Proslogion* is a philosophical work of the first order; its philosophical integrity is constituted by the relation between two ideas of God. The first is the idea affirmed by faith—what God is for God; the second is the idea conveyed by the human understanding—what God is for man. The idea of faith is the idea of that being who is what he is only through himself, the idea of that being who alone contains nothing which is dissimilar with himself, the idea of God as the only being who fully is what he is and who he is. This is the idea of God as the Trinity in which each person is simply what the unity of the persons is. This idea of faith is positive; it is the idea of something greater than can be thought by man, the idea of a being who is fundamentally impervious to man's comprehension—the idea of the God of Abraham, Isaac, and Jacob who is hidden, a "deus absconditus."

Anselm, however, does not operate exclusively with the idea of faith, nor does he infer, from the ineradicable hiddenness of God as he is in himself, that God is unknowable by reason. God can be thought by man insofar as he can be thought to be in terms of what he is for man; and this idea of the understanding (which in the usual interpretation of the Ontological Argument is taken to be its heart) is the idea of "id quo maius cogitari non potest." It is proposed by Anselm not only in the mode of language which he addresses to God (i.e., prayer) but also in the mode of language which is a response to the situation of the "insipiens." What is heard in the formulation of this idea can be understood by the fool even though the *thing* (the "aliquid") to which this idea refers cannot be fully understood. Man thus thinks the inconceivable in the mode of negativity, although he cannot fully think the *what* or the *whom* to which this inconceivability applies. This idea of understanding is purely negative and amounts to whatever can be thought as better for the divine being to be than not to be.

Insofar as the Ontological Argument is construed exclusively in terms of this negative idea of the understanding (which exists *for* the understanding of man), it is primarily a disclosure about man's access to him*self* by means of the "via negativa." Insofar as the argument is held to be solely about this negative idea, it amounts to a *moral* argument for God's existence, and its primary logical significance is an injunction for man to desire the simple good which contains every good—the "unum est necessarium."[*] Its significance here is not, as such, metaphysical but is, rather, a moral description of a joy to which the human mind cannot be equal. If, in fact, the negative idea of God has as its object what God is for man, i.e., if the idea here is not, as such, and by itself, a participation in God's self-knowledge, then it would follow that this idea is primarily directed to man's natural desire for God rather than to an ontological truth about God as he is in himself. The instructiveness of this

---

[*] See p. 80 above.

negative idea is thus primarily in the human sphere rather than in the metaphysical realm addressed by first philosophy.

The misunderstanding of the Ontological Argument by philosophical modernity is essentially the treatment of this negative idea as if it were positive or descriptive of what God is for God. Fundamentally, the modern treatment of the Ontological Argument is, by and large, in terms of an idea which man possesses, a positive content of his mind, an idea among ideas. Here Descartes' appropriation of the argument in his fifth meditation is a case in point. But this misconstrual of the negative idea of the understanding which pertains to what God is for man, as if it were a positive idea of the understanding which pertains to what God is in himself, is precisely what enables philosophical modernity in its early stages (particularly in Descartes) to treat the idea of God as a kind of support of the notion of man as the finite subject who is constituted as an *ego* by his infinite aspiration.

This idea of man as an infinitely aspiring *ego* is seen to come first in the order of discovery; this idea is viewed as that which modernity discovers by itself by means of the materials of modernity alone. Philosophical modernity interprets itself as unconditioned, as an absolutely new beginning of first philosophy, as a declaration of autonomy and liberation from the categories of a theology which is predicated on Christian faith. The content of Anselm's negative idea is now addressed as positive and descriptive of what God is for himself. Yet, what God is for himself is seen to consist essentially in its relevance for man and modern culture. The modern notion of the subject as a finite "res cogitans" with an aspiration to infinity is predicated on the infinite value of particularity. Since this value cannot be derived from anything in ancient or classical thought, it must be said that it is the claim of Christian faith, with the scandal of the particularity of God in Christ, which underlies the modern invention of philosophical subjectivity.[12] But since modern philosophy claims to be an autonomous philosophical activity, an activity which brackets off theology and the data of faith, it must somehow appropriate the claim of Christian faith without admitting that faith as data or evidence for its conclusions. Paradoxically, it is chiefly its misunderstanding of Anselm's Ontological Argument, that is, its obliviousness to the two ideas of God constituting the philosophical integrity of that argument, which enables philosophical modernity to appropriate the infinite value of particularity entailed by Christian faith without consciously admitting that faith as data or evidence for its invention of subjectivity.

What precisely is the philosophical integrity constituted by the relation of the two ideas of God in Anselm's Ontological Argument? The answer would seem to be that the philosophical argument of the *Proslogion* in its integrity is a faith seeking understanding by which the assent of faith to the positive idea of what God is for God is a search for an identity or oneness with the knowledge of what God is for man (the negative idea accessible to man by understanding). Man is not simply the being who has or can have these two ideas, but he is the being who is the very act of seeking the identity of what God is for God and what God is for man. Man is the very being who is constituted by the thinking of God, by the striving for the identity of what God is in himself and what God is for man. Man is the sign of God in the mode of negativity. Man is defined in terms of seeking (quaerens) an identity of God as he is in himself and God as he is for man—an identity which man does not make or even attain by himself but which is entirely the work of God. Man is defined in terms of a radical contingency, a fundamental finitude, which is a striving or aspiration to exist *in* the infinite. The identity of God in himself and God for man—an identity which man aspires to comprehend—is reflected in the concern of the infinite (God) for reconciliation with the finite. In this way, the Ontological Argument in its philosophical integrity is a raising of the human mind to participation in God's self-knowledge—a self-knowledge which this mind does not possess by its nature. The Ontological Argument in its philosophical integrity is a raising of the human mind by God to a comprehension of the identity of what God is in himself and what God is for man.

But what we find in modern philosophical subjectivity is the primacy of the finite (human) *ego* as an aspiration for infinity *without* the raising of the human mind to God by God. It is almost as if the very dynamics of modern philosophical subjectivity lie hidden in Anselm's Ontological Argument, only awaiting their being raised into the dimension of one-sidedness by modern philosophy—awaiting their "invention," as if that invention were simply a "discovery" by moderns within the theoretical contents of modernity alone. Modernity, to its core, is about more than itself, but its primary notion of subjectivity can emerge only to the extent that it can perceive itself as exclusively about itself—only to the extent that it can misperceive the philosophical integrity of the identity of God in himself and God for man in Anselm's single and self-sufficing argument.

For both the positive idea of faith and the negative idea of human understanding, in Anselm, God is an "aliquid," a preeminently particular being, an absolutely unique being, and not a universal intellect or mind. God cannot be conceived except as a unique being, so that nothing else can be thought to be like him.[13] What joins the positive and negative ideas of God—both in terms of the identity which God gives and the identity which man seeks—is the particularity of God, God as the absolutely unique and unconditional subject of being. It is here that the Ontological Argument in its philosophical integrity is seen to be not simply a moral argument but a metaphysical argument, an "ontological" argument, an argument which establishes the existence of a real "aliquid" independently of man's understanding and his moral needs. What man needs and *what ought to be there*, if man is to exist and to exist well, *is*, in fact, *what exists*. Only because God exists is man the utterly contingent, finite desire for the infinite. Man *is* the desire for God; and the desire for God is the seeking for what binds together what God is for man and what God is for and in himself. Man, then, in his particularity, i.e., the "mens mea," *is* the Ontological Argument for God's existence.

It is thus not without cause that Hegel spoke of Anselm's argument as the "first properly metaphysical proof of the existence of God," which contains the "depth of the Idea in the modern world."[14] But philosophical modernity's appropriation of the depth of this notion of God as the subject of being is one-sided by virtue of modernity's attempt to absorb the Anselmian idea of the human mind as a finite aspiration for infinity, while transforming the Anselmian negative idea of human understanding into a positive content of the human mind, an idea among ideas within the human mind. The development of the dynamics of modern philosophical subjectivity requires this one-sidedness. But if the source of the dynamics lies in the depth of Anselm's Ontological Argument, it would seem that philosophy should henceforth be committed to overcoming this one-sidedness—notwithstanding Feuerbach's attempt to remove this one-sidedness by dissolving the ontological claim implicit in the source of the dynamics of modern philosophical subjectivity.

Both the Cartesian attempt to put Anselm's idea of faith outside of first philosophy and the attempt by Feuerbach to reduce this idea to the alienation of man's nature—in their own peculiar ways—display an obliviousness to Anselm's realization that it is not the nature of God to be unhidden, a forgetfulness of the repentance involved in the exercise of human understanding, a loss of balance between "aenigmata" and rational lucidity*—in sum, a progressive exclusion of mystery from first philosophy. And yet it is precisely the mystery of an absolutely singular God made an object of reason in Anselm's first philosophy which functions as the dynamic principle for the invention of a human subject—that transcends nature and cannot be made an object among objects—and for the systemization of that subjectivity. Reason's attempt to confront and uphold the mystery of God, the hiddenness of God, in Anselm's first philosophy, is precisely what must be used and misunderstood in order to overcome mystery programmatically in nature and man (thus the early modern refounding of first philosophy) and in order to dissolve the mystery of God (thus the late modern reduction of first philosophy to anthropology). Once again, the sign of the Christian mystery's being used and misunderstood in order to exsect—progressively and (very nearly) completely—mystery from philosophy is an inexpungible residue of

---

* See pp. 43, 211 above.

mystery haunting modern philosophical subjectivity—the "problem" of evil.

### iii. The Cartesian Regulative Notion

The second consideration for reflection on the Anselmian vortex of the historical travail of first philosophy is the operative presence of Anselm's so-called Ontological Argument as a regulative notion for the development of modern philosophical subjectivity. Our previous remarks on the first consideration (namely, the modern misinterpretation of this argument) suggest that both the misinterpretation of the argument and the argument's capacity to serve as a regulative notion for modern philosophical subjectivity have their source in Anselm's first philosophy where reason makes the mystery of the Christian God an object while, at the same time, reason never removes or dissolves the mystery that is made an object. The regulative notion for modern philosophical subjectivity, then, is a mystery addressed and upheld by reason. This mystery, the mystery of God and God alone, which is at the center of Anselm's notion of faith, is precisely the mystery of the Trinity. It is the mystery of the Trinity, operative *in* Anselm's first philosophy, which operates *outside* the categorical material of the Cartesian invention of subjectivity while, nonetheless, regulating that invention. No less is this regulative notion extrinsically present, largely as an unspoken dynamism, in Feuerbach's systemization of modern philosophical subjectivity. At this point, however, we will deal with the trinitarian dynamics of the *Cartesian* invention of subjectivity.

The medieval theological development of the mystery of God's triune nature—which Anselm inherited and incorporated into his first philosophy—attempts to articulate divine being as a paradigmatic self-consciousness. The generation of the Son (the Word) posits the otherness of the "self" of God to itself, while the spiration of the Holy Spirit from both Father and Son posits the oneness of God with himself. This otherness returning to oneness in God—this divine unity which transcends the very distinction between oneness and plurality—is at once analogized to nature (thus, the generation of the Son from the Father) and yet is held to transcend any analogy with nature (thus the spiration of the Holy Spirit which, although it is a metaphor drawn from nature, viz., breath, functions in the Trinity with no clear correspondence to the way in which it functions in nature). The procession of the Son or Word from the Father is a likeness-producing operation which proceeds by intellectual activity, whereas the procession of the Holy Spirit from both the Father and the Son is neither generation nor likeness-producing activity but is, instead, a kind of delectation or willing, i.e., a loving of the Father and the Son. The mystery of the Trinity, then, functions in terms of, as well as beyond, the confines of analogy to the operations of nature—at once pointing to a distinction between the understanding and the will as well as an identity of the understanding and the will in God. It is precisely the sense in which the Trinity transcends analogy to nature, i.e., the spiration of the Holy Spirit, that permits the trinitarian life of God, in the order of grace, to will itself outwardly and freely to man. The Holy Spirit, by operating in man and truly sanctifying and uniting man to himself, elevates man into a partaking of the divine trinitarian nature.[15]

Of all the medieval Christian mysteries, the Trinity appears to be the most fundamental; and of all medieval Christian doctrines, the Trinity appears to be the most purely theological—the one least explicitly founded in Scripture and yet seemingly least accessible to (philosophical) reason as such. However, the relation of the finite human self to itself—treating itself as other than itself while remaining one with itself—which is to be found in the Cartesian invention of metaphysical subjectivity might well be said to have had its first anticipation in the generation and spiration conceived as obtaining in the Trinity and absorbed by Anselm into his transformation of the Aristotelian founding of first philosophy. The otherness to self which is yet not different from the self in the mystery of the Trinity suggests itself as the paradigm for the Cartesian discovery of the finite self's ability to stand outside of itself as spectator of itself in the midst of its ineradicable identity with itself as *ego*.

## The Historical Travail of First Philosophy

The Cartesian "I think" appears to be a kind of generation of the "I" from the activity of thinking—a thinking which is of "one substance" with the "I." The Cartesian "I exist" appears to proceed from both the primal activity of thinking-as-doubting and the "I" itself and is, therefore, *of* both equally. The "I think" is an othering of the "I" which returns to unity with itself in the "I exist." In othering itself in *doubt*, the finite self returns to unity with itself in *certainty*: doubt and a fundamental certainty are other and yet one. Thus, the Cartesian *cogito* appears to be implicitly triadic—"at once a reflexive discernment of thought by itself and an immediate inference of existence by way of the discernment of a necessary connection between this case of thought and this case of existence."[16]

But if the Christian mystery of the Trinity is a kind of pre-structuralization of the development of Cartesian subjectivity, this mystery operates in a different way than the various explicit categories\* of Cartesian first philosophy operate and without being attended to by Descartes himself. The point is not simply that Descartes is unconscious of the trinitarian regulative notion for his thought; for, in a way, he can be said to have disavowed consciously this regulative operation to the extent that he brackets off theological categories from his autonomous first philosophy. The point is rather that his denial of his "genetic heritage" here is entirely consistent with its being *there* in full force—that Cartesian subjectivity requires as its paradigm something like trinitarianism. In Cartesian first philosophy, the notion of the Trinity does not operate among other categories (as it did in Anselm's first philosophy), but it is operative as a non-verbalized paradigm for the invention of subjectivity. This can be made explicit in several ways.

First of all, the Cartesian possibility of a world-encompassing doubt requires the assumption by the finite subject of a divine perspective capable of encompassing the world. This divine perspective could actually *inhere* only in a God who encompasses within himself a dialectic of self and "othering" of self. Some kind of preworldly "othering" of God within God—which, nonetheless, returns

---

\* See pp. 152 above.

to a unity (which was never lost) with itself—would have to be presupposed by the assertion of the otherness of world and God. In this way, the dialectic of otherness and identity immanent in the Trinity is the opera*tive* paradigm for the opera*ting* category of universal doubt in the method of Cartesian first philosophy.

Secondly, the possibility of the Cartesian *cogito* is implicitly modeled on the identity of essence and existence which is (later) applied by Descartes exclusively to God. But the inseparability of essence and existence in God is implicitly an identity which presupposes a distinction between the "what" of essence and the "that" of existence. The inseparability of essence and existence in God, in other words, presupposes a subject of being, a "whom" in which the distinction between "what" and "that"* is really an identity—a God who is a personal subject and not simply an impersonal substance. Once again, the identity of substance with person found in the Trinity, in terms of a dialectic of otherness and oneness, seems to be the tacit paradigm for the explicit category of the *cogito*.

Thirdly, there is Descartes' purported demonstration of God's existence not as an impersonal mind or universal essence but as a supremely particular entity who is the only member of its logical class and, therefore, exhausts the perfection of that class. But it is precisely the Trinity which first articulates the insight that God is not to be identified with a unity that excludes plurality,° that God is not to be identified with a pure universality or an impersonal mind. Of course, the use of the Trinity as a tacit paradigm and not as a verbalized category in Descartes' demonstration of God's existence would have to be maintained in such a way that God is not identified with the finite subject as such. And since thinking and existence are identical in the finite subject (as well as in God), the only point of difference between God and the finite subject is in the non-identity of thinking and willing in the finite subject and the identity of thinking and willing in God.** But the ground of the

---

\* See pp. 1, 18 above.

° See p. 38 above.

\*\* See pp. 139-140, 212 above.

identity of thinking and willing in God is precisely the unity in difference of spiration (modeled on volition) and generation (modeled on intellection) in the Trinity.

All of this suggests that the Cartesian finite subject, although analogous to nature, transcends analogy to nature, much as the relationship of the Son to the Father in the Trinity is analogous to nature, while that of the Holy Spirit to both the Father and the Son transcends analogy to nature. The sense in which the Cartesian "natural light" of reason is a shining-forth of a more-than-natural consciousness in the finite subject would thus appear to be the sense in which the finite *ego* proceeds from itself and not from the world—a kind of infinitely *spirating* (or aspiring) finite subject.

Of course, there is something missing in Cartesian subjectivity which is characteristic of the Trinity, viz., the pure activity of contemplation itself, i.e., the contemplation of mystery. There is no seventh day of meditation (no return to contemplation of mystery) on Descartes' part but only the six days of the divine triune work of Creation now assumed as the perspective of the Cartesian meditator. The final end of Cartesian and modern philosophy is no longer the contemplation of mystery proper to the unending seventh day, the "perpetuum sabbatum," which is the beatific vision of the triune God, but which has already begun to be observed in this life, according to St. Augustine, by virtue of God's grace. The final end is now practical knowledge, the knowledge which enables man to gain mastery over nature. The human mind, consequently, is not turned outward in contemplation of the mystery of God who is above that mind in being present within that mind, but is turned inward in meditation,[17] drawing out from within itself its own intelligibility, much as within the triune inwardness of God, the Word is generated from the speaker of that Word, and the divine will proceeds from both the Word and the speaker of that Word, while each utters himself and the other two.[*]

The intelligibility of forms within the world has vanished entirely for Descartes and for modern philosophy. There is no mystery in

---

[*] See p. 41 above.

the world or in the clear and distinct ideation of the subject. Yet, the non-verbalized dynamics of the Cartesian meditator still reside in the medieval attempt (epitomized in Anselm's first philosophy) to derive the structure of the human soul from the relations obtaining in the Trinity. The *will* of the Cartesian meditator, after all, presupposes the notion of the self-identity of the *ego* at the center of knowing and acting—something that cannot be found in ancient philosophy. For Aristotle, for example, the knowing and acting agent is a knower and actor *within* what is known and within the action itself: man can have no domination over that natural world of which he is merely a part.[18] There is, then, as F. Edward Cranz points out in his stimulating treatment of Anselm's novelty as a thinker, a single order where understanding and thing are inseparably conjoined, for ancient philosophy. But Anselm breaks with the ancients here as, seemingly for the first time, he finds an explicit distinction between what is *in* the understanding and what is *in* the order of things;* and the whole force of the Ontological Argument depends on this distinction. Whereas the ancient emphasis is entirely on the being of being*s* and on the mind only insofar as it contains beings, for Anselm the emphasis is on meaningfulness and meanings and on the things outside the mind only insofar as they are taken into the realm of meanings.[19]

It is Descartes who completes and finalizes Anselm's departure from the ancient notion of a single order where understanding and things are inseparably conjoined in knowledge. In this way, Descartes addresses human thought meditating on itself and drawing out from within itself its own intelligibility. In doing this, the tacit Cartesian model is Anselm's attempt to ponder the human mind in terms of the relations holding within the Trinity. The dialectic of otherness and selfsameness, of unity and plurality, of intellection and volition, of analogy to nature and transcendence of nature within the Trinity is precisely the dialectic in terms of which the "mens mea" as an image of the Trinity is examined by Anselm. The distinction between what is *in* this "mens mea" and what is *in*

---

* See pp. xiv, 60, 86 above.

the order of things finds its model in what is *in* the trinitarian life of God and what is *in* the order of created things. In Anselm, however, there are profound disanalogies between the trinitarian life of God and the human mind; that mind, after all, is still part of the order of nature. But in Descartes these disanalogies have dwindled and, in a sense, only one significant disanalogy remains, the absence of an identity of knowing and willing in the human subject.

Of course, in its later stages, most especially in Feuerbach, modern thought reverses the Anselmian procedure and attempts to derive the dynamics of what it calls the "God-hypothesis" from the triadic structure of the Cartesian *ego*.*[20] But such a reversal—if, in fact, the "genetic heritage" of the Cartesian *ego* lies hidden in its development and destiny—might be an index of the consummate subtlety with which the very attempt of modern thought to exclude mystery from philosophy was preconditioned by the Christian notion of mystery. The *production* by human thought of its objects in the same activity by which it understands these objects,[21] which Descartes proposes and Feuerbach upholds, is not, after all, something discoverable by unaided reason but requires a paradigm that could not have been discovered by that reason alone—requires the proposal of a mystery extrinsic to unaided human reason as such. An activity that is at once contemplative or theoretical *and* productive or creative would not be—in and of itself—a properly human or natural activity, accessible to human reason as such or capable of being found in nature. The proof here is that such an activity is not even a possibility for Aristotle's first philosophy. For Aristotle, God is in no way productive, and the human act of knowing is never simultaneously contemplative and productive.

### iv. The "Essence" of Feuerbach

The regulative notion constituted by the trinitarian mystery is no less present extrinsically to Feuerbach's systemization of subjectiv-

---

* C. G. Jung remarks that the "medieval mind finds it natural to derive the structure of the psyche from the Trinity, whereas the modern mind reverses the procedure."

ity than it was to Descartes' invention of subjectivity. The difference, however, is that in Feuerbach the Trinity is explicitly treated as an alienation of the triadic essence of the Cartesian *ego*. Feuerbach, in other words, presupposes the triadic essence of the Cartesian finite *ego*. But in presupposing it, he also presupposes, although he never adequately articulates, the significance of the Christian mystery of the Trinity in relation to the Christian mysteries of Creation "ex nihilo" and the Incarnation. We should, in the first place, consider, apart from Feuerbach, the relation of these mysteries.

It is the mystery of the Trinity, in which God is first conceived as father and not as maker, which permits God to be conceived in the doctrine of Creation as maker and not as father.[*] These two operations, which Plato, in proposing the "demiurge" in the *Timaeus*, had conceived somewhat confusedly as terminating upon the same matter, are each held, by traditional Christian theology, to terminate with a distinct "object"; the father imparts his own essence to what he generates, but the artificer or creator does not. It is precisely this distinction which permits modern philosophy and science to assume that the things of nature, which it investigates, are artificial (i.e., products) and not ensouled, animate, or "personal" forces. It is, in other words, the notion of God's mind as freed from the limitation of the Platonic demiurge—viz., the limitation of being directed to a matter which exists alongside the divine—which permits the human mind to be conceived by modern philosophy as freed from this limitation.[22]

Creation "ex nihilo," then, presupposes a God who is absolutely unique, who would exist if there were no world, i.e., a pre-worldly Trinity, in order to postulate the otherness of the Creator and his creation. This otherness finds its expression in the ineradicable temporality of creation and the absolute timelessness of the Creator. The temporality of creation is willed by a God who is absolutely timeless. This means that the infinite distance separating God and creation does not preclude God's willing to communicate

---

[*] See p. 39 above.

the mystery of his trinitarian life—although it does not necessitate this communication—to man as the measurer of the temporality of creation. Far from entailing a merely potential and possibly meaningless status for time—a status which is intimated by ancient philosophy where, as Aristotle makes clear, becoming is the revelation of a defect—the temporality of creation entails for human life, as the measure of time, the character of an intense temporal struggle concerning what existence in time *ought* to mean and, therefore, does mean. But it is in the Christian mystery of the Incarnation—where Christ is true God (and not merely the appearance of God) and true man (and not merely the appearance of man)—that the significance of temporality and man's measuring it are theologically secured by virtue of a freely willed entrance of divine timelessness into time.[23]

The mystery of the Trinity thus operates theologically as the ground for the doctrines of Creation "ex nihilo" and the Incarnation. Creation "ex nihilo" requires a fruitful God with his own unique kind of life and relation to himself who can at once produce, distinguish, and find good a created being which need not have existed, which contains no matter that could be eternally co-existent with God, and which is absolutely other than God. And God's becoming man in the Incarnation is permitted and saved from pantheism (i.e., God's becoming his creation) by a trinitarian theology which allows God to remain God—the God who *is* his own life and not the life to be found in the world—while becoming a particular member of his creation. It is thus the import of the personality of God affirmed by the mystery of the Trinity which runs through Creation "ex nihilo" (where God's freely willed creative activity terminates upon particular entities and not upon universal essences) and the Incarnation (where the scandal of particularity and of the meaningfulness of time is boldly asserted).

It is the significance afforded particularity by the Trinity, then, which lies behind Anselm's conception of "that than which nothing greater can be conceived" *and* that which is greater than can be conceived. As Karl Barth points out, Gaunilo's failure to comprehend the true nature of Anselm's ontological claim is due to the fact that he took God to be a general concept and he presupposed the existence of God to be that of a universal. Gaunilo failed to recognize that if God exists, he exists as the only being who really *fully* exists, so that all that is not God exists only within the purpose of God's willing, i.e., only by the Word of God's trinitarian being. Gaunilo failed to see, in other words, that God exists as an absolutely unique particular being whose essence can only be sought in prayer and known by a knowledge that is permeated and circumscribed by mystery and divinely bestowed on man. It is his failure to appreciate this which leads him to fear—in Anselm's notion of the negative idea of God (which Gaunilo misperceives as positive) as a particular thing had in the understanding—something akin to what Feuerbach asserted, namely, the notion of man as the creator of God.[24]

Feuerbach's failure might very well be said to be the same as Gaunilo's failure. Feuerbach seems to conceive God, as such, as a universal\* and is blind to the absolutely unique existence of God posited by Anselm, in which God does not exist in the way that created things exist. Gaunilo's criticism of Anselm presupposes that Anselm's notion of the impossibility of God's nonexistence is grounded on the necessity of certain universal ideas. Gaunilo even intimates that Anselm's argument might be able to be applied to the necessity of Anselm's own existence. In this way, Gaunilo seems to anticipate as a possibility what Descartes asserted as a necessity. What Gaunilo fails to appreciate is also precisely what Descartes and Feuerbach fail to appreciate, namely, Anselm's realization that all thinking *about* God has to begin as a thinking *to* God.[25] Thinking about God must begin with reason's confrontation with the absolutely unique, particular, being of God, with the mystery of the particularity of God presented by the Trinity. Nonetheless, Feuerbach must tacitly presuppose the notion of the Christian mystery of the Trinity in relation to the Christian mysteries of Creation "ex nihilo" and the Incarnation in order to argue that the triadic essence of the human *ego* is the logic of this mystery

---

\* See pp. 169 above.

and, therefore, that this mystery is no longer a mystery. But it is only by removing the mystery of particularity from the Christian triune God that Feuerbach can claim to have demystified "God" and to have uncovered the "secret" of theology as anthropology.

The intellectual landscape of first philosophy has never quite been the same since Feuerbach set foot on it. What had been called "natural theology" is now seen to be a landscape framed by anthropology. Yet, despite all the fundamental changes of this landscape set forth in the map he constructed, Feuerbach would be the first to admit that he was only a listener and interpreter—that he was following footsteps already left upon the speculative terrain of first philosophy. Feuerbach's charting of this terrain, his attempt to bring the travail of first philosophy to a halt in atheism, produced a new map only to the extent that it turned the old one upside down. For the seemingly unprecedented wanderings of Feuerbach have their precedent in Gaunilo's defense of the "insipiens" and in Gaunilo's failure to take into account the mystery of divine particularity. If it is the case, however, that Feuerbach has surpassed Gaunilo in defending the "fool," Feuerbach has not been able to reach beyond Anselm. Feuerbach, in the end, is a response *to* Anselm.

If Feuerbach's claim—that at the heart of Christian theology lies a self-contradiction and a kind of inverted atheism—cannot be sustained by him because he fails to recognize the particularity of the divine, the absolute uniqueness of God, entailed by the mystery of the Trinity, then his contemporary readers would be called back—in a way and to a degree not experienced by Gaunilo or Descartes or even Feuerbach himself—to a reflection on *Anselm's claim* in first philosophy. Anselm's claim is that at the heart of atheism—as a lived and not merely a speculative denial of God's existence—lies a self-contradiction and an inversion of Christian theology. In the medieval world—given Anselm's reply to Gaunilo's defense of the fool—it is the believer who has the last word. But in the modern world—given Feuerbach's response to Anselm's reply—it would seem to be atheism which has the last word. The question, however, is whether or not in contemporary or so-called post-modern culture the word of atheism is truly last. The question is whether or not the travail of first philosophy has been truly brought to a close in atheism or merely removed by eliminating first philosophy itself.

In referring to modern subjectivity as found in Hegel, Heidegger remarks that the "I" is, to begin with, a "unity" which relates itself to itself not immediately, but through abstracting from its content and determination, and returning to the freedom of its unbounded equality (schrankenlosen Gleichheit) with itself. In this way, the "I" is both "universality" and "particularity."[26] Modern subjectivity would thus seem to model itself on Anselm's notion of God as the subject of being, except that, unlike the human "I," the divine subject of being is immediately related to itself, i.e., its relation to itself is not mediated by time but is eternity as such, viz., the timeless processions of the Trinity. Descartes absorbs the timeless processions of the Trinity into the "I," the finite subject, but this subject, he admits, cannot perpetually and timelessly hold itself fixed to one thought,* and to this extent the processions become temporally mediated in the human *ego*. This *ego* is the temporal subject, the subject who measures time, whereas God is thought by this subject as the timeless, i.e., infinite, substance. Feuerbach's reduction of God to the human essence alienating itself from itself, presupposing Cartesian subjectivity as it does, is thus the reduction of timelessness to temporality as measured by man. The timelessness of the trinitarian processions is seen to be nothing more than the human self's consciousness of being a measure of time. The whole thrust of Anselm's dialectic, on the other hand, is that temporality is unintelligible unless it has an internal relation to the timelessness of the trinitarian processions in God—to that than which no greater can be conceived *and* that which is greater than what can be conceived. This would mean that for Anselm the divine subject of being is the being of timelessness that has freely willed to enter into time, i.e., a kind of "timed-timelessness." The human mind is the

---

\* See p. 132 above.

being of time that has entered into or, rather, been raised into timelessness, i.e., a kind of "timeless-time."

Heidegger asks "Whether time itself discloses itself as the horizon of being?"[27] The travail of first philosophy, in its historical journey from substantiality to subjectivity, raises the question of whether temporal subjectivity is the horizon of the timeless being of God. For Anselm, it would seem, God is the horizon for what would later be called subjectivity, whereas for Feuerbach, subjectivity is the horizon for what had earlier been called "God." But for Descartes, subjectivity as the horizon of divinity has an explicit priority, while the idea of God as the horizon of subjectivity has an implicit priority. Anselm begins with God and ends with the issue of man's desire, i.e., with his joy. Descartes begins with his own doubt and ends with God, i.e., the idea of God. But Feuerbach holds the beginning, midpoint, and end to be entirely human. Feuerbach thus claims that what Anselm begins with and what Descartes ends with are in essence nothing more than that with which Anselm ends and that with which Descartes begins.

The logic of first philosophy as theology, for Feuerbach, is thus anthropomorphism; and the trinitarian dynamics of modern subjectivity is nothing but the dynamics of the self in its imagined extraworldly processions. The human self which exists "as a force counter to what is—society, education, the past, indeed, all of nature"[28]—is the sole content of this trinitarianism. But what is decidedly absent from Feuerbach's contention here is precisely a sustained and critical analysis of the logic of anthropomorphism itself. If there is a genuinely *historical* travail undergone by first philosophy, i.e., if first philosophy is in some fundamental fashion a history of itself in which the movement from substantiality to subjectivity is effected, then the logic of anthropomorphism itself is an absorption of what we might be inclined to call "theomorphism." "Theomorphism" is taken here to mean the projection of the attributes of a God who is absolutely unique, who is the very mystery of particularity, onto the human subject. In this way, what Descartes begins with—the *ego*—is historically permitted as a starting point precisely by virtue of that with which Anselm began.

Human subjectivity is at once an invention and a discovery,* but as such it is historically situated within a series of *ontological* claims. These ontological claims are effectively banished by Feuerbach's reduction of first philosophy to anthropology; and this reduction (with its anthropomorphic logic) effectively subverts the invention and discovery of subjectivity. The condition here for the invention or discovery—namely, the mystery of God as a procession within himself which transcends analogy to this world—cannot simply be cast off as a scaffolding which is no longer necessary after the fact of the invention or discovery. God is not really a scaffolding for the discovery of subjectivity but is nothing less than an ontological ground for its invention. And if the term "God" entails no ontological claims, then the radical subject that is man has no ontological supports. Intersubjectivity in and by itself cannot be a ground for subjectivity but only a superstructure imposed on Cartesian subjectivity. Subjectivity cannot be its own ground. A God who personally proceeds from himself, without requiring the being of the rest of nature, is either the principle of subjectivity for the modern human subject or else there is no principle of subjectivity for that subject. Take away the ontological claim of God's existence and all that subjectivity is left to be is an entirely "private self-defining impulse, a *feeling* of self, beyond law, above time, and without limit,"[29] an ontologically unanchored "res." And this may be, notwithstanding the attempt which he made to situate this "res" intersubjectively, what subjectivity has become in Feuerbach and for many who follow in the wake of his thought.

The disappearance for all practical purposes of the debate between atheism and theism in the contemporary world does not alter this outcome. It may very well be that both atheism and theism can only attempt to function today in a culture which is fundamentally uninterested in their debate precisely because the human subject and its presupposition of the infinite worth of the human individual only function, in the present context, on the level of feeling or sentiment. Yet, the disappearance of the nineteenth-

---

* See pp. xiv, 54, 97-98, 146, 150, 161, 220-221 above.

century debate and the reduction of subjectivity to the status of feeling do not as such mean the evaporation of the question of the ground of subjectivity. This question is there to be recalled to the extent that the historical travail of first philosophy is there to be appropriated. The question of the ontological ground of the radical human subject will not be able to be dissolved. It must be raised or—in the tradition of "avoidance-thinking*—ignored.

The question which underlies all of medieval culture, namely, the question of the relation of faith and reason, has its medieval solution put outside of modern thought by modern thought itself. But it can do this only by attempting to carry "medieval principles to a higher level of comprehension."[30] Feuerbach's attempt here does not yield a higher level of comprehension; it yields only one variety or another of reductionism—ultimately a reduction of language about God to the language of intersubjectivity. And yet, Feuerbach's attempt—the attempted break with the speculative dimension of philosophy—is itself significant in terms of its reductionism. The real "essence" of Feuerbach's reductionism lies outside the confines of Feuerbach's thought in his attempt to re-defend the "fool," in the ontological claim to which he responds—namely, that the denial of God's existence presupposes the existence of something affirmed by faith—which Anselm made an object for first philosophy. Feuerbach—when considered properly in the context of the travail of first philosophy—summons us back to this ontological claim. But this "return" to Anselm is not simply a return to Anselm. It is, rather, a question of what will be done with the logic of the so-called Ontological Argument and modern philosophical subjectivity by contemporary philosophy *if* (and *as*) it reassesses its tasks at the end of the twentieth century and reevaluates its relation to its own past.

### v. That by which Man is Man

Western Civilization, as our inheritance, has proven to be a civilization with two beginnings and, in a sense, two lives. Its first and

---

* See p. 91 above.

absolute beginning is in Greece and finds its consummation in Rome: Western Civilization as the civilization of the Mediterranean world. Its second and derivative beginning is in Rome: Western Civilization facing outward on the Atlantic, the civilization of medieval and modern Europe. Essential for the two lives of Western Civilization—for its absolute beginning and its very continuance—is the notion of the world, of the *cosmos* and, therefore, the question of the nature of being itself such that it can constitute a world. The beginning of philosophy and the absolute beginning of Western Civilization are very nearly coeval; and ever since, the question of first philosophy, the question of being *qua* being, has been tied up with the two lives of Western Civilization. Corresponding to the historical travail of the values of Western Civilization, then, is the historical travail of first philosophy. And first philosophy too has had more than one life.

The first life of the question of being is in terms of what is by nature—being as the realization of form in nature—and corresponds to the absolute beginning of Western Civilization, to the emergence of Athens. The second life of the question of being is permitted by the reciprocal influence of Jerusalem and Athens and results in the transformation of the meaning of Rome—the unity in difference of Athens and Jerusalem in Rome. This second life of the question of being is in terms of the relation between the contingent being of nature and supranatural being—being as the uncreated subject for what is contingently realized in nature. This second life of the concept of being corresponds to the medieval European *phase* of the second life or second beginning of Western Civilization. The third life of the question of being is in terms of the more-than-natural being of man and the "naturalization" of that being—being as the finite subject constituted by an aspiration to infinity. This third life of the question of being corresponds to the modern European phase of the second life of Western Civilization: modern culture with its seemingly infinite aspirations. Facing outward, as it does, on the Atlantic Ocean, this second life of Western Civilization issued in the "discovery" of America which seems to be nearly coeval with the "invention" of subjectivity.

The third life of the question of being, in a sense, raises the question of a possible third life for Western Civilization, namely, the absorption of that civilization, for better or for worse, in a world-wide technological order. A planetization of the values of Western Civilization—to the extent that these values permitted (and, therefore, are somehow locked inside) a technological social order—could, of course, mean the destruction of these values in favor of a purely technological culture (made possible by these values but no longer requiring these values). But it could also mean a third life for Western Civilization, a maintenance of this civilization on new terms, provided, that is, the third life of the question of being can be sustained on new terms.

It would seem that at the present juncture of Western Civilization, the humanization of being, the *subjectivization* of being, could just as easily lead to the *subjection* of being to human technical consciousness—to a realm of pure instrumentality and technique—as it could lead to something quite different, viz., technical consciousness in the *service* of values that are more-than-technical and congruent with the highest dignity of human being. This second alternative is probably a good deal more difficult to spell out than the first. But if the lives of the question of being are so intimately tied up with the lives of Western Civilization, then the possibility of this second alternative has a lot to do with the possibility of a rebirth of first philosophy out of its own ashes, out of the residue of the travail of first philosophy which still remains in the reduction of that philosophy to anthropology.

If the travail of first philosophy involves, in some fundamental sense, a "quarrel between the ancients and the moderns" that is concerned, perhaps even from the beginning, with the "status of 'individuality',"*"[31] then any contemporary reappropriation of the significance of that travail would have to pay a great deal of attention to what intervenes between antiquity and modernity. The binding of being to time in the late modern and contemporary

---

* Thus, e.g., the εκαστος in Aristotle (see pp. 1, 3 above) and the "mens mea" in Anselm and Descartes (see pp. 204, 160-161, 114, 71, 59, 42, 36-37 above).

world—a world obsessed with novelty—if it can lead to the attempt to reduce first philosophy to anthropology, is nevertheless dependent on a "new" view of time and novelty which first suggested itself in the notion of "creatio ex nihilo" (with its trinitarian context) during the medieval European phase of the second life of Western Civilization. In this way, the attempt to reduce first philosophy to anthropology poses, for philosophy in the contemporary setting, the possibility of finding a path for philosophy in the future which is quite different from this reduction but the elements of which are underneath and presupposed by this attempted reduction.

The modern sense of what Whitehead called "the infinity of the possibilities that confront humanity," the notion of what William James called the "everlasting coming of concrete novelty into being,"[32] seems to be inconsonant with the idea that something stands fast in being. Fairly constant throughout the travail of first philosophy has been the notion that being is somehow *there* and is subsequently spoken about. Language is a kind of be-speaking of what is *there* independently of language. This notion survives even when, in medieval theology, the Word of God is posited as bringing contingent being out of nothingness. To propose that language itself is the primordial mode of being, so that without saying of some kind, there can be no being, and to take this proposal as a central program for first philosophy would seem to pose enormous difficulties for the notion that there is something that stands fast in being. The notion that language is a bespeaking of a being that is already *there* would have to be a primary stance—a persistently held position—in the fortunes of first philosophy. We see this, from the beginning, in the classical Greek interpretation of language as oriented into stating something about *things*. Common to both the first philosophy of Aristotle and that of Anselm is the supposition that language is not simply a work of man, but that language itself "speaks" as a being that is more fundamental than man and more fundamental than *human* language.

But if there must always be a sense in which language is a bespeaking of a being that is there, could there also be another sense in which language is a coming into being of something which is not-yet (and which could or could-not be)? This would mean that being is *there* for language, but that being also speaks in the "space" of non-being or nothingness. Language is a bespeaking of being, but being is a primordial saying. In this way we might speak of the emergence of new being, of "concrete novelty." But to think this way would be to see both language *qua* being and being *qua* language as mysteries intimately related to each other. Interestingly enough, the attempt to push language to a confrontation with its ground, the insight that the *verbum dei* is the very condition of human language,* the attempt to make the inconceivability of this *verbum* the object of conception—all of these features of Anselm's transformation of the Aristotelian founding of first philosophy—represent an attempt to see both language and being as mysteries profoundly related to each other. It is precisely the notion which Heidegger articulates, viz., that something can be inconceivable (unbegreiflich) and not primarily "disclosed," without thereby excluding from itself some kind of conceptual "mounting" (begriffliche Fassung),[33] which makes possible the task of theology embodied in the first philosophy of Anselm. For Anselm, language itself proceeds from and ultimately leads to the conceivability of the inconceivable.

The modern philosophical sense of man as a more-than-natural or supra-substantial subject, in the midst of man's being a body-soul composite in the context of nature, would seem to be predicated on the way in which the conceivability of the inconceivable underlies language. Man speaks because man *is* the desire for God, and this desire is the desire for the infinite, for something not of this world.° Speech, in other words, has its source in what "comes from without and not from within the order of nature, though nature is glorified and transfigured" by this source.[34]

The very significance that late modernity and the contemporary world afford philosophically to temporality and novelty would thus seem to be built upon the correlativity of the mystery of language

---

\* See pp. xvi, 63-64, 90 above.

° See pp. 221, 94, 67, 59, 52 above.

and being, notwithstanding the modern attempt to exsect mystery from philosophy. This correlativity finds its most salient expression in the notion of "creatio ex nihilo" with its roots in the trinitarian Word of God. Here is to be found the condition for the emergence of novelty in a contingent and temporal being, namely, the notion of a temporal beginning of being, a beginning unknown to the first philosophy of Aristotle. Here is also to be found the stumbling block for any attempt to afford novelty a metaphysical significance; for the notion of a temporal beginning of being, to the extent that it is entailed by "creatio ex nihilo," seems to be inaccessible to reason as such and, therefore, to first philosophy.

And yet, strangely enough, for all of the emphasis in Aristotle's first philosophy on the status of nature as older and larger than man, the assertion of an eternal and finished order of being might very well be a subtle projection of a human perspective on the being of nature—on the nature of being itself. In other words, the limitation of being in the human realm, i.e., the limitation of human things as experienced in the ancient world, might have been projected onto the fabric of being *qua* being. The notion of a beginning of being, on the contrary, for all the difficulty posed by its inaccessibility to first philosophy, suggests a nonhuman or more-than-human source for the being of nature and for the meaning of being as such. And the sense of this supranatural source would itself have to haunt any attribution of a metaphysical status to novelty and temporality by a humanism that has discarded the supranatural.

Behind the efforts of such a humanism to eliminate mystery stands the mystery of being and language: always and everywhere, the silence of what is; what is lies forever hidden and mute. And yet, being, always and everywhere, yearns to speak but needs the void (nothingness) to say what is hidden in itself. Thus it is that being makes an "inside" for itself by encompassing nothingness and replicating itself in this void within. Being "others" itself in speech, and insofar as being speaks out of itself and nothingness, being manifests itself as man. Being as manifested in this human subject need no longer be absent from what is other than itself. Having spoken itself, being erupts into the never-before, into the new, into the once-and-only-once, and proceeds to pass, frozen for the moment only in speech.

Being speaks about its speaking, and this act which is philosophy speaks about itself in first philosophy which, in turn, confronts the finitude of man and the limits of philosophy. And this means that being could not begin to be as man unless it could somehow speak at and before this beginning. Being as being is a beginning without beginning. It is not man as such that makes speech possible, but the primordial possibility of being's saying which makes man possible. There must be and have always been a Word to being, a mirroring of being within being, a mirroring of being in language within being. The being beyond beings, *who* says and is not silent, is as such hidden, the only mystery *per se*. But this Being beyond the beings of nature has freely disclosed itself in the context of the beings of nature. At the beginning without beginning of being, then, stands the being which permits being's coming to speak in and *as* man.

If the particularity, the subjectivity of man means anything, then, it *means* by virtue of a divine speaker of being. The attempt to reduce first philosophy to a pure anthropology is thus the negation of first philosophy, the forgetfulness of first philosophy. Such a negation is a negation of the human awareness of that *by* which man is man. If the "first" philosophy is to be anthropology, then man has ceased to wonder about that by which he is man. And to cease to wonder about this is to be left to affirm his dignity as an individual or a subject only in terms of the intensity of the feeling underlying the affirmation. Subjectivity without a rational ground can lead anywhere that feeling can lead. The malleability of the human subject can lead as readily to the gas chamber as it does to the lunar surface.

### vi. The Mystery of Evil

The last remaining hope in the face of an assertion of subjectivity and the "dignity" of the human individual which can only appeal to feeling is reflection on where the malleability of this individual can lead. This means reflection on the problem of evil which in its own subdued way runs through, as the least visible thread, the travail of first philosophy. Material for such a reflection is provided in passages from St. Augustine's *De Libero Arbitrio Voluntatis*. These passages set the tone for the appearance of the problem in Anselm's first philosophy and (to that extent) in the Cartesian refounding of first philosophy and Feuerbach's reduction of first philosophy to the categories of anthropology.

Whatever in nature has form, according to Augustine, has it by virtue of having number, so that providence can be seen in all things, in the entire number of creatures (universam creaturam). All good things, however great or small, are not able to exist except from God. Whatever in nature is praiseworthy is to be referred to the unutterable praise, the "ineffabilem laudem," of its framer. Such moral virtues as prudence, fortitude, and temperance cannot be "used" for evil. So why wasn't free will given to us in such a way that it could not be used except rightly? The answer is to be found in the fact that both greater and lesser goods do not exist unless from God.\*

We should not be tricked, then, Augustine admonishes, by virtue of the fact that the "intermediate and lowest" goods are able to be used for "evil," into forgetting that not only the great goods but also the least ones can be from no other source than from him from whom all good things derive, namely, God. The "abundance and

---

\* This could not become fully clear, according to Augustine, until the objection of the fool (who said in his heart, "There is no God") had been met. All good things exist from God. Much as the eye in the body is something good, although to lose it is not to be prevented from living rightly, "recte vivendum," even though it can be used for evil, so also free will is something good, and no one can live rightly without it, even though it can be used for evil. If, in fact, even the hairs of our heads are numbered (see p. 216 above), so that every species and form of body is derived from the supreme form of all things, the "rerum forma," i.e., from truth, and if, in fact, number has "supremacy" in nature, so that when we count the hairs of our head, however "lowly" they may be, they can be attributed to no other author than God as the Creator of all good things, then how can we not judge free will as a gift from God and as a good?

greatness of the goodness of God" are responsible not only for the great goods but also for the intermediate and lowest goods. If it is the case that the goodness of God ought to be praised more in the great goods than in the intermediate goods, and more in the intermediate than in the lowest goods, it is nonetheless the case that his goodness is to be praised more in *all* goods than it is to be praised were God not to have bestowed *all* goods.³⁵ For, as Augustine says in another of his works, everything that exists, however lowly it is, is rightly praised when it is compared with nothingness.³⁶

Even the sinner, whose will is "turned away" from immutable and commonly-shared goods toward a private good (proprium bonum) which is external or inferior to the will itself, is "ruled by the administration of divine providence" which ordains all things to their proper places (congruis sedibus). If follows that neither the goods which are desired by sinners nor the free will itself are "in any way evil." The "movement itself" of this will in sin is certainly evil, but this movement cannot be from God. Augustine must confess, then, that he is "ignorant" of the origin of this movement, for that which is nothing is not able to be known (sciri). When one takes away from nature what can be measured, counted, and ordered, there is absolutely nothing which remains. This means that there is nothing in nature which occurs that is not from God.³⁷

These considerations by St. Augustine set the tone for what St. Anselm calls the distinctions appropriate to freedom (dividas eandem libertatem) in his *De Libertate Arbitrii*. If the movement of the will to sin, St. Anselm remarks, to the extent that it originates from nothingness, is to be distinguished from the freedom of the will itself, then that will which is not able to be turned away (declinare nequit) from the rectitude of not sinning is more free than that will which is able "to desert" this rectitude. Therefore, neither freedom nor a part of freedom consists in the "power of sinning"; the "power" of sinning, when added to the will, "diminishes" the will's freedom.*

---

\* Those who sin, sin through their own choice (arbitrium suum) which is "free," but not through that by which it is free, namely, the power to be able "not to

But even God, who is able to reduce every substance that he has made from nothing back into nothing, is not able to separate rectitude from a will having it. Man is not able to be "deprived" of his freedom in any way—either by himself or by another. When the human will has rectitude, it does not have that powerlessness or incapacity for not sinning (impotentiam non peccandi).[38] The power of sinning is really the incapacity for not sinning.

The incapacity for not sinning, however, as the antithesis of the capacity for not sinning, is the antithesis of the power to be or exist, a power which finds its source only in God. As Anselm indicates in his *De Casu Diaboli*, there is a sense in which before (antequam) there was a world, it was impossible for the world to be, since the world itself could not have the power to be. But there is another sense in which before there was a world, it was possible for the world to be since in God there was the power for the world to be.

The power and powerlessness for not sinning, in fact, are best examined in the case of the good and bad angels. The fallen angel had not "deserved" to suffer evil because of any preceding sin. The fallen angel's sin was followed by the elevation of the "bonus angelus," through the merit of that angel's perseverance, so that he can no longer see anything more to want. The good angel thus has no need of the Ontological Argument since there is nothing more for him to desire. The fallen angel, however, willed to be like God (similis deo); yet, if to will to be like God were evil, the Son of God would not have willed to be like the Father (similis patri). The devil, then, must have willed *inordinately* to be like God in the sense that he willed what God did not wish him to will. The fallen angel presumed to have his own "private will" in the sense in which God alone ought to have his own will, namely, a will which "follows no superior will."[39]

---

sin." Freedom, then, is had precisely *for* the rectitude of the will, "rectitudinem voluntatis." Freedom of choice is the power of serving the rectitude of the will for the sake of that rectitude itself. Nonetheless, the will is not able to be overcome unless through its own power. The powerlessness of the will (impotentiam voluntatis) is precisely the will's "not being able to adhere perseveringly to its rectitude."

Now, just as nothing comes from the highest good unless it itself is good, so also nothing comes from the supreme essence unless it itself is an essence. But since the highest good is the highest essence, it follows that every good is an essence and "every essence is good." Nothingness or nonexistence, "non esse," being neither essence nor good, is not from God. This means that no thing can be called evil except an evil will (malam voluntatem) or on account of an evil will. If whatever is evil is not from God, evil would seem to "be" from created willing or the movement of the created will. But neither the will nor the turning (conversionem) of the will is able to be denied to be something (aliquid), Anselm thinks, for although neither is a substance, it cannot be proved that either is not an essence. Therefore, neither the evil will nor the "depraved turning of the will" as such is the *evil itself* by which the angel or the man became evil. The consequence is that an evil will is not itself what makes evil things evil, just as a good will is not itself what makes good things good.* But if the fallen angel willed with the will which God gave him, how did he sin? And if he had this will *from himself*, then he had something good which he *did not receive* from God, which is impossible.[40]

Since every essence is from God and is good, the will of the fallen angel and its orientation or "conversio," since they cannot be denied to be essences, cannot be denied to be from God. This means that the "disordered" will which is had by the fallen angel is itself characterized not only by the will to be equal to God (esse aequalis deo), but also by the will to be greater (maior) than God by willing what God did not will him to will. But since nothing greater than God can be conceived, the will of the fallen angel is at bottom the desire for nothingness. And Anselm, like Augustine before him, confesses that he is ignorant of what this nothingness is.

Anselm's ignorance here is facilitated by the ordinary usage of language, the "usus loquendi," in which things are sometimes said

---

\* See, in contrast, Kant's *Foundation of the Metaphysics of Morals*, First Section.

"improperly" and which leads him to ask how evil can be *nothing* if what the name signifies is *something*. If something or "aliquid" is not signified by this name, then it does not signify something, and if it truly does not signify anything, then it is not a name or "nomen." But "evil" is a name, and no one can deny that the name "nothing" is "significative." It must be the case, then, that these terms signify the removal of something but not in accordance with the thing (secundum rem) removed but in accordance with the form of speaking (formam loquendi). Evil, then, truly is nothingness, and nothingness is not something.* Yet we speak of evil or nothingness as if it were something. "Evil" is not said about that which is something but about that which is *spoken* of *as if* it were *something* (quasi aliquid dicitur).°

Much as the term "being" or "existence" must be predicated of God but does not as such signify God, so also the term "evil" or "nothingness" can be predicated of a movement of the will found in a fallen angel or a fallen man; yet what this term signifies is not as such evil or nothing but that which is not truly something (non vere aliquid)—a "quasi aliquid." Even the will of the fallen angel is from God "from whom is everything which is something."[41]

But if the problem of evil proves to be the problem of a nothingness which is spoken of as a *quasi-something*, then we must conclude that the problem of evil is insoluble within the confines of the very "creatio ex nihilo" which raises evil into a problem. The "problem" of evil is thus more than a mere problem. It is the inverse reflection of the mystery of a God who is absolutely unique and who created the world freely "out of" nothingness. And it is this "problem"—which is more than a problem—that moves uneasily in the background of the efforts of Anselm, Descartes, and Feuerbach. It is this "problem" which is at the bottom of the travail of first philosophy in its historical journey from substance to subject. It is this "problem" which is, paradoxically, the last hope for contemporary or so-called post-modern thought in order to move be-

---

* Malum igitur vere est nihil, . . . et nihil non est aliquid
° See pp. 68, 172 above.

yond the futility of "grounding" subjectivity on the non-ground of feeling.

What is common to Anselm's transformation of Aristotle's founding of first philosophy *and* Descartes' refounding of first philosophy is the denial of the rule of fate, the impossibility of an irrational substrate (matter itself) in nature* which is implicit to Aristotle's first philosophy, for which there is no problem of evil. In attempting to move beyond Aristotelian substantiality, in attempting to move to the being of the subject, first philosophy, in its travail, has assumed that every last iota of being is intelligible and good because God has made it. And even when there is no belief left that God has made it (as in Feuerbach), it is "creatio ex nihilo" (with its roots in the mystery of the Trinity) which is the non-verbalized paradigm in terms of which the denial of God's existence (or the reduction of God to an alienation of human excellences) is made. Evil can no longer be a flaw or failing in being, or a fate in nature, or a kind of irrationality, a resistance on the part of particularity to being governed by universality. Evil can only be, for the travail of first philosophy, an absolute nothingness which is spoken of *as if* it existed, as if it were something. Evil is a powerlessness which is absolute negation but which is spoken of as if it were a power, the power of nothingness. It is speech—created speech—which "loans" being to nothingness.

Since reason as such could never attribute being to nonbeing, the ultimate source of the attribution must be the will, but not the will as such (which comes from God) but the will's capacity in the realm of contingent being to will nothingness as if it were something. Behind the "power" of created speech to "loan" being to nothingness, then, stands the will. And it is the will which lies at the center of modern philosophical subjectivity—at the heart of the *ego* which, in contradistinction to the classical and even medieval notion of the soul, is spoken of as if it were more-than-natural, as if it would exist even if there was no world. This means that any attempt in first philosophy to maintain the existence of this *ego* (even

---

* See pp. 215, 212, 190, 108, 47, 13 above.

Feuerbach's version of intersubjectivity), in order to be consistent with itself, would have to confront the will's capacity to orient itself into nothingness, i.e., the problem of evil. But the problem of evil is a problem only in the context of a creationist and trinitarian view of existence, a view in which being is the divine power *to be* without being over against anything, i.e., the power to be over against nothing.

There can, then, be no ontological ground for radical human subjectivity other than that provided by the existence of a more-than-natural divine subject of being absolutely untouched in its essence by the powerlessness of nothingness. The rejection of this God's existence, consequently, entails the rejection or subversion of modern philosophical subjectivity and intersubjectivity. The only metaphysical way in which Feuerbach could have brought the travail of first philosophy to a halt would have been either to return to reflection on the "quiet eye" of Anselm's first philosophy *or* to reject subjectivity entirely and return to the Aristotelian God as a νοῦς* immanent in nature. Only by returning to Aristotelian first philosophy as the only "adequate" first philosophy could Feuerbach have been consistent in returning to the irrational substrate in nature, returning to one or another version of evil as a fate which stands above even the gods.

But Feuerbach could not entirely fail to realize that the "fate" of modern man is to be without fate—that the gods have departed, and that his burden, his travail, is to be free. Such a burden is not incompatible with a recurrent yearning for the return of the gods and an animated nature, and is proving more and more not to be incompatible with diverse political collectivizations in which the burden of individual freedom simply becomes too much for segments of society and even for whole societies. But "You are gods" addressed to men is not simply an occasion for joy but for woe as well, not simply a "plowshare" but a "sword" and a two-edged one at that. "You are gods" is not only not inconsistent with, but it is only

---

\* See pp. 16, 60, 81, 155 above.

plausible in terms of, "Thou alone art God."[*] The problem of the "power" of the powerlessness of evil—in its very inconsistency with the existence of the absolute power to exist of the Creator-God—is only *there* by virtue of belief (and the ontological claim entailed by such belief) in that God. The travail of first philosophy from substance to subject can make no ultimate sense out of the power of nothingness precisely because that travail cannot, in the final analysis, manage to make any sense out of the non-existence of the God of infinite *power* and wisdom—the God of Abraham, Isaac, Jacob, and Anselm.

Remove the ontological claim to the existence of this God and, in one anthropological motion, the problem of evil is removed, lifted from the heart of man. But in the same motion is removed the *metaphysical* ground of modern philosophical subjectivity and intersubjectivity and, with it, the overwhelming burden of the freedom of the individual. Feuerbach's attempt to cut this motion in half and to maintain subjectivity, while rejecting the ontological claim inherent in the notion of the God of infinite power and wisdom, *is* precisely its own philosophical falsification: the proclamation of the death of first philosophy, the end of philosophy as connected with wonder and mystery, and, therefore, the end of philosophy as such. If Descartes attempts to explain why first philosophy *need not* be done (but only physical science) by those who follow him, then Feuerbach's efforts amount to an attempt to explain why philosophy in its speculative and critical majesty *cannot* be done any longer in an intellectual milieu where the ontological claim entailed by belief in the existence of the God of infinite power and wisdom is no longer taken seriously.

The travail of first philosophy, consequently, brought to a stop by Feuerbach, raises the question of whether philosophy in its speculative and critical integrity can be done any longer. Certainly if it can still be done, it cannot be done without wonder; and wonder requires the confrontation with mystery. But mystery is not of man's making. The travail of first philosophy from substance to

---

[*] Psalms 82:6 and 86:10. Cf. John 10:34; Isaiah 41:23, 37:16, 2:4; Joel 3:10.

subject would seem to suggest that the description of philosophy as purely "unaided" reason is not entirely to the point, although, in the end, philosophy and *revealed* theology are not the same. In fact, the really intriguing thing about the modern philosophical invention and systemization of subjectivity is that its break with theology is itself conditioned by theology—a revealed theology, a theology operating with revealed data. And the really intriguing thing about the present age in which we live is that the beginning of a confrontation with the issue of *God and* subjectivity—with no residue of divinity in either nature or man's reason—might very well appear to be a confrontation with the issue of *nothingness and* subjectivity. If, then, there is to be an authentically *speculative and* critical philosophy in our times, it might very well come out of the relation of the human subject to what is perceived as nothingness—a nothingness which is dimly apprehended as what Sartre calls "an abrupt break in continuity" within the human subject which "can not in any case *result* from prior affirmations," an original and irreducible "consciousness of negation."[42]

Some relation to nothingness, some noticeably vacant space in the cognitive spectrum where God should be (and where he was in the travail of first philosophy) would now begin to be evident in the fabric of radical human subjectivity. In the midst of man's projects to control and master nature would appear what for the contemporary mind—conditioned as it has been for several hundred years by the project to extrude mystery progressively from philosophical consciousness—would have to be a surprise: a nothingness at the "eye" of the will which constitutes the center of the radical human subject or "I" who is controlling and mastering nature. The surprise would be the discovery, as Alexsandr Solzhenitsyn so masterfully articulates it, that the line dividing good and evil passes through the center of each human heart and that the struggle is with the evil *inside* the "I."[43] The surprise would be the discovery that beneath the will to power, the power of being, which modern man has appropriated for himself in his particularity, is the sense, as Heidegger puts it, in which man is holding a place open in his subjectivity for the negation of being, the sense in which "Der

Mensch ist der Platzhalter des Nichts," the sense in which man is the seat-holder, the "stand-in" for nothingness.[44]

Of course, this sense is already had by Descartes; and even Leonardo da Vinci could say that "among the great things which are to be found among us, the being of nothingness is the greatest." But this was for early modernity—for da Vinci and Descartes—no surprise, because Christian theology (even though put outside of Descartes' first philosophy) was still very much *there*—and with that theology the problem of evil. But for late modernity the "being" of nothingness—given the removal of theology—would have to be a surprise. Could it be that we today are now in the position to see the "problem" of evil as more than a problem—as the inverse reflection of *a* Being that has brought being*s* "out of" nothingness? If nothingness and the mystery of evil are thus able to put in an appearance in the contemporary world, the question is whether the theological dimension which is pervasive of all first philosophy (even when it renounces its theological character) is now "putting in an appearance."[45] The present age, after all, is what it is by virtue of the conjunction of biblical faith and Greek philosophy[46]—by virtue of the unity in difference of Athens and Jerusalem in Rome.

# Epilogue

The modern invention and systemization of subjectivity have "naturalized" in man a more-than-natural consciousness—melted down the supra-natural claims of Christianity into this-worldly alloy and minted it into a secularized coin. The dynamics of modern philosophical subjectivity has led to the refurbishment of the Protagorean "man-as-measure-of-all-things" but in an un-Protagorean and un-classical world where the measure is nonetheless infinite and every particular thing is meaningful. And this philosophical subjectivity is not as "easily shrugged off as Protagoreanism was," if the "'man' in question, each one of us in fact, is *imago dei* and personally related (though at some remove, in most cases) to the incarnate Word, the intelligibility of God."[1]

But in the world that modern subjectivity wove for itself, the divine has seemingly become another name for what is perceived as an infinite human capacity to create meaning out of the bare sensible manifold, with the resultant exaltation of human experience into its own ground of intelligibility.* William James had provided the codification here when he said that "truth grows up inside of all the finite experiences" which depend on each other, but the totality of these experiences depends on nothing. This means that "all

---

\* "When, in antique times, we held the universe to be finite," John McDermott remarks, "we also held that it was eternal. Human life had a fixed and natural place in this version of the world, and only *sub specie aeternitatis* could it play a permanently meaningful role in the cyclically repetitive flow of time." The cosmology of modernity largely interprets reality as "infinite and, on behalf of the doctrine of relativity, denies that we have a natural and fixed place. The paradox is that in the modern view time has no ultimate meaning, yet it does take on profound human meaning, for it is both unrepeatable and the distinctive way in which human life asserts its presence and significance in the context of infinite reality. Infinite space becomes increasingly domesticated by being subjected to human time."

'homes' are in finite experience," but this experience itself is "homeless," for "nothing outside of the flux secures the issue of it," and it "can hope salvation only from its own intrinsic promises and potencies."[2]

With the removal of a transcendent divine measure and ground, the absence of God becomes conditional for the autonomy of man. The historical task of naming God—which seems to define the significance of medieval theology—finds its bizarre fruition in a kind of namelessness of the divine *or* in a name which designates the human subject or modern culture's infinite aspirations. Thus the echo of Feuerbach's "Homo homini deus est" can be heard in our own times. We seem to inhabit a "world" that is really several worlds, since man is now a maker of worlds in which the measure of intelligibility is infinite and yet human. The unbounded will of man attempts to dictate the shape of reality, and the highest pursuit is that of individuality; and *yet*, human nature itself is perceived as infinitely malleable, and the meaning of the human as such is fundamentally in doubt.

Nonetheless, the problem of how we are to read the dynamics of modern philosophical subjectivity still remains. How can the modern philosophical negation of medieval theology—a negation which does not simply put aside this theology but incorporates it as well—be permitted to disclose its innermost significance? The pages of the contemporary text on the names of God seem to be blank. Is this a text that can no longer be written? Or is this a book, Feuerbach notwithstanding, that has yet to be written?

The invention and systemization of modern philosophical subjectivity constitute the strangest of all "glasses," at once distorting and faithfully rendering, reducing and magnifying, the medieval theological spectrum. St. John of the Cross once remarked that the sun's rays coming through a window are "less clearly visible" the purer and freer they are from dust and specks; and the more dust and specks there are in the air, the "brighter is the light to the eye." This is because the light itself is not seen but is only that by which the things that it strikes are seen, although the light itself comes to be seen through its reflection in the things it strikes.³ Thus might we raise the question of whether the very development of medieval reflection on the names of God and the absorption of that development by the invention and systemization of modern philosophical subjectivity have provided a clearer medium for the "light"—for what Scripture called the "lux inaccessibilis."*

Could it be that the ultimate consequence of the dynamics of modern philosophical subjectivity is not as such man's emergence into a condition where he perceives himself as divine but one where he can more clearly recognize the divine as something absolutely beyond human things? Could it be that the logical progression of the modern invention and systemization of subjectivity is really a progressive purification of the "specks and dust" surrounding the "optical instrument" capable of clearly disclosing the more-than-human ground of the intelligibility of what is—even and precisely when that intelligibility is held to be purely human? And if the medium for man's naming God has been so purified of anthropomorphic "impurities" that the purity of the light of understanding God has a medium which is truly fitting, would it not follow that the immediate consequence of the provision of such a medium would be a clouding of the vision of the light of understanding God—perhaps even an obsession with the new medium itself, with the "Licht des Geistes"°?

In this way, it might be suggested that the modern entrancement with the human subject as the measure of all things would itself be a sign of the discovery of a purer medium with which to name the divine, a discovery entailing a myopic vision in which what is seen is the "nothingness" of the divine. In this sense, one of the most subtle but reliable signs of a purified medium for naming God would be a love of and delight in the medium for its own sake—perhaps even an interpretation of the medium as the very meaningfulness of the light that shines through it. This medium, after all, makes the ontological claim to God's existence the proof of God's exis-

---

* See pp. 75, 78, 94 above.
° See p. 183 above.

tence: it proceeds from within the claim of faith, of the human heart. Faith here is made an object for human reason—a faith whose proper object (God) is beyond human reason. The primary meaning of Being here is to be independent of context, even the context of discursive thought itself—an infinite agency, a particular subject, God, who would exist even if there were *no* being of nature. The "proof" here, in fact, *is* the human self.[*] And this would mean that the autonomy of that self in the modern world is a byproduct of—perhaps even identifiable with—a new mode of discourse about God.

The ultimate purpose of this study of God and subjectivity has been to provide the beginning of a philosophical reflection on the meaning of the present age. If part of the meaning of the present age turns out to be the availability of a new medium for naming God, then the theoretical nature of this study of God and subjectivity proves to have certain practical implications.

A new medium for naming God is useless for those who are not concerned with or do not know how to use it. If the contemporary world has been singularly gifted, by virtue of its historical inheritance, it has not yet found its own version of the education that would permit it, on a significant scale, to be concerned with and to know how to use this new medium. It has not yet found its own peculiar version of the monasticism which issued in the birth of the medieval university. The place apart from its own time provided by medieval monasticism for an education in the very *meaning* of its own time and experience found its inspiration in the linguistic wealth of the Psalms, a wealth clearly in evidence in the first philosophy of Anselm. Both linguistic wealth and a place which is truly apart from its own time[4] appear to be what is lacking in our present age.

But what we lack is not unaccompanied by great wealth. We have behind us an extensive and rich history; our faith in the human individual has been shaped by the language spoken in a "conversation" among the great minds of the ancient, medieval, and

---

[*] See pp. 96, 221 above.

modern past of our civilization. Our attempt to enter this conversation is decisive. The alternative is to converse *only with* our contemporaries, *only in* the worlds that have been built in the last hundred years, and *only about* the electronic images of ourselves. What is needed, in sum, is an education in the more-than-technological conditions of our technology, the more-than-utilitarian conditions of our utilitarianism, the more-than-modern conditions of our modernity, and the more-than-subjective conditions of our subjectivity.

But though of the utmost importance, these practical implications are secondary in *this* study of God and subjectivity. What remains of primary importance for this study is a report on the history of the concept of being, a theoretical consideration of the possibility for approaching the profound relation of God to subjectivity in the contemporary world.

Our point of departure in this epilogue, namely, the metaphor of light, does, of course, have its limitations, if only that it seems to suggest that the way we go about naming God is a subclass of the way in which we name other things. If the medium for naming God has undergone a purification in the modern assimilation of the medieval theological heritage, an essential aspect of this purification would be a *distinct recognition* that we name God in a radically different way than we name all other things. Yet, this distinct recognition does not seem to be present in contemporary thought. On the contrary, the name of God seems to have become a name among names, much as the idea of God became an idea among ideas.* All names, it would seem, are now perceived as arbitrary, and so the name of God has become a psychological epithet.°

This would seem to be a telling criticism of the possibility that the contemporary world now has before it a new and purer avenue for approaching God. Unless, that is, we are too readily conflating the story and the story-teller, too readily assuming that the message of the contemporary psychologization of the Cartesian *ego* lies en-

---

\* See pp. 137, 149-150, 219 above.

° Cf. p. 2 above.

tirely in the psychological modality itself. Could the significance of contemporary psychologism, behaviorism, and relativism ultimately be something quite different from the psychological, the behavioral, and the relative? Perhaps we can raise this question through a somewhat indirect approach, that of a kind of fable.

Suppose, for a moment, that my words were somehow able to speak. Undoubtedly, they would note the existence of each other and thus name each other. But it would not occur to them that they themselves were words. After a while, the more intelligent of my words would take cognizance of the fact that they are speaking, and so they would begin to speak about their speaking itself. These more intelligent words would soon perceive that their speaking has a grammar. But they would presume that this grammar is nothing extrinsic to their speaking. This grammar would be seen as a "member" of their discourse.

But, suppose that I now enter the conversation of my words with one another, disclosing to them that they—all of them—are none other than my words. In doing this, I would have to speak about myself as the speaker of them. Some of them might accept me at my "word," while others might argue that I am simply another speaker like themselves—a speaker among speakers, so to speak. My departure from their conversation would likely occasion a debate which would last for a considerable length of time. Eventually some of my words might infer from my speaking about myself that they too can speak about themselves. And when the memory of my intrusion in their conversation became quite faint, some of them might infer that I myself am simply a word among their words, a kind of idealization of themselves. My words would be inclined to forget that their speaking about themselves—their absorption in and distancing from themselves—was something they could not have discovered by themselves.

Yet, their entrancement with the imaging of themselves would conceal a new kind of avenue for speaking about me as their original speaker. For in the midst of their denial of my existence, the one thing they would know is that if by chance I do really exist, I cannot be a speaker among speakers. If I am real, I must be a person who spoke them and not simply a vanishing-point toward which all their words are drawn—not simply the grammar which has membership in their discourse. On the one hand, their denial of my existence would be assumed, would be a given, in the fact of their fascination with their own powers of self-reflection. On the other hand, the linguistic avenue for their approach to my existence and to my relationship with them would be less clouded by hypotheses which they entertained about themselves prior to my intrusion in their conversation. The options would become more clearly defined. Either I exist and I spoke (and would exist without) them *or* I do not exist since they speak themselves and I could not exist without them. Either I am a word which they speak about themselves *or* I really exist as their speaker. Either I do not exist and the conditions for their self-consciousness lie entirely in that self-consciousness *or* I exist and there are more-than-psychological conditions for their self-consciousness.

Eventually the entrancement of my words with their own self-consciousness would wear off as that self-consciousness became more and more of a commonplace. The debate about the two options would be declared to have outlived its usefulness. As self-consciousness became less and less marvelous and more and more of a given (and not something to be wondered at), my existence as their speaker would seem less and less plausible and more and more preposterous. The faint memory of my intrusion in their conversation would now be perceived as their dream—their collective dream. Their name for me would now become simply a designation of how they would be if, in fact, they could bring words into existence which were capable of uttering words.

But the place in their consciousness once occupied by my intrusion into their conversation would never quite be filled by the positive assertions they make about their self-consciousness. Instead there would be a void in this place, a kind of nothingness that persistently refused to be filled up. For those of my words willing to reflect upon this nothingness, willing to wonder at the place they keep open for it, it will appear to be "something" that should not be *there* if the conditions for their self-consciousness lie entirely in that self-consciousness.

As this fable suggests, in a world where the name of God has become a psychological epithet, an epithet for designating the capacity of man's speaking to address itself, the medium for naming God becomes clearest at precisely that point where the vision of God becomes most proximate to seeing only darkness or nothingness. The possibility of a reborn search for naming the more-than-psychological reality of God, that is, the reborn search not only for the "nomen proprium" but for the "nomen personae" of God,[*] would have to proceed from the claim (and, most importantly, the conditions for that claim) of modern atheism—the claim that only darkness can enter the apertures of religious and metaphysical discourse.

The darkness, the nothingness, the absence of God in our time—an absence which, as Sartre said, is discerned everywhere, as the aloneness of man[5]—have, of course, been amply addressed by others and are presupposed by this study of God and subjectivity. But the question is what this nothingness and absence mean. It has only been recently that the gods of antiquity have departed, vanished entirely, not only from ordinary experience but from literature and art as well. In being left with a world without gods, in being left with *the* world, with *this* world and its temporality, we are left with a being which has an ineradicable nothingness as a residue at the center of its "power" to be. Any attempt, then, to ground our hope in *this* world or to conceive of God spatially or pantheistically is now decisively excluded. God can no longer be conceived to be *there* in any operative denotation of the word "there." Those who have claimed that God is only a name, a name with opiatic or narcotic effects, have shown, unknown to themselves, that we no longer need this kind of opiate, this kind of name.

In the most paradoxical of ways, we have narrowed the motives for wanting to name God. The only motive that can now effectively operate in desiring to know and investigate the name of God

---

[*] See pp. 207, 182, 64, 40-41, 39, 24 above.

is the quest for truth and the will to love the truth. Our contemporary confrontation with the being of time involves a confrontation with the nothingness at the center of time. But this nothingness should not be there if there *is* only human subjectivity, if there is nothing for subjectivity to be conjoined with. Radical subjectivity makes sense only as a mean between *God* and nothingness.* Radical nothingness makes sense only if there is a radical "something" or "aliquid" on the other side of human subjectivity. To confront this nothingness as the mystery it is and to make this mystery an object for metaphysical reflection, for first philosophy, is to raise again the question of God's existence—the question of the existence of "something" that is reducible to no other thing. The "eclipse of the light of God," Martin Buber reminds us, "is no extinction; even tomorrow that which has stepped in between may give way," namely, the human "selfhood that has become omnipotent" and that is now "the lord of the hour."[6] The place held for nothingness by the "imperial ego"[7] that has stepped in between is already the giving way of what has stepped in between. "To-morrow" has already begun.

Proclaiming the "death" rather than the eclipse of God in our own time, Nietzsche had said: "Is not the greatness of this deed too great for us? Must we ourselves not become gods simply to appear worthy of it?"[8] The preceding remarks, however, imply a reversal of Nietzsche's logic. Is not the greatness of our having become gods—of our having vanquished the gods—too great for us? Must we ourselves not proclaim the non-existence of the God we can now properly name and call upon in order to appear worthy of our having vanquished the gods? Having probed the Pascalian "silent" infinite spaces with his radio telescopes, contemporary man is nostalgic for the gods and listens for their messages. In his more reflective moments, he is frightened by his replication of the explosions of the sun and his impending manipulation of his own genetic code. What may be even more frightening is the possibility of being in the position to *know* God's existence as the necessary and

---

* See pp. ix, 128, 133, 146, 151, 152-153, 157, 206, 252 above.

ontological condition for the modern human subject in its status as the negative idea of that existence.

To be in this position is not at all inconsistent with or destructive of the *mystery* of God, the hiddenness of God, nor is being in this position a pretext for smugness or "dogmatism." On the contrary, being in the position to know is to think not like comfortable, disinterested observers on the shore but like drowning sailors. The history of the concept of being has been a travail. And the travail is *not yet* over.

Of all ironies, the greatest might be that after nine-hundred years, Anselm's single and self-sufficing "proof in prayer," which first explicated the necessity of the absolutely unique way in which God is named—an argument which, although largely unrecognized to be so, was the gateway to modern philosophical subjectivity—has come home to square away its debts with the "fool" *in all of us* who says in his heart "There is no God." The late modern attempt to name man as God ("Homo homini deus est"[*]) has turned out to be—in its very effort to use Anselm's insight against the conclusion of his "solo et brevi argumento"[9]—the occasion for thinking through the insight of Anselm in a way and to a degree that were not accessible to Anselm himself. It has taken nine-hundred years to remove painstakingly and fully the "specks and dust" surrounding the optical instrument for naming God which constitutes the "quiet eye," the "vortex," of the travail of first philosophy. But if the *Geschichte*, the travail, of the concept of being is not yet over, then any report on the life of the concept, at this point in time, must remain incomplete.

It is with this *sobering* realization that we must end—much as we had begun—our report on the life of the concept of being. The trivialization and anti-metaphysical stance of philosophy in recent times may have been an indispensable respite. But its hour is now over and it is time to think greatly, but "to think with sober judgment,"[°] and to think about the innermost meaning of the age, the

---

[*] See pp. 256, 184 above.
[°] Romans 12:3.

time, in which we live. We can only arrive at such thinking; we can never successfully start from it. For although we can only think about the meaning of the present as dwellers within that present, it is *not* merely *we* who understand this meaning *but a past* that permits this meaning to be understood.[10]

# Primary Texts and Translations

AB  *Saint Anselm: Basic Writings*. Translated by S. N. Deane. Introduction by Charles Hartshorne. LaSalle, Illinois: Open Court, 1962, Second Edition. (Contains translations of the *Monologion, Proslogion*, and *Cur Deus Homo*.)

AC  *Anselm of Canterbury*. Edited by Jasper Hopkins and Herbert Richardson. Six Volumes. Toronto and New York: Edwin Mellen Press, 1974-1976. (Volume One contains translations of the *Monologion* and *Proslogion*.)

AM  Aristotle. *The Metaphysics*. Greek text with an English translation by Hugh Tredennick. Loeb Classical Library. Volumes XVII and XVIII. London: William Heinemann Ltd. Cambridge: Harvard University Press, 1933; reprinted 1975.

AO  *S. Anselmi, Cantuariensis Archiepiscopi, Opera Omnia*. Edited by Franciscus Salesius Schmitt, O.S.B. Six Volumes. Edinburgh: Thomas Nelson and Sons, 1946-1961.

AP  Saint Anselm. *Proslogion*. Translated with philosophical commentary by M. J. Charlesworth. Oxford: At the Clarendon Press, 1965.

AT  Adam, Charles and Tannery, Paul, editors. *Oeuvres de Descartes*. Twelve volumes and supplement. Paris: Leopold Cerf, 1897-1913.

BS  *Biblia Sacra, Vulgatae Editionis*. Edited by Augustini Arndt, S. J. Vetus Testamentum (two volumes); Novum Testamentum (one volume). Regensburg, Rome, New York, Cincinnati: Fr. Pustet & Co., 1914.

DB  *Descartes' Conversation with Burman*. Translated with introduction and commentary by John Cottingham. Oxford: Clarendon Press, 1976.

Primary Texts and Translations

DG  *De Grammatico* by St. Anselm. Text and translation in *The De Grammatico of St. Anselm: The Theory of Paronymy*. Edited by Desmond P. Henry. "Publications in Mediaeval Studies." The University of Notre Dame. Volume XVIII. Notre Dame: University of Notre Dame Press, 1964.

DM  "Die Metaphysik als Geschichte des Seins" by Martin Heidegger. Chapter Eight of Heidegger's *Nietzsche*. Two Volumes. Verlag Günther Neske Pfullingen, 1961, Third Edition. Volume II, pp. 399-457.

EC  *The Essence of Christianity* of Ludwig Feuerbach. A translation by George Eliot of *Das Wesen des Christentums*, with an introductory essay by Karl Barth. New York: Harper and Row, 1957.

EF  *The Essence of Faith According to Luther* by Ludwig Feuerbach. A translation by Melvin Cherno of *Das Wesen des Glaubens im Sinne Luthers*. New York: Harper and Row, 1967.

EG  "Entwürfe zur Geschichte des Seins als Metaphysik" by Martin Heidegger. Chapter Nine of Heidegger's *Nietzsche*. Volume II, pp. 458-480.

EP  *The End of Philosophy* by Martin Heidegger. Translated by Joan Stambaugh. New York: Harper and Row, 1973. (Contains translations of DM, pp. 1-54, and EG, pp. 55-74.)

HR  Haldane, Elizabeth S. and Ross, G.R.T., translators. *The Philosophical Works of Descartes*. Two Volumes. Cambridge: At the University Press, 1911, reprinted 1977.

LE  *Lectures on the Essence of Religion* by Ludwig Feuerbach. A translation by Ralph Manheim of *Vorlesungen über das Wesen der Religion*. New York: Harper and Row, 1967.

OL  *Oeuvres et Lettres* de René Descartes. Textes présentes par André Bridoux. "Bibliothèque de la Pléiade." Paris: Editions Gallimard, 1953. (Contains the text of the Objections to the Meditations, Descartes' replies, and Descartes' Conversation with Burman.)

PP   *Principles of the Philosophy of the Future* by Ludwig Feuerbach. A translation by Manfred H. Vogel of *Grundsätze der Philosophie der Zukunft*. New York: The Library of Liberal Arts, Bobbs-Merrill, 1966.

RL   Rodis-Lewis, Geneviève, editor. Rene Descartes. *Meditationes de Prima Philosophia: Méditationes Métaphysiques*. "Bibliotheque des Textes Philosophiques." Paris: Librairie Philosophique J. Vrin, 1963. (Contains the Latin text, appearing in Vol. VII of AT, and the French translation by the Duc de Luyn, supervised by Descartes, in 1647, appearing in Vol. IX of AT.)

SW   Ludwig Feuerbach, *Sämtliche Werke*. Edited by Wilhelm Bolin and Friedrich Jodl, 1903-1910, with additional material selected and arranged by Hans-Martin Sass. Thirteen Volumes. Stuggart-Bad Cannstatt, 1960-1964.

TD   *Thoughts on Death and Immortality* by Ludwig Feuerbach. A translation by James A. Massey of *Gedanken über Tod und Unsterblichkeit*. Berkeley: University of California Press, 1980.

TF   *Truth, Freedom, and Evil: Three Philosophical Dialogues* by Anselm of Canterbury. Edited and translated by Jasper Hopkins and Herbert Richardson. New York: Harper and Row, 1967. (Contains translations of *De Veritate, De Libertate Arbitrii,* and *De Casu Diaboli*.)

WC   *Das Wesen des Christentums* by Ludwig Feuerbach. Edited by Werner Schuffenhauer. Volume Five (projected sixteen volumes) of Feuerbach's *Gesammelte Werke*. (East) Berlin: Akademie-Verlag, 1973.

WG   *Why God Became Man and The Virgin Conception and Original Sin* by Anselm of Canterbury. A translation, with introduction and notes, by Joseph M. Colleran of *Cur Deus Homo* and *De Conceptu Virginali*. Albany: Magi Books, Inc., 1969.

# Notes

## Prologue

1. Gerald J. Galgan, *The Logic of Modernity* (New York and London: New York University Press, 1982), pp. xi, xii, 401.

2. Ibid., p. 401.

3. See Martin Heidegger, *The Basic Problems of Phenomenology*, trans. Albert Hofstadter (Bloomington: Indiana University Press, 1982), pp. 111, 119.

4. Galgan, p. 346.

5. See F. Edward Cranz, "1100 A.D.: A Crisis for Us?," in *De Litteris: Occasional Papers in the Humanities*, ed. Marijan Despalatovic (New London Conn., 1978), p. 89.

6. Hegel is a far more formidable and significant systemization and completion of the logic of philosophical subjectivity than Feuerbach and is treated as such in Galgan, pp. 274-350.

7. See DM, p. 409.

8. Galgan, p. 401.

9. See Elmer O'Brien, S.J., ed., *Varieties of Mystic Experience: An Anthology and Interpretation* (New York: Holt, Rinehart and Winston, 1964), p. 282.

10. Martin Heidegger, *The Question of Being*, trans. William Kluback and Jean T. Wilde (New York: Twayne Publishers, 1958), p. 97.

## Chapter One

1. DM, pp. 399, 401-404, 406, 409. See EP, pp. 4, 5, 9.

2. AM, Vol. XVII, Book A, 988a, 35 to 988b, pp. 48, 50; 991b, 1-3, p. 68; 993a, 15, p. 80; 992b, 29-30, 19-20, p. 78.

3. AM, Vol. XVII, Book A ΕΛΑΤΤΟΝ, 993b, 9-11, p. 84; 995a, 3, p. 94; 993b, 27-28, p. 86; 995a, 13-14, p. 94; Book B, 997a, 8-9, p. 108; Book Γ, 1003a, 33-34, p. 146; 1003a, 21-22, 31-32, p. 146.

4. AM, Vol. XVII, Book Γ, 1003b, 5, pp. 146, 148; 1003b, 18-19, p. 148; 1004b, 26, p. 156; 1005b, 12-13, 19-20, 22, p. 160; 1005b, 33, p. 162.

5. AM, Vol. XVII, Book Γ, 1006a, 29-30, p. 164; 1007a, 35-36, p. 170; Book Δ, 1015a, 34-36, p. 224; 1015b, 12-13, pp. 224, 226; 1016b, 1-4, p. 230; 1016b, 20, p. 232; 1017a, 8, p. 234; 1017b, 24-26, p. 240; 1020a, 5-6, p. 254.

6. AM, Vol. XVII, Book E, 1025b, 1-3, 8-10, p. 292; Book Z, 1028a, 14-15, p. 310; 1028b, 3-5, p. 312; 1028a, 30-31, p. 312; 1028b, 34 to 1029a, 2, pp. 314, 316; 1029a, 29-30, p. 318; 1029b, 20-21, p. 320; 1030a, 21-23, p. 324; 1031b, 20-21, p. 334; 1032b, 15, p. 340.

7. AM, Vol. XVII, Book Z, 1034a, 6-8, p. 348; 1036a, 2-8, pp. 360, 362; 1039b, 28-31, p. 386; 1040b, 26-28, p. 392; 1041a, 4-6, p. 392; 1041b, 25-27, p. 398; Book θ, 1051b, 7-9, pp. 468, 470. AM, Vol. XVIII, Book I, 1054a, 13-19, pp. 14, 16.

8. AM, Vol. XVIII, Book K, 1059a, 18-19, p. 52; 1060a, 11-13, p. 58; 1060a, 25-26, p. 60; 1060b, 20-23, pp. 62, 64; 1060b, 31-33, p. 64; 1061b, 26-27, p. 70; 1061b, 34 to 1062a, 2, p. 70. AM, Vol. XVII, Book E, 1026a, 31-32, p. 298; 1026a, 19-20, p. 296.

9. AM, Vol. XVIII, Book K, 1064a, 31-35, p. 86; 1064a, 37 to 1064b, 1, p. 86; 1064b, 4-5, p. 88; 1066b, 12-13,. p. 102; Book Λ, 1070a, 8, p. 128; 1071b, 5-6, p. 140; 1072a, 24-27, pp. 144, 146; 1072b, 3-5, p. 146; 1072b, 14-31, pp. 148, 150; 1073a, 3-5, p. 150.

10. AM, Vol. XVIII, Book Λ, 1073a, 5-12, pp. 150, 152; 1074b, 1-4, 9-10, p. 162; 1074b, 34-35, p. 164; 1075a, 3-5, 8-16, p. 166; Book M, 1086a, 31-34, p. 248; 1086b, 11-13, p. 248; 1087a, 24-25, p. 254.

11. Joseph Owens, *The Doctrine of Being in the Aristotelian "Metaphysics": A Study in the Greek Background of Mediaeval Thought* (Toronto: Pontifical Institute of Mediaeval Studies, 1951), pp. 6, 61, 122, 132, 134, 153, 168, 176, 179-180.

12. Ibid., pp. 219, 233, 236, 274, 280, 281, 285.

13. Franz Brentano, *On the Several Senses of Being in Aristotle*, trans. Rolf George (Berkeley: University of California Press, 1975), pp. 131, 148.

14. Owens, pp. 290, 291, 293-294, 295, 296, 297, 298.

15. Giovanni Reale, *The Concept of First Philosophy and the Unity of the "Metaphysics" of Aristotle*, trans. and edited from the third edition by John R. Catan (Albany: State University of New York Press, 1980), pp. 18-19, 122, 123, 165, 207, 210, 217, 222, 223, 224, 296-297, 356.

16. The formulation here is that of William J. Richardson, S. J., *Heidegger: Through Phenomenology to Thought* (The Hague: Martinus Nijhoff, 1963), p. 631.

17. Werner Marx, *The Meaning of Aristotle's 'Ontology'* (The Hague: Martinus Nijhoff, 1954), pp. 17, 18, 23, 25, 26, 33-34, 36.

18. Ibid., pp. 41, 45, 49, 51, 55, 57, 62, 63.

19. Christopher Stead, *Divine Substance* (Oxford: At the Clarendon Press, 1977), pp. 71, 74-75, 1 (note).

20. Ibid., pp. 162, 159, 272-273.

21. DM, pp. 412, 414, 415-416. See EP, pp. 12-15.

22. See Thomas A. Losoncy, "Anselm's Response to Gaunilo's Dilemma—An Insight into the Notion of 'Being' Operative in the *Proslogion*," *The New Scholasicism*, Vol. LVI, No. 2 (Spring 1982), pp. 207, 213.

23. W.K.C. Guthrie, *A History of Greek Philosophy*, Six Volumes (Cambridge: Cambridge University Press, 1962-1981), Vol. VI, *Aristotle: An Encounter*, pp. 258, 253-254.

24. See WG, p. 65 and R.W. Church, *Saint Anselm* (London: Macmillan, 1888), pp. 353-355. See also Étienne Gilson, *History of Christian Philosophy in the Middle Ages* (New York: Random House, 1955), pp. 139, 619 (note 68).

## Chapter Two

1. DG, 4.411, 4.412, p. 39.

2. AO, Vol. I, Prologus, pp. 7-8. Ch. 1, lines 3, 9-10, 11, 14, 16, p. 13; lines 1-4, p. 14. WG, p. 67.

3. AO, Vol. I, Ch. 1, lines 5-13, p. 14; lines 5, 7, 11-12, p. 15. Ch. 2, lines 15-23, p. 15. Ch. 3, lines 25-30, p. 15; lines 2-4, 6-7, 10-12, 21-22, 26-28, p. 16.

274    *Notes*

4. AO, Vol. I, Ch. 4, lines 31-32, p. 16; lines 1, 4-10, 17-18, 30, 32-33, p. 17; lines 1-2, p. 18. Ch. 5, lines 5-6, p. 18. Ch. 6, lines 20, 21, 25-26, p. 18; lines 1-24, 28-31, p. 19; lines 3-4, 11-19, p. 20.

5. AO, Vol. I, Ch. 7, lines 22-23, 32-33, p. 21; lines 1, 8-10, p. 22. Ch. 8, line 12, p. 22; lines 27, 31-33, 24, p. 23; lines 2, 6, p. 24. Ch. 9, lines 14-15, p. 24. Ch. 10, lines 24-25, 28-29, 31, p. 24; lines 1, 21-25, p. 25. Ch. 11, lines 20-23, p. 26. Ch. 12, lines 25-27, p. 26. Ch. 13, lines 8-9, 14, p. 27. Ch. 14, lines 19-20, 24-26, p. 27.

6. AO, Vol. I, Ch. 15, lines 2, 6-16, 18-22, p. 28; lines 10-12, 20-21, 26-33, p. 29. Ch. 16, lines 10-11, 14-16, p. 30; lines 1-2, p. 31. Ch. 17, lines 10, 13-15, 23-24, 30-32, p. 31; line 1, p. 32.

7. AO, Vol. I, Ch. 18, lines 16-20, p. 32; lines 9-10, 14-18, 22-23, p. 33. Ch. 19, lines 28-29, p. 33; lines 1, 8-11, 18-22, 26-27, p. 34; lines 1-3, p. 35.

8. AO, Vol. I, Ch. 21, lines 26-27, p. 37. Ch. 22, lines 21-23, 29, p. 39; lines 1-2, p. 40. Ch. 20, lines 9-12, p. 35. Ch. 22, lines 18-19, 27-33, p. 40; lines 1-2, 4-10, 15-18, p. 41.

9. AO, Vol. I, Ch. 24, lines 12-13, 16, 18-20, p. 42. Ch. 25, lines 6-10, 21-24, 29-30, p. 43. Ch. 26, lines 4-5, 7-11, 15-19, p. 44. Ch. 27, lines 8-9, 13-15, 19, p. 45. Ch. 28, line 26, p. 45; lines 1-3, 7-8, p. 46.

10. AO, Vol. I, Ch. 28, lines 17-18, 15-16, 20-21, 25-26, 29-31, p. 46. Ch. 29, lines 1, 4-5, 8-11, 14-16, 20-22, p. 47; lines 2-4, p. 48. Ch. 30, lines 7, 12, p. 48.

11. AO, Vol. I, Ch. 31, lines 14, 22-23, p. 48; lines 3, 6-8, 10-11, 15, 20-21, p. 49; lines 1-3, 8-13, p. 50. Ch. 32, lines 12-13, 15-18, p. 51. Ch. 33, line 20, p. 51; lines 1-6, p. 52. Ch. 32, lines 9-10, p. 51.

12. AO, Vol. I, Ch. 33, lines 13-15, 17-19, 24-29, p. 52; lines 1-2, 4-6, p. 53. Ch. 34, lines 15, 21-26, p. 53. Ch. 36, lines 16-19, p. 54; lines 1-2, 5-6, p. 55. Ch. 37, line 18, p. 55.

13. AO, Vol. I, Ch. 37, lines 16-17, p. 55. Ch. 38, lines 14-16, 30-31, p. 56. Ch. 39, lines 7-9, p. 57. Ch. 41, lines 10-11, p. 58. Ch. 43, lines 15-17, p. 59; lines 5-7, p. 60. Ch. 39, lines 10-11, p. 57. Ch. 40, lines 4-5, p. 58. Ch. 42, lines 2, 10-12, p. 59. Ch. 44, lines 22-23, 27, p. 60; line 1, p. 61.

14. AO, Vol. I, Ch. 46, lines 17-20, 25-26, p. 62. Ch. 47, lines 4-7, p. 63. Ch. 48, lines 16-17, 19-20, 22-24, p. 63; lines 5-6, 12-13, 3, p. 64. Ch. 49, lines 16-18, p. 64. Ch. 50, lines 4-6, p. 65. Ch. 51, lines 16-18, p. 65. Ch. 52, lines 22-24, p. 65. Ch. 53, lines 10-11, p. 66. Ch. 54, lines 24-25, 27-29, p. 66.

15. AO, Vol. I, Ch. 55, lines 13-14, p. 67. Ch. 56, lines 24-25, p. 67; lines 7-8, p. 68. Ch. 57, lines 13, 22, 24-25, p. 68; lines 6-7, 9-10, p. 69. See Sancti Thomae Aquinatis, *Summa Theologiae*, Five Volumes (Matriti: Biblioteca De Autores Cristianos, 1961), Vol. I, Prima Pars, Qu. 36, Art. 1, p. 259.

16. AO, Vol. I, Ch. 59, lines 3-4, p. 70. Ch. 60, lines 1, 5, p. 71. Ch. 61, lines 19, 23, p. 71; line 1, p. 72. Ch. 62, lines 7-10, 12-17, p. 72. Ch. 63, lines 10-12, 17-18, 24, 28, p. 73; lines 5, 8-9, 16-17, p. 74.

17. AO, Vol. I, Ch. 64, lines 29-31, p. 74; lines 1-7, 11-12, p. 75. Ch. 65, lines 21-22, p. 75; lines 3-8, 12-22, 27-31, p. 76; lines 1-3, p. 77.

18. AO, Vol. I, Ch. 66, lines 5-6, 12, 14, 18-19, 22-24, p. 77. Ch. 67, lines 26-28, p. 77; lines 1, 9-11, p. 78. Ch. 68, lines 14-16, 20, p. 78; lines 2-3, 5-6, p. 79.

19. AO, Vol. I, Ch. 69, lines 11, 14, 26-27, p. 79; lines 5-6, p. 80. Ch. 70, lines 18, 24-25, 30-31, p. 80; line 1, p. 81. Ch. 71, lines 1-3, p. 82. Ch. 72, lines 7-8, p. 82. Ch. 74, lines 5-6, p. 83. Ch. 75, lines 11-12, p. 83.

20. AO, Vol. I, Ch. 76, lines 16-25, 27, 29, p. 83. Ch. 78, line 24, p. 84; lines 7-9, p. 85.

21. AO, Vol. I, Ch. 79, lines 16-17, 13, 22, p. 85. Ch. 80, lines 18, 20-21, p. 86; lines 12-13, 1-2, 5-7, p. 87.

22. AO, Vol. I, Ch. 80, lines 17-18, p. 86.

23. Robert Sokolowski, *The God of Faith and Reason: Foundations of Christian Theology* (Notre Dame: University of Notre Dame Press, 1982), pp. 5-6, 12, 15-16, 19.

24. Ibid., pp. 33, 36, 38, 43, 50, 107.

## Chapter Three

1. See Paul Vignaux, *Philosophy in the Middle Ages*, trans. E. C. Hall (London: Burns & Oates, 1959), p. 47.

2. C. S. Lewis, *The Pilgrim's Regress: An Allegorical Apology for Christianity, Reason, and Romanticism* (New York: Bantam Books, 1981 reprint), p. xii.

3. DM, pp. 421, 422. See EP, p. 20.

4. See Desmond Paul Henry, *The Logic of Saint Anselm* (Oxford: At the Clarendon Press, 1967), pp. 230-231.

5. AO, Vol. I, Prooemium, lines 2-21, p. 93; lines 1-2, 6-13, p. 94.

6. See R. W. Southern, *St. Anselm and his Biographer: A Study of Monastic Life and Thought, 1059-c.1130* (Cambridge: Cambridge University Press, 1963), pp. 333-335.

7. See Dom David Knowles, *The Monastic Order in England: A History of its Development from the Times of St. Dunstan to the Fourth Lateran Council, 943-1216* (Cambridge: At the University Press, 1949), pp. 682-683, 509.

8. AO, Vol. I, Ch. 1, lines 3-9, p. 97; lines 1-4, p. 98; lines 12-19, p. 100. BS, Novum Testamentum, p. 21.

9. *Augustine: Later Works*, Selected and Translated by John Burnaby (Philadelphia: Westminster Press, 1955), p. 129. BS, Vetus Testamentum, Vol. II, p. 544.

10. AO, Vol. I, Ch. 2, lines 3-7, p. 101. BS, Vetus Testamentum, Vol. II, p. 19.

11. Joseph J. Carpino, "A Study of Negation in Hegel," Doctoral Dissertation, Department of Philosophy, Fordham University, N.Y., 1960, p. 101.

12. See Andre Hayen, "The Role of the Fool in St. Anselm and the Necessarily Apostolic Character of True Christian Reflection," in *The Many-Faced Argument: Recent Studies on The Ontological Argument for the Existence of God*, ed. John Hick and Arthur McGill (New York: Macmillan, 1967), p. 172. See also Thomas O'Loughlin, "Who Is Anselm's Fool?", *The New Scholasticism*, Vol. LXIII, No. 3, Summer 1989, pp. 313-325.

13. AO, Vol. I, Ch. 2, lines 7-10, p. 101. See Jasper Hopkins, *A Companion to the Study of St. Anselm* (Minneapolis: University of Minnesota Press, 1972), p. 72.

14. AO, Vol. I, Ch. 2, lines 10-13, p. 101.

15. AO, Vol. I, Ch. 2, lines 13-18, p. 101; lines 1-3, p. 102. See Jasper Hopkins, "On Understanding and Preunderstanding St. Anselm," *The New Scholasticism*, Vol. LII, No. 2 (Spring 1978), p. 259.

16. Charles Hartshorne, *Anselm's Discovery: A Re-examination of the Ontological Proof for God's Existence* (La Salle, Ill.: Open Court, 1965), p. 241.

17. Carpino, *op. cit.*, "Defense Outline," pp. 6-7.

18. See Robert S. Hartman, "Prolegomena to a Meta-Anselmian Axiomatic," *The Review of Metaphysics*, Vol. 14 (1961), p. 671.

19. Boethius, De Consolatione Philosophiae, III, 23-28, in *Boethius: Tracts and De Consolatione Philosophiae*, with a translation by H.F. Stewart and E.K. Rand, revised by S.J. Tester, Loeb Classical Library, p. 277. Lucius Annaeus Seneca, *Opera Omnia*, ed. F. Haase, i, 159, cited by R.W. Southern, *op. cit.*, p. 59. *St Augustine's Confessions*, with a translation by William Watts, two volumes, Loeb Classical Library (1912, reprinted 1968), Vol. I, p. 344 (Book VII, ch. iv).

20. Jasper Hopkins, *A Companion to the Study of St. Anselm*, p. 19. Jasper Hopkins, "On Understanding and Preunderstanding St. Anselm," p. 251.

21. See G.R. Evans, *Anselm and Talking about God* (Oxford: Clarendon Press, 1978), p. 52. See also Josef Pieper, "The Meaning of 'God Speaks'," *The New Scholasticism*, Vol. XLIII (1969), pp. 212-213.

22. Robert S. Hartman, pp. 655, 657, 663, 667.

23. AO, Vol. I, Ch. 3, lines 5-10, p. 102; lines 1-2, p. 103.

24. See Carpino, *op. cit.*, p. 101, "Defense Outline," pp. 6-7.

25. AO, Vol. I, *De Veritate*, Ch. 4, lines 6-7, p. 181. Ch. 5, line 12, p. 181; lines 4-7, p. 183. Ch. 9, lines 10-16, 24-25, p. 189. Ch. 11, lines 19-20, p. 191. Ch. 12, lines 19-24, p. 196.

26. See Aimé Forest, "St. Anselm' Argument in Reflexive Philosophy," trans. Arthur C. McGill, in *The Many-Faced Argument*, pp. 285, 286.

27. Robert S. Hartman, p. 674.

28. AO, Vol. 1, *Proslogion*, Ch. 3, lines 3-7, p. 103. See Charles Harteshorne, pp. 66, 85, 88.

29. See David Platt, "What the Ontological Proof Can and Cannot Do," *The New Scholasticism*, Vol. XLVII (1973), p. 464.

30. AO, Vol. I, *Proslogion*, Ch. 3, lines 7-9, p. 103. See J.N. Findlay, "Can God's Existence be Disproved?," in *The Ontological Argument from St. Anselm to Contemporary Philosophers*, ed. Alvin Plantinga (New York: Doubleday Anchor, 1965), p. 117.

31. St. Anselm, "Philosophical Fragments," p. 42 (line 22ff) and p. 43 (line 14ff) of the Latin text in *Ein neues unvolendetes,* trans. Jasper Hopkins in *A*

*Companion to the Study of St. Anselm*, pp. 239-240. AO, Vol. I, *Proslogion*, Ch. 3, lines 9-11, p. 103.

32. AO, Vol. I, *Proslogion*, Ch. 4, lines 14-21, p. 103; lines 1-4, p. 104.

33. See Charles Hartshorne, p. 234.

34. AO, Vol. I, *Proslogion*, Ch. 4, lines 5-7, p. 104.

35. AO, Vol. I, Ch. 5, lines 9, 11-17, p. 104. Ch. 6, line 22, p. 104.

36. AO, Vol. I, Ch. 7, lines 9-11, 25-27, p. 105; lines 1-2, p. 106.

37. AO, Vol. I, Ch. 8, lines 5, 9-14, p. 106. Ch. 9, lines 16-17, p. 106; lines 4-8, p. 107. BS, Novum Testamentum, p. 782.

38. AO, Vol. I, Ch. 9, lines 8-12, 15-18, 20-21, 26-27, p. 107; lines 1-9, 11-15, p. 108. Ch. 10, lines 23-24, 27-28, p. 108; lines 1-2, p. 109. Ch. 11, lines 15-17, p. 109.

39. AO, Vol. I, Ch. 11, lines 11-12, 17-24, p. 109. Ch. 12, lines 6-8, p. 110. Ch. 13, lines 13-15, p. 110. Ch. 14, lines 7, 12-17, 20-25, p. 111; lines 1-11, p. 112. Ch. 15, lines 14-17, p. 112.

40. AO, Vol. I, Ch. 16, lines 20-24, 27, p. 112; lines 1-4, p. 113. Ch. 17, lines 8-15, p. 113. Ch. 18, lines 18-19, p. 113; lines 2-13, p. 114.

41. AO, Vol. I, Ch. 18, lines 14-17, 19-24, p. 114; lines 3-4, p. 115. Ch. 19, lines 13, 15, p. 115. Ch. 20, lines 17-18, 21-22, p. 115. Ch. 19, lines 13, 15, p. 115. Ch. 20, lines 17-18, 21-22, p. 115; lines 2-3, p. 116. Ch. 21, lines 7-8, 11, p. 116. Ch. 22, lines 15-21, 23, p. 116; lines 1-2, p. 117. Ch. 23, lines 4, 10, 15-20, p. 117. Ch. 24, line 2, p. 118.

42. Robert S. Hartman, p. 644.

43. AO, Vol. I, Ch. 24, lines 4-9, p. 118. Ch. 25, line 17, p. 118; lines 2-3, 17-20, p. 120. Ch. 26, line 25, p. 120; lines 1, 3-4, 7-8, 14-18, 22-24, p. 121; lines 1-2, p. 122.

44. AO, Vol. I, Gaunilo, *Quid ad haec respondeat quidam pro insipiente*, # 4, line 30, p. 126; lines 17-21, p. 127. # 5, line 29, p. 127; lines 1-2, 11-13, p. 128. # 6, lines 14-19, 21-26, 30-32, p. 128. #7, lines 7-8, 14-19, p. 129. # 8, lines 22-24, p. 129. # 7, lines 10-12, p. 129.

## Notes

45. AO, Vol. I, St. Anselm, *Quid ad haec respondeat editor ipsius libelli*, lines 3-5, p. 130. #I, lines 2-13, p. 131; lines 5-7, p. 132. # II, lines 17-20, 25-27, 30, p. 132; lines 1-2, p. 133.

46. Ibid., # III, lines 6-14, 19, p. 133. # IV, lines 7-8, 10-17, p. 134. # V, lines 27-28, p. 134; lines 14-16, 18-20, 26-28, p. 135.

47. Ibid., # VI, line 5, p. 136. See Hans Verweyen, "Faith Seeking Understanding: An Atheistic Interpretation," *The New Scholasticism*, Vol. XLIV (1970), p. 390.

48. AO, Vol. I, St. Anselm, *Quid ad haec respondeat editor ipsius libelli*, # VII, lines 30-31, p. 136; lines 1, 3-5, p. 137. # VIII, lines 27-28, 16-18, p. 137. # IX, lines 6-11, 15-27, p. 138. # X, lines 28-31, p. 138; lines 1-4, 6-7, 9-12, p. 139.

49. Parmenides, Fragment 8, lines 35-36, in G.S. Kirk and J.E. Raven, *The Presocratic Philosophers: A Critical History with a Selection of Texts* (Cambridge: At the University Press, 1960), p. 277.

50. Vincent J. Ferrara, "Some Reflections on the Being-Thought Relationship in Parmenides, Anselm, and Hegel," in *Analecta Anselmiana: Untersuchungen über Person und Werk Anselms von Canterbury*, ed. F.S. Schmitt, Five Volumes (Frankfurt am Main: Minerva, 1969), Vol. III, pp. 96, 99, 100, 102, 103, 105, 106.

51. See Edward J. O'Toole, "Anselm's Logic of Faith," in *Analecta Anselmiana*, Vol. III, p. 152.

52. Vincent J. Ferrara, "Hegel's Logic: A Dialectical Substantiation of Anselm's Ontological Argument," in *Analecta Anselmiana*, Vol. IV, pp. 263, 265.

53. DM, p. 422. See EP, p. 21.

54. F. Alquié, in *La Decouverte métaphysique de l'homme chez Descartes* (Paris: Presses Universitaires de France, 1950), pp. 236-237, remarks: "L'homme n'a pas l'idée de Dieu, il est l'idee de Dieu, le signe de Dieu . . . ."

55. Aimé Forest, p. 294.

## Chapter Four

1. DM, pp. 423, 424, 425, 426. See EP, pp. 21-22, 23.

2. See Walter J. Ong, *The Barbarian Within and Other Fugitive Essays and Studies* (New York: Macmillan, 1962), pp. 69-70.

3. See David Platt, pp. 464-465.

4. AT, VII, pp. 1-4; IX, p. 6. RL, pp. 1-3. See HR, I, pp. 133-135.

5. AT, VII, pp. 4-9; IX, p. 8. RL, pp. 4-8. See HR, I, pp. 135-139.

6. AT, VII, pp. 12-16; IX, pp. 9, 11. RL, pp. 14-17. See HR, I, pp. 140-143.

7. AT, VII, pp. 17-18; IX, p. 13. RL, pp. 18-19. See HR, I, pp. 144-145. See AO, Vol. I, lines 3, 5-6, p. 97.

8. AT, VII, pp. 18-20; IX, pp. 14-16. RL, pp. 19-21. See HR, I, pp. 145-147.

9. AT, VII, pp. 21-22; IX, pp. 16, 17. RL, pp. 21-23. See HR, I, pp. 147-148.

10. AT, VII, pp. 22-23; IX, pp. 17, 18. RL, pp. 23-24. See HR, I, pp. 148-149. Richard Kennington, "The Finitude of Descartes' Evil Genius," *Journal of the History of Ideas*, Vol. 32 (1971), p. 445.

11. AT, VII, pp. 23-25; IX, p. 19. RL, pp. 24-25. See HR, I, pp. 149-150.

12. AT, VII, pp. 25-27; IX, p. 21. RL, pp. 26-28. See HR, I, pp. 150-152.

13. AT, VII, pp. 28-31; IX, p. 22. RL, pp. 29-32. See HR, I, pp. 152-155.

14. AT, VII, pp. 32-34; IX, pp. 25, 26. RL, pp. 32-34. See HR, I, pp. 155-157.

15. See L.J. Beck, *The Metaphysics of Descartes: A Study of the Meditations* (Oxford: At the Clarendon Press, 1965), p. 294.

16. AT, VII, pp. 34-36; IX, p. 27. RL, pp. 34-36. See HR, I, pp. 157-159.

17. AT, VII, pp. 37-39; IX, pp. 29, 31. RL, pp. 36-40. See HR, I, pp. 159-161.

18. AT, VII, pp. 39-40; IX, pp. 31, 32. RL, p. 40. See HR, I, pp. 161-162. Descartes, "Réponses de l'auteur aux Secondes Objections contre les précédentes Méditations," in OL, p. 390; see HR, II, p. 52.

19. AT, VII, pp. 40-46; IX, pp. 32, 36. RL, pp. 40-46. See HR, I, pp. 162-166.

20. AT, VII, pp. 46-50. RL, pp. 46-50. See HR, I, pp. 166-169.

21. AT, VII, pp. 51-52; IX, pp. 41, 42. RL, pp. 51-52. See HR, I, pp. 170-171.

22. AT, VII, pp. 53-55; IX, pp. 42-44. RL, pp. 53-55. See HR, I, pp. 171-173.

23. AT, VII, pp. 55-57; IX, p. 45. RL, pp. 55-57. See HR, I, pp. 173-175.

24. AT, VII, pp. 58-62; IX, pp. 48, 49. RL, pp. 58-62. See HR, I, pp. 175-179.

25. AT, VII, pp. 64-66; IX, pp. 51, 52. RL, pp. 63-65. See HR, I, pp. 179-181.

26. AT, VII, pp. 66-71; IX, p. 56. RL, pp. 65-70. See HR, I, pp. 181-185. See *St. Augustine's Confessions*, Loeb Classical Library, Vol. II, pp. 92, 94.

27. AT, VII, pp. 71-79; IX, p. 62. RL, pp. 70-72, 74-77. See HR, I, pp. 185-190.

28. AT, VII, pp. 79-83; IX, pp. 63, 64. RL, pp. 77-81. See HR, I, pp. 191-194. Descartes, "Réponses de l'auteur aux Secondes Objections," in OL, p. 391.

29. AT, VII, pp. 83-90; IX, p. 66. RL, pp. 81-87. See HR, I, pp. 194-199.

30. AT, VII, p. 90; IX, p. 71. RL, p. 87. See HR, I, p. 199.

31. Descartes, "Réponses de l'auteur aux Premières Objections," OL, pp. 348, 350, 352, 353, 355. "Secondes Réponses," OL, pp. 375-376.

32. Descartes, "Secondes Réponses," OL, pp. 394, 395. "Troisièmes Réponses," OL, pp. 413, 414.

33. Descartes, "Quatrièmes Réponses," OL, p. 440. "Cinquièmes Réponses," OL, pp. 512, 478. "Quatrièmes Réponses," OL, p. 447.

34. Descartes, "Cinquièmes Réponses," OL, pp. 482, 496, 498.

35. Descartes, "Sixièmes Réponses," OL, pp. 532, 539, 544-545.

36. Descartes, "Entretien avec Burman," OL, pp. 1357, 1360, 1365-1366, 1368, 1370, 1371, 1372. See DB, # 5, p. 5; # 9, p. 8; #19, p. 13; # 21, pp. 14-15; # 24, p. 17; # 28, pp. 18-19; # 29, p. 19; # 30, p. 20; # 31, pp. 20-21.

37. Descartes, "Entretien avec Burman," OL, pp. 1374, 1375, 1377, 1380, 1373, 1381. See DB, # 33, p. 22; # 34, p. 23; # 35, p. 24; # 40, # 41, p. 26; # 45, p. 29; # 32, p. 21; # 48, pp. 30-31. Jacques Maritain, *Three Reformers: Luther, Descartes, Rousseau* (New York: Thomas Y. Crowell, 1929, reprinted 1970), pp. 68, 83.

38. Hiram Caton, *The Origin of Subjectivity: An Essay on Descartes* (New Haven: Yale University Press, 1973), pp. 3, 10.

39. Descartes, letter to Mersenne, Jan. 28, 1641, in AT, III, pp. 297-298. See Caton, p. 10.

40. See Caton, pp. 20-21, 33, 34, 124, 62, 125, 135, 141, 142, 155-156, 15. See Descartes, "The Search After Truth by the Light of Nature," AT, X, p. 525, HR, I, p. 325. See also Klaus Oehler, *Die Lehre vom Noetischen und Dianoetischen Denken bei Platon und Aristoteles* (München: Ch. Beck 'sche Verlagsbuchhandlung, 1962), pp. 1, 2, 260.

41. See Caton, p. 62.

42. Michael B. Foster, "The Christian Doctrine of Creation and the Rise of Modern Natural Science," *Mind*, N.S., Vol. XLIII (Oct. 1934), pp. 450, 465.

43. Descartes, letter to Mersenne, Dec. 1640, in OL, p. 1102. See also Étienne Gilson, *Études sur le Rôle, de la Pensée Médiévale dans la Formation du Système Cartésien*, "Etudes de Philosophie Médiévale," Vol. XIII (Paris: Librairie Philosophique J. Vrin, 1951), p. 221.

44. Jean La Croix, *Maurice Blondel: An Introduction to the Man and his Philosophy*, trans. John C. Guinness (New York: Sheed and Ward, 1968), p. 78.

45. DM, pp. 426-427. See EP, p. 24.

46. DM, pp. 433-434, 427, 429, 431-432. See EP, pp. 30-31, 25, 26. EG, p. 472. See EP, p. 67.

47. Erich Frank, *Wissen, Wollen, Glauben* (Zurich: Artemis-Verlag, 1955), p. 169.

48. Edmund Husserl, *Die Krisis der Europäischen Wissenschaften und die Transzendentale Phänomenologie*, herausgegeben von Walter Biemel, in *Husserliana*, Edmund Husserl, *Gesammelte Werke* (Haag: Martinus Nijhoff, 1950-), Band VI, pp. 83-84. Husserl, *Cartesianische Meditationen und Pariser Vorträge*, herausgegeben und eingeleitet von S. Strasser, in *Husserliana*, Edmund Husserl, *Gesammelte Werke*, Band I, pp. 61, 45. See Edmund Husserl, *The Crisis of European Sciences and Transcendental Phenomenology*, trans. David Carr (Evanston: Northwestern University Press, 1970), pp. 81-82, and *Cartesian Meditations: An Introduction to Phenomenology*, trans. Dorion Cairns (The Hague: Martinus Nijhoff, 1969), pp. 21, 3.

## Chapter Five

1. DM, pp. 452, 453, 454; see EP, pp. 47-48, 49. EG, p. 467; see EP, p. 63.

Notes                                                                                          283

2. See Karl Löwith, *From Hegel to Nietzsche: The Revolution in Nineteenth-Century Thought* (New York: Doubleday, Anchor, 1967), pp. 74, 75, 335, 336.

3. Sidney Hook, *From Hegel to Marx: Studies in the Intellectual Development of Karl Marx* (Ann Arbor: University of Michigan Press, 1962), pp. 225, 232, 256, 260, 259. See PP, p. 5. See also SW, II, pp. 211, 263, 339.

4. See C.A. van Peursen, *Body, Soul, Spirit: A Survey of the Body-Mind Problem* (London: Oxford University Press, 1966), p. 54. See Eugene Kamenka, *The Philosophy of Ludwig Feuerbach* (New York: Praeger Publishers, 1970), pp. 49, 50-51, 57, 80, 72-73, 77, 87, 129, 116, 100. See also SW, VI, p. 180; II, pp. 254, 214-215, 162, 315-316.

5. LE, Lecture I, p. 7; XIX, p. 176; XXX, p. 276; III, p. 19; II, pp. 10-11, 13-14; III, pp. 22-23. PP, p. 5.

6. LE, IV, pp. 25-26, 27-28, 29-30, 31; V, pp. 33, 34; XXIII, p. 207; VII, pp. 53-54, 55, 56-57; VIII, p. 62; IX, p. 80; XI, pp. 95-96, 97-98; XII, p. 101; XIII, p. 111. See SW, X, p. 22; II, p. 83.

7. LE, XIII, pp. 115-116, 116-117, 119-120; XIV, pp. 121, 122-123, 129; XV, pp. 131, 135, 136; XVI, pp. 142, 143; XVIII, p. 153.

8. LE, XVI, p. 149; XVIII, pp. 160, 163-164, 168; XIX, p. 175; XX, p. 186; XXII, pp. 199, 204; XX, pp. 178-179; XXVII, p. 251; XXVIII, p. 264; XXIX, pp. 267, 269, 274-275; XXX, pp. 279, 282-283; Notes, pp. 343-344.

9. WC, pp. 14, 15, 16-17, 17-18, 20. See EC, pp. xxxiii, xxxiv, xxxv, xxxvi, xxxvii, xxxix.

10. WC, pp. 28, 29, 30, 36, 40-41, 42, 45-46, 47-49, 51, 53, 54, 56. See EC, pp. 1, 2-3, 6, 9, 10-11, 12, 13-14, 16, 17, 18, 19.

11. WC, pp. 56, 57, 59, 60, 64, 65, 72-73, 75, 79-80, 81, 82, 84. See EC, pp. 19, 21, 22, 23, 26, 27, 30, 31, 33, 35, 36, 37, 38, 40.

12. WC, pp. 86, 89, 114, 118, 119, 121-122, 126, 128, 131-132. See EC, pp. 42, 44, 56, 59, 60-61, 62, 63-64, 65.

13. WC, pp. 163-164, 159, 186-187, 188, 190, 191, 198, 199, 200, 205, 215. See EC, pp. 81, 78, 98, 99, 101-102, 106-107, 108, 111, 118.

14. WC, pp. 220, 221, 223, 226, 228, 229, 237-238, 241, 247, 248-249, 255, 256. See EC, pp. 121, 122, 123, 125, 126, 127, 133, 135, 140, 141, 144-145.

15. WC, pp. 257, 259, 261, 262, 269, 270, 293, 296, 299, 301, 309, 310, 312-313. See EC, pp. 146, 147, 148, 149, 150, 153, 154, 170, 172, 173-174, 181-182, 183.

16. WC, pp. 314-315, 318, 328, 329, 334, 338, 339, 342. See EC, pp. 184, 186, 193, 197, 198, 199, 201.

17. WC, pp. 340-341, 346, 347, 350, 351-352, 376, 385, 397, 410. See EC, pp. 200, 204, 206, 207, 225, 230-231, 239, 247.

18. WC, pp. 410-411, 436, 439, 442-443, 444. See EC, pp. 247-248, 264, 266, 269, 270-271. See G.W.F. Hegel, *Lectures on the Philosophy of Religion*, trans. E.B. Speirs and J. Burdon Sanderson, Three Volumes (London: Routledge and Kegan Paul; New York: The Humanities Press, reprinted 1974), Vol. III, p. 13, and *Philosophy of History*, trans. John Sibree (New York: P.F. Colier, 1902), Part Three, pp. 408-409.

19. WC, pp. 448, 453, 454, 455, 475, 459, 532, 601, 600. See EC, pp. 273, 277, 278, 281, 285, 283, 307, 337, 336.

20. EF, pp. 41, 46, 48, 50, 51-53, 54, 62, 64, 65, 68-69.

21. EF, pp. 77, 78, 89, 90, 92, 93, 94, 95, 98, 107.

22. EF, pp. 109, 115-116, 125, 126, 127, 105. Luther, *Briefwechsel* (Weimar), Vol. 8, p. 328, cited by Feuerbach.

23. TD, # 183, p. 190; # 26, p. 27; # 71, p. 67; # 103, p. 95; # 127, p. 116.

24. PP, # 13, pp. 18-19; # 15, p. 23; # 17, pp. 27-28; # 18, pp. 30-31.

25. PP, # 29, pp. 44, 45; # 25, p. 39; # 33, p. 53; # 36, p. 54; # 52, p. 68; # 63, p. 72.

26. Ernst Bloch, *Atheismus im Christentum: Zur Religion des Exodus und des Reichs* (Frankfurt am Main: Suhrkamp Verlag, 1968), pp. 281-283. See Ernst Bloch, *Atheism in Christianity: The Religion of the Exodus and the Kingdom*, trans. J.T. Swann (New York: Herder and Herder, 1972), pp. 210-211.

27. See Patrick Masterson, *Atheism and Alienation: A Study of the Philosophical Sources of Contemporary Atheism* (Dublin: Gill and Macmillan, 1971), pp. 72, 76, 9-10.

28. Karl Löwith, *Gott, Mensch, und Welt in der Metaphysik von Descartes bis zu Nietzsche* (Gottingen: Vanderhoeck & Ruprecht, 1967), p. 29.

29. See Richard T. Murphy, *Hume and Husserl: Towards Radical Subjectivism* (The Hague: Martinus Nijhoff, 1980), p. 136.

30. See Roger Poole, *Towards Deep Subjectivity* (London: Penguin Press, 1972), p. 6.

31. See Harry G. Frankfurt, *Demons, Dreamers and Madmen: The Defense of Reason in Descartes's Meditations* (New York: The Bobbs-Merrill Co., Inc., 1970), pp. 26, 166, 175-176.

32. Albert Einstein, "Science and Religion," in *Science, Philosophy and Religion: A Symposium* (New York: Conference on Science, Philosophy and Religion in their Relation to the Democratic Way of Life, Inc., 1941), p. 212.

33. See John L. Navickas, *Consciousness and Reality: Hegel's Philosophy of Subjectivity* (The Hague: Martinus Nijhoff, 1976), p. 274.

34. See John McIntyre, *St. Anselm and His Critics: A Re-interpretation of the "Cur Deus Homo"* (Edinburgh: Oliver and Boyd, 1954), pp. 42, 51.

35. St. Anselm, "Commendatio," *Cur Deus Homo*, in AO, Vol. II, p. 40, lines 10-12.

36. St. Anselm, *Epistola de Incarnatione Verbi*, in AO, Vol. II, p. 9, lines 5-6.

37. See J. Heywood Thomas, *Subjectivity and Paradox* (Oxford: Basil Blackwell, 1957), p. 51.

38. Jules Vuillemin, *Le Dieu D'Anselme et les Apparences de la Raison* (Paris: Aubier Montaigne, 1971), p. 15.

39. See G.R. Evans, *Anselm and a New Generation* (Oxford: Clarendon Press, 1980), pp. 86, 90.

40. Desmond Paul Henry, *Commentary on "De Grammatico": The Historical-Logical Dimensions of a Dialogue of St. Anselm* (Dordrecht, Holland: D. Reidel Publishing Co., 1974), p. 12.

41. See Walter J. Ong, *Fighting for Life: Contest, Sexuality, and Consciousness* (Ithaca: Cornell University Press, 1981), p. 195.

42. See Herbert Marcuse, *Eros and Civilization: A Philosophical Inquiry into Freud* (Boston: Beacon Press, 1974), pp. 109-110.

## Chapter Six

1. Michael B. Foster, *Mystery and Philosophy* (London: SCM Press, 1957), pp. 19, 22(note), 31, 34-35, 37, 41, 42.

2. Ibid., pp. 44, 58, 60, 61, 46, 27-28, 49, 73, 83, 90, 91.

3. See Richard R. LaCroix, *Proslogion II and III: A Third Interpretation of Anselm's Argument* (Leiden: E.J. Brill, 1972), p. 10.

4. St. Anselm, "Oratio ad Sanctam Mariam pro Impetrando Eius et Christi Amore," AO, Vol. III, p. 22. See Sokolowski, *The God of Faith and Reason*, p. 102.

5. See Bernard J.F. Lonergan, S.J., *Method in Theology* (New York: Herder and Herder, 1972), pp. 95-96.

6. See Richard Foster Jones, *Ancients and Moderns: A Study of the Rise of the Scientific Movement in Seventeenth-Century England* (Berkeley and Los Angeles: University of California Press, 1965), p. 49.

7. See Amintore Fanfani, *Catholicism, Protestantism and Capitalism* (London: Sheed and Ward, 1935; reprinted by Arno Press, New York, 1972), p. 86.

8. Descartes, letter to Mesland, May 2, 1644, in AT, IV, pp. 118-119. See Descartes, *Philosophical Letters*, trans. and ed. Anthony Kenny (Oxford: Clarendon Press, 1970), p. 151.

9. See Paul Henry, *Saint Augustine on Personality* (New York: Macmillan, 1960), pp. 5, 6.

10. See Peter Geach, *Providence and Evil* (Cambridge: Cambridge University Press, 1977), pp. 108, 116.

11. See Alasdair MacIntyre, "The Debate About God: Victorian Relevance and Contemporary Irrelevance," in Alasdair MacIntyre and Paul Ricoeur, *The Religious Significance of Atheism* (New York and London: Columbia University Press, 1969).

12. See Galgan, *The Logic of Modernity*, pp. 311-313. On the modern misconstrual of the negative idea as positive, see Jorge J.E. Gracia, " 'A Supremely Great Being'," *New Scholasticism*, Vol. 48, 1974, pp. 371-377. For the relevant modern texts, see Alvin Plantinga (ed.), *The Ontological Argument: From St. Anselm to Contemporary Philosophers* (New York: Doubleday, Anchor, 1965).

13. Anselm, *De Casu Diaboli*, ch. iv, AO, Vol. I, p. 241, lines 31-32.

14. *Hegel's Lectures on the History of Philosophy*, trans. E.S. Haldane and Frances H. Simson, Three Volumes (London: Routledge and Kegan Paul, 1892; New York: The Humanities Press, reprinted 1968), Vol. III, p. 63.

*Hegel's Philosophy of Right*, trans. T.M. Knox (London, Oxford, New York: Oxford University Press, 1967), # 280, p. 185.

15. See Cyril of Alexandria, "Thesaurus on the Holy and Consubstantial Trinity," cited by Edmund J. Fortman, *The Triune God: A Historical Study of the Doctrine of the Trinity* (Philadelphia: Westminster Press, 1972), p. 90.

16. Julius R. Weinberg, "The Sources and Nature of Descartes' 'Cogito'," in Julius R. Weinberg, *Ockham, Descartes, and Hume: Self-Knowledge, Substance, and Causality* (Madison: University of Wisconsin Press, 1977), p. 90.

17. St. Augustine, *De Genesi ad Litteram*, Bk. IV, Ch. xiii, 24, in J.P. Migne, ed., *Patrologiae Cursus Completus*, Series Prima, Latina, 1845, Vol. XXXIV, Column 305. Michael B. Foster, "Christian Theology and Modern Science of Nature (II)," *Mind*, Vol. XLV, No. 177 (Jan. 1936), p. 10.

18. See Timothy J. Reiss, *The Discourse of Modernism* (Ithaca and London: Cornell University Press, 1982), pp. 59, 68-69.

19. See F. Edward Cranz, *op. cit.*, pp. 89, 91. See also F. Edward Cranz, "The Renaissance Reading of the *De Anima*," in $XVI^e$ *Colloque International de Tours: Platon et Aristote a la Renaissance* (Paris, 1976), p. 370.

20. C.G. Jung, "A Psychological Approach to the Dogma of the Trinity," in *The Collected Works* (Princeton: Princeton University Press), Vol. 11 (1958), p. 147.

21. Michael B. Foster, "Christian Theology and Modern Science of Nature (II)," p. 10.

22. Ibid. Michael B. Foster, "Christian Theology and Modern Science of Nature (I)," *Mind*, Vol. XLIV (1935), pp. 445, 447, 465-466.

23. See Anton Hermann Chroust, "The Metaphysics of Time and History in Early Christian Thought," *The New Scholasticism*, Vol. XIX, No. 4 (Oct. 1945), pp. 333, 341, 344, 349, 351.

24. Karl Barth, *Anselm: Fides Quaerens Intellectum*, trans. Ian W. Robertson (Richmond, Virginia: John Knox Press, 1960), pp. 95, 98, 102, 121.

25. Ibid., pp. 129-130, 137, 169.

26. Martin Heidegger, *Sein und Zeit* (Frankfurt am Main: Vittorio Klostermann, 1977), Band 2 of Heidegger, *Gesamtausgabe* (I. Abteilung: Veroffentlichte Schriften, 1914-1970), p. 572 (pp. 433-434 of original German text). See

Martin Heidegger, *Being and Time*, trans. John Macquarrie and Edward Robinson (New York and Evanston: Harper and Row, 1962), p. 484. Cf. Hegel, *Encyklopädie*, Section 257, Hoffmeister's Critical Edition (1949).

27. Heidegger, *Sein und Zeit*, p. 577 (p. 437 of original German text). See Heidegger, *Being and Time*, p. 488.

28. John O. Lyons, *The Invention of the Self: The Hinge of Consciousness in the Eighteenth Century* (Carbondale: Southern Illinois University Press, 1978), p. 197.

29. Ann Hartle, *The Modern Self in Rousseau's Confessions: A Reply to St. Augustine* (Notre Dame: University of Notre Dame Press, 1984), p. 152.

30. Mortimer Adler, "God and the Philosophers," in *Science, Philosophy and Religion: A Symposium*, pp. 132-133.

31. Leo Strauss, *Natural Right and History* (Chicago: The University of Chicago Press, 1953), p. 323.

32. Alfred North Whitehead, *Dialogues of Alfred North Whitehead*, as recorded by Lucien Price (New York: The New American Library, Mentor, 1956), p. 134. William James, *Some Problems of Philosophy: A Beginning of an Introduction to Philosophy* (New York: Greenwood Press, reprinted 1968), p. 149.

33. Martin Heidegger, *Phänomenologie und Theologie* (Frankfurt am Main: Vittorio Klostermann, 1970), pp. 44, 28. See *The Piety of Thinking: Essays by Martin Heidegger*, trans. with notes and commentaries by James G. Hart and John C. Maraldo (Bloomington: Indiana University Press, 1976), pp. 28, 17.

34. E.L. Mascall, *Christian Theology and Natural Science: Some Questions in Their Relations* (London: Longmans, Green & Co., 1956), p. 307.

35. St. Augustine, *De Libero Arbitrio Voluntatis*, Book Two, Chapters xvi to xix, in *Obras de San Agustin*, published under the direction of P. Felix Garcia, O.S.A. (Madrid: Biblioteca de Autores Cristianos, 1950), Vol. III, pp. 380, 386, 388, 390, 392, 394. See St. Augustine, *On Free Choice of the Will*, trans. Anna S. Benjamin and L.H.. Hackstaff (New York: Library of Liberal Arts, Bobbs-Merrill, 1964), pp. 76, 77, 78, 79, 80, 81.

36. St. Augustine, *Of True Religion*, trans. J.H.S. Burleigh (South Bend, Indiana: Gateway Editions, 1959), p. 75.

# Notes

37. St. Augustine, *De Libero Arbitrio Voluntatis*, Book Two, Chapters xix, xx, pp. 396, 398. See St. Augustine, *On Free Choice of the Will*, pp. 82, 83, 84.

38. St. Anselm, *De Libertate Arbitrii*, in AO, Vol. I, Ch. 14, line 1, p. 226; ch. 1, lines 26-27, 11, p. 208, and lines 4-5, p. 209; ch. 2, lines 6-10, p. 210; ch. 3, lines 13-14, p. 211, and lines 19-20, p. 212. Ch. 5, line 31, p. 216, and line 1, p. 217; ch. 6, lines 17-18, p. 217; ch. 8, lines 13-15, p. 220; ch. 11, lines 9-10, p. 223; ch. 12, lines 24-26, p. 223, and lines 1-2, p. 224. See TF, pp. 143, 123, 122, 124, 126, 127, 132, 133, 136, 140, 141, 143.

39. St. Anselm, *De Casu Diaboli*, in AO, Vol. I. Ch. 12, lines 13-17, p. 253; ch. 21, lines 23-24, p. 268; ch. 25, lines 25, 29-30, p. 273; ch. 13, line 10, p. 257; ch. 19, lines 8-10, p. 264; ch. 4, lines 29-30, p. 241, and lines 5-6, 8-9, p. 242. See TF, pp. 170, 187, 192, 193, 174, 182, 156, 157.

40. St. Anselm, *De Casu Diaboli*, in AO, Vol. I. Ch. 1, lines 29-30, p. 234, and lines 1-5, p. 235; ch. 19, lines 15-16, p. 264; ch. 20, line 28, p. 265; ch. 8, lines 21-23, p. 245, and lines 15-16, 5-8, p. 246; ch. 7, lines 18-20, p. 244. See TF, pp. 148-149, 182, 183, 161, 162, 160.

41. St. Anselm, *De Casu Diaboli*, in AO, Vol. I. Ch. 7, lines 16, 13-15, p. 244; ch. 4, lines 8-10, p. 242; ch. 11, lines 8-9, p. 248; ch. 12, lines 18-20, p. 253; ch. 10, lines 20-21, p. 247; ch. 11, lines 15-16, 17-19, 27-28, p. 248. Ch. 11, lines 19-22, p. 249 and lines 3-4, 8-10, 15-16, p. 251. Ch. 11, lines 17-20, p. 250; ch. 26, lines 11-13, p. 274; ch. 27, lines 32-33, p. 275; ch. 28, lines 7-9, p. 276. See TF, pp. 159, 157, 164, 170, 163, 165, 166, 167, 168, 193, 195.

42. Jean-Paul Sartre, *Being and Nothingness: An Essay on Phenomenological Ontology*, trans. Hazel E. Barnes (New York: Washington Square Press, 1966), Part One, ch. 1, section ii, p. 13.

43. Aleksandr I. Solzhenitsyn, *The Gulag Archipelago*, trans. Thomas P. Whitney (New York: Harper and Row, 1975), Vol. II, p. 615.

44. Martin Heidegger, *The Question of Being*, p. 97.

45. Leonardo da Vinci, *Diaries and Notes*, ed. T. Lucke, 1940, p. 4, cited by Heidegger, ibid., p. 69.

46. See Leo Strauss, "Jerusalem and Athens: Some Preliminary Reflections," in Leo Strauss, *Studies in Platonic Political Philosophy*, with an introduction by Thomas L. Pangle (Chicago and London: University of Chicago Press, 1983), p. 147.

## Epilogue

1. Joseph J. Carpino, Review of F. D. Wilhelmsen's *Christianity and Political Philosophy*, in *Interpretation: A Journal of Political Philosophy*, Vol. 8, no 2/3 (May 1980), p. 220.

2. William James, "Pragmatism and Humanism," in *"Pragmatism" and Four Essays from "The Meaning of Truth"* (New York and Cleveland: The World Publishing Co., Meridian Books, 1955), p. 169. John J. McDermott, "The Inevitability of Our Own Death: The Celebration of Time As a Prelude to Disaster," in John J. McDermott, *Streams of Experience: Reflections On The History and Philosophy of American Culture* (Amherst: The University of Massachusetts Press, 1986), p. 165.

3. Saint John of the Cross, *Complete Works*, trans. and ed. E. Allison Peers, Three Volumes (London, 1953), Vol. I. p. 395. See Elmer O'Brien, S.J., ed., *Varieties of Mystic Experience*, p. 283.

4. See Michael Oakeshott, "A Place of Learning," in *Thinking: The Journal of Philosophy for Children*, Vol. III, No. 3, 4 (April 1982), pp. 65-75.

5. See Sartre's conversation with Simone de Beauvoir in 1974, "A Conversation about Death and God," in *Harper's*, Vol. 268, No. 1605 (Feb. 1984), p. 39.

6. Martin Buber, *Eclipse of God: Studies in the Relation between Religion and Philosophy* (New York: Harper and Row, 1957), p. 129.

7. Langdon Gilkey, *Society and the Sacred: Toward a Theology of Culture in Decline* (New York: Crossroad Publishing Co., 1981), p. 129.

8. Friedrich Nietzsche, *The Gay Science*, trans. Walter Kaufmann (New York: Random House, Vintage Books, 1974), Book III, # 125, p. 181.

9. *The Life of St. Anselm, Archbishop of Cantebury*, by Eadmer, edited with introduction, notes, and translation by R.W. Southern (Oxford: Clarendon Press, 1972 reprint), Ch. XIX, Book I, p. 29.

10. See Hans-Georg Gadamer, "On the Problem of Self-Understanding," in Gadamer, *Philosophical Hermeneutics*, trans. and ed. David E. Linge (Berkeley: University of California Press, 1976), p. 58.

# Index

Anselm
    Aristotle and, 17-21
        in *Monologion*, 49-52
    Descartes and, 157-163
        in *Proslogion*, 90-96
    dialogue of, in first philosophy, 53-96. *See also Proslogion* of Anselm
    inversion of, in Feuerbach's reduction of first philosophy to anthropology, 192-201
    as medieval philosopher, xv-xvi
    meditation of, on first philosophy, 23-52. *See also Monologion*
    modern misunderstanding of, 217-223
    response of, to criticism, in *Proslogion*, 81-90
    significance of, xiii-xiv
Anselmian transformation of Aristotelian founding of first philosophy, ix-xviii
Anthropology
    Feuerbach's reduction of first philosophy to, 165-201
        being beyond God in, 179-186
        inversion of Anselm in, 192-201
        negativity in, 172-179
        religion and logic of subjectivity in, 167-172
        from subjectivity to intersubjectivity in, 186-192
    as theology, Feuerbach on, 183-186
Aristotelian founding of first philosophy, viii, 1-21
    Anselm and, 17-21
    being of beings in, 14-17
    divine substance in, 4-8
    essence as substance in, 1-4
    first philosophy as theology in, 8-13
    transformation of, by Anselm, 17-21
Aristotle
    Anselm and, in *Monologion*, 49-52
    Cartesian refounding of first philosophy and, 158
Aquinas, 41
Augustine
    Anselm and, xv, 24, 57, 58, 63, 82
    Descartes and, 137, 212, 227
    on evil, 244-245

Bacon, Francis, 209-210, 211-212
Barth, Karl, 231-232
Being
    among beings in Anselm's *Monologion*, 24-29
    in ancient founding of first philosophy, viii
    of beings, Aristotle on, 14-17
    beyond beings in Anselm's *Monologion*, 45-49
    beyond doubt in Cartesian refounding of first philosophy, 111-117
    beyond God in Feuerbach's reduction of first philosophy to anthropology, 179-186
    and intelligibility, Anselm on, xiv
    *qua* being as substance, 8-9
Bloch, Ernst, 192-193
Body-soul system, Descartes on, 147-148
Boethius, 20, 33, 63
Buber, Martin, 263

Cartesian refounding of first
philosophy, viii-ix, 97-163
   addressing the self alone in, 117-128
   being beyond doubt in, 111-117
   Descartes and Anselm in, 157-163
   Descartes' response to criticism of, 148-157
   divorce of first philosophy and theology in, 98-104
   first philosophy as foundation of physical science in, 140-148
   negativity in, 104-111
   supra-substantial human subject in, 128-135
   truth as certitude in, 135-140
Cartesian regulative notion in historical travail of first philosophy, 223-229
Christianity
   contradiction in, Feuerbach on, 182
   essence of, Feuerbach on, 172-179, 181-182
Cicero, 169
Comprehension and incomprehensible in *Proslogion*, 71-78
"Conversation with Burman" (Descartes), 152
Created essence in Anselm's *Monologion*, 35-39
Creation, God's, Ontological Argument and, 73
Criticism, Anselm's response to, in *Proslogion*, 81-90

Dante, 20
Dependency as origin of religion, Feuerbach on, 168
Descartes
   Anselm and, 157-163
   in *Proslogion*, 90-96
   refounding of first philosophy by, 97-163. *See also* Cartesian refounding of first philosophy
   response of, to criticism, 148-157
Divine subject, supra-substantial, in *Proslogion*, 78-81
Divine substance, Aristotle on, 4-8
Divine Trinity, Anselm on, 39-45
Doubt
   being beyond, in Cartesian refounding of first philosophy, 111-117
   methodic, in Cartesian refounding of first philosophy, 104-111
Duns Scotus, xv

Eadmer, 56-57
*Ego*
   Descartes on, 147-148, 158-159, 161-162
   in Descartes' replies to criticism, 156-157
   in historical travail of first philosophy, 206-208
Einstein, Albert, 196
Error, Descartes on, 128-135
Essence
   created and uncreated, in Anselm's *Monologion*, 35-39
   of Feuerbach in historical travail of first philosophy, 229-237
   as substance, Aristotle on, 1-4
   substance as, in Anselm's *Monologion*, 29-35
*Essence of Christianity, The* (Feuerbach), negativity in, 172-179
*Essence of Faith in Luther's Sense, The* (Feuerbach), 186-189
Evil
   God and, contradictoriness of, in historical travail of first philosophy, 214-217

mystery of, in historical travail of
  first philosophy, 243-253
Existence
  of God, denial of, in *Proslogion*,
    59-64
  as problematic for first
    philosophy, 25-26

Faith
  Anselm on, xiv-xv, 46
  in God, Feuerbach on, 179-180,
    181
  versus love, Feuerbach on, 184,
    198
  Luther's notion of, Feuerbach on,
    186-190
  and philosophy, separation of, by
    Descartes, 103
  and reason, antithesis of,
    Feuerbach on, 189-191
Feuerbach
  "essence" of, in historical travail
    of first philosophy, 229-237
  on first philosophy, xi, 208
  mystery of Trinity and, 230-234
  reduction of first philosophy to
    anthropology by, 165-201. *See
    also* Anthropology,
    Feuerbach's reduction of first
    philosophy to
First philosophy
  Anselm's dialogue in, 53-96. *See
    also Proslogion*
  Anselm's meditation on, 23-52.
    *See also Monologion* of
    Anselm
  Aristotelian founding of, viii, 1-
    21. *See also* Aristotelian
    founding of first philosophy
  Cartesian refounding of, 97-163.
    *See also* Cartesian refounding
    of first philosophy
  divorce of theology from, in
    Cartesian refounding of first
    philosophy, 98-104

Feuerbach's reduction of, to
  anthropology, 165-201. *See
  also* Anthropology, reduction
  of first philosophy to
as foundation of physical science
  in Cartesian refounding of first
  philosophy, 140-148
historical travail of, 203-253. *See
  also* Historical travail of first
  philosophy
history of, xi
as theology, Aristotle on, 8-13
as trinitarian theology in Anselm's
  *Monologion*, 39-45
Form, Aristotle on, 9-10
Foster, Michael B., 209, 210
Frank, Erich, 161

Gaunilo's criticism of Anselm, 83-84
  reply to, 84-90
  Feuerbach and, 232-233
God
  Aristotle's versus Anselm's, ix-x,
    203-204
  being beyond, in Feuerbach's
    reduction of first philosophy to
    anthropology, 179-186
  essence and existence in,
    Descartes on, 138-140
  existence of, denial of, in
    *Proslogion*, 59-64
  naming of
    medium for, 257-259
    motives for, 262-263
  as triune, Anselm on, 80
  veracity of, Descartes on, 107-108
  will of, in Descartes' replies to
    criticism, 155-156

Hegel, xv, 185, 221, 234
Heidegger
  on Aristotle, 1, 17, 18
  on Christianity, 54-55, 93, 97
  on subjectivity, 160, 161, 165-166,
    234, 235, 252-253

Historical travail of first philosophy, 203-253
  Cartesian regulative notion in, 223-229
  "essence" of Feuerbach in, 229-237
  modern misunderstanding of Anselm in, 217-223
  mystery of evil in, 243-253
  removal and perdurance of mystery in, 208-217
  that by which man is man in, 237-243
Human subject, supra-substantial
  in Cartesian refounding of first philosophy, 128-135
  in Descartes' replies to criticism, 151, 152-153
Husserl, Edmund, 161

Ideas, kinds of, in Descartes' meditations, 119-123
Imagination
  understanding and, Descartes on, 141-142
  will and, Descartes on, 146-147
Incomprehensible, comprehensible and, in *Proslogion*, 71-78
Intersubjectivity, from subjectivity to, in Feuerbach's reduction of first philosophy, 186-192

James, William, 240, 255-256
John of the Cross, xvii, 256-257
Jung, C.G., 229
Justice as rectitude of will, 74

Kant, 247
Kennington, Richard, 110

Language in historical travail of first philosophy, 240-243
*Lectures on the Essence of Religion* (Feuerbach), religion and logic of subjectivity in, 167-172

Leibniz, 180
Leonardo da Vinci, 253
Lewis, C. S., 54
Love versus faith, Feuerbach on, 184, 198
Löwith, Karl, 194
Luther, Martin, notion of faith of, Feuerbach on, 186-190
Maritain, Jacques, 155
Marx, Leo, 14, 15-16, 17
McDermott, John, 255
Meditation on first philosophy, Anselm's, 23-52. *See also Monologion*
*Meditationes de Prima Philosophia* of Descartes, 97-163. *See also* Cartesian refounding of first philosophy
Metaphysics, Descartes and, 140, 156, 160-161
Methodic doubt in Cartesian refounding of first philosophy, 104-111
*Monologion* of Anselm, 23-52
  Aristotle and, 49-52
  Being among beings in, 24-29
  Being beyond beings in, 45-49
  created and uncreated essence in, 35-39
  first philosophy as trinitarian theology in, 39-45
  substance as essence in, 29-35
Mystery
  of evil in historical travail of first philosophy, 243-253
  removal and perdurance of, in historical travail of first philosophy, 208-217
  of Trinity
    Feuerbach and, 230-234
    in historical travail of first philosophy, 223-227

Nature, de-mystification of, in historical travail of first philosphy, 209-210

Negativity
  in Cartesian refounding of first philosophy, 104-111
  in Feuerbach's reduction of first philosophy to anthropology, 172-179
  in *Proslogion*, 59-64
Nietzsche on God, 263
Ontological Argument of Anselm
  Creation and, 73
  Feuerbach on, 182-183
  human reason and, 95
  ideas of God in, philosophical integrity constituted by, 220-222
  misunderstanding of, by philosophical modernity, 219-220
Owens, Joseph, 8-9, 10, 11, 17

Parmenides, 91
Perception, sensory, veracity of, Descartes on, 105-106
Physical science, first philosophy as foudation of, in Cartesian refounding of first philosophy, 140-148
Plato, 12, 230
Platonic Forms, 8,9
Prayer, Feuerbach on, 179
*Proslogion* of Anselm, 53-96
  Anselm's response to criticism in, 81-90
  comprehension and incomprehensible in, 71-78
  Descartes and, 90-96
  negativity in, 59-64
  submergence and emergence of self in, 55-59
  supra-substantial divine subject in, 78-81
  truth as rectitude in, 64-71
Protagoreanism, 255

Reale, Giovanni, 12-13, 17

Reason
  and faith, antithesis of, Feuerbach on, 189-191
  human, Ontological Argument and, 95
Regulative notion, Cartesian, in historical travail of first philosophy, 223-229
Religion
  dependencey as origin of, Feuerbach on, 168
  logic of subjectivity and, Feuerbach on, 167-172
"Replies to Objections Urged Against The Meditations" (Descartes), 148-152

Sartre, 252, 262
Scholasticism, Anselm as father of, 20
Self
  addressing, in Cartesian refounding of first philosophy, 117-128
  submergence and emergence of, in *Proslogion*, 55-59
Seneca, 63
Sensations, existence and, Descartes on, 142-147
Sense perception, veracity of, Descartes on, 105-106
Sin, will and, in historical travail of first philosophy, 245-247
Sokolowski, Robert, 49-50, 51
Solzhenitsyn, Aleksandr, 252
Subjectivity
  Descartes and, 148, 160-161, 162-163
  in historical travail of first philosophy, 236
  to intersubjectivity in Feuerbach's reduction of first philosophy to anthropology, 186-192
  logic of, religion and, Feuerbach on, 167-172

Substance
　being *qua* being as, 8-9
　divine, Aristotle on, 4-8
　essence as, Aristotle on, 1-4
　as essence in Anselm's
　　*Monologion*, 29-35
　in founding of first philosophy, viii
　primary signification of, 10-11

Theology
　anthropology as, Feuerbach on,
　　183-186
　as anthropomorphic, Feuerbach
　　on, 172-179
　divorce of first philosophy from,
　　in Cartesian refounding of first
　　philosophy, 98-104
　first philosophy as, Aristotle on,
　　8-13
　trinitarian, first philosophy as, in
　　Anselm's *Monologion*, 39-45
Theomorphism in historical travail
　of first philosophy, 235
Transformation of Aristotelian first
　philosophy by Anselm, 17-21
Trinitarian theology, first philosophy
　as, in Anselm's *Monologion*, 39-
　45
Trinity
　Feuerbach on, 177-178

　mystery of
　　Feuerbach and, 230-234
　　in historical travail of first
　　　philosophy, 223-227
Truth
　Anselm on, xvi-xvii
　as certitude in Cartesian
　　refounding of first philosophy,
　　102, 135-140
　as rectitude in *Proslogion*, 64-71

Uncreated essence in Anselm's
　*Monologion*, 36
Understanding, imagination and,
　Descartes on, 141-142

Western Civilization, lives of, 237-
　240
Whitehead, A. N., 240
Will
　God's, in Descartes' replies to
　　criticism, 155-156
　human
　　in Descartes' replies to
　　　criticism, 154-155
　　errors and, Descartes on, 130-
　　　134
　　sin and, in historical travail of
　　　first philosophy, 245-247

## DATE DUE

| MAR 23 1998 | | | |
|---|---|---|---|
| | | | |
| | | | |
| | | | |
| | | | |
| | | | |
| | | | |
| | | | |
| | | | |
| | | | |
| | | | |
| | | | |
| | | | |
| | | | |
| | | | |
| | | | |
| | | | |

HIGHSMITH   # 45220